Going Rouge:

Sarah Palin—

An American Nightmare

GOING ROUGE:
Sarah Palin—
An American Nightmare

Edited by Richard Kim and Betsy Reed

First published by OR Books, New York 2009
© the collection: Richard Kim and Betsy Reed
© individual pieces: the contributors
(see credits, page 333)

OR Books
www.ORbooks.com

ISBN 978-0-9842950-0-5 (paperback)
ISBN 978-0-9842950-1-2 (e book)

Library of Congress Cataloging-in-Publication Data
A catalog record for this book is available from
the Library of Congress

British Library Cataloguing-in-Publication Data
A catalog record for this book is available from
the British Library

Printed by Book Mobile, USA

INTRODUCTION
Richard Kim and Betsy Reed

On the evening of November 4, 2008, progressives were in an ebullient mood. After eight long years of Republican rule, Barack Obama had been elected president. Accompanying our shouts of joy were audible sighs of relief. The prospect of a John McCain presidency had filled us with dread. But to imagine Sarah Palin—a conservative Christian with a penchant for folksy warmongering who flaunted her ignorance as a virtue—separated from the red button in the Oval Office only by a 72-year-old cancer survivor... *that* was beyond terrifying. Palin, we hoped, would slink back to Alaska, where her corrosive influence could be contained and perhaps ultimately extinguished, as her candidacy, historic in its way, became a footnote in an election filled with other, more galvanizing political developments.

As we write, it has been one year since that memorable night, and if the hard realities of governing a nation engulfed in two wars and a deep recession have somewhat dampened the hopes Obama raised during his campaign, another gnawing realization has crept in: The story of Sarah Palin is far from over. Her abrupt announcement over the July 4 weekend that she was quitting the governorship of Alaska may have removed her from public office, but it did little to diminish her presence in the public eye. Her memoir, *Going Rogue*, with a first printing of 1.5 million copies, became a best seller thanks to preorders before it even hit the stores. While her approval rating among all voters hovers around 40 percent, among Republicans it still stands at the 70 percent mark. Disgruntled former McCain staffers continue to snipe at her in the press, but she consistently ranks in the top tier of Republican presidential hopefuls. McCain's campaign manager Steve Schmidt—who sanctioned her selection as McCain's running mate—has said that a Palin presidential bid would be "catastrophic," but McCain himself recently acknowledged that Palin is a "formidable force in the Republican Party" and a strong contender for the party's nomination in 2012. Compared to the all-male also-rans and might-have-beens that pop up in Republican straw polls— Mitt Romney, Mike Huckabee, Tim Pawlenty, Bobby Jindal, Ron Paul, and Rudy Giuliani—Palin is a bona fide celebrity. She transcends politics. As *New York Times* columnist Frank Rich puts it, Palin is "not just the party's biggest star and most charismatic television performer; she is its *only* star and charismatic performer."

What explains this enduring allure? Her gender? Good looks? Her small-town Alaskan roots? Her fascinating biography and family drama? Undeniably, these are all part of the Sarah Palin mystique. Her name instantly conjures up a pungent brew of images, phrases and associations: just an average hockey mom of five, a pit bull with lipstick, beauty queen, moose hunter, long-distance runner, sexy librarian, winker, rogue—you betcha! But for those who care to look, beneath these shimmering surfaces there lies both a crude ideology and an alarmingly potent strategy for selling it. Like Nixon, Reagan, and George W. Bush, Palin has managed to become a brand unto herself, quite a feat for a failed vice presidential candidate. No one speaks of McCainism or Dole-ism, but Palinism signals not just a political position but a political style, a whole way of doing politics.

Palinism works by draping hard-right policy in a winning personal story and just-folks rhetoric, delicately masking the extremism of her true positions and broad-ening the audience for them. Its genius rests in its ability to magically absorb inconvenient facts and mutually contradictory realities into an unassailable personal narrative. In the Palin universe, her unwed pregnant teenage daughter Bristol is somehow a poster child for abstinence-only education; hence criticism of Palin's sex-ed policies is an attack on her family. While Palin says tolerantly that members of her own family disagree about abortion, that there are "good people" on both sides, and that she would "personally" counsel a pregnant 15-year-old who'd been raped by her father to "choose life," she actually believes that a child in that situation should not have the legal option to terminate her pregnancy. Although Palin is an aggressive advocate for opening up the United States' oil reserves to drilling instead of investing in renewable energy, she labels herself "pro-environment," a stance exemplified by her love of shooting animals or her husband's hobby of racing snowmobiles across the tundra. And who'd dare question Palin's foreign policy credentials, when her son Track shipped out to Iraq after high school?

To grasp the persistent power of Palinism, consider the "death panel" hysteria that hijacked the debate over health care reform in the summer of 2009. It began on July 24, when Betsy McCaughey, the former lieutenant governor of New York and Clinton health care antagonist, took to the pages of the *New York Post* to vilify Dr. Ezekiel Emanuel, the brother of White House chief of staff Rahm Emanuel and a health policy adviser to the Obama administration. Dr. Emanuel, McCaughey wrote, had advocated rationing health care away from the elderly and disabled, and the Democrats' health care reforms would "put the decisions about your care in the hands of presidential appointees" like him. McCaughey's claims were easily debunked, and they initially failed to break into the mainstream. That changed on August 7, when Sarah Palin posted a screed against health care reform on her Facebook page that included this classic Palinism: "The America I know and love is not one in which my parents or my baby with Down Syndrome will have to stand in front of Obama's 'death panel' so his bureaucrats can decide, based on a subjective judgment of their 'level of productivity in society,' whether they are worthy of health care. Such a system is downright evil." With remarkable economy of prose, Palin cast health care reform as an assault on the country, put a face on its supposed victims (her baby Trig), coined the expression "death panel" (linking it directly to Obama), raised the specter of euthanasia in the service of a state-run economy, and rallied the troops around a fight against "evil." In short, she personalized, popularized, and polarized the debate. Never mind that Democratic health care reform bills merely funded optional end-of-life consultations that had heretofore been almost universally acknowledged as a good. (Indeed, Palin herself once championed them in Alaska.) The madness exploded. Astroturf groups funded by the health insurance industry began pumping up the base of tea party protesters, who laid siege to town hall meetings, heckling elected officials from both parties. Fights broke out. Armed zealots began showing up at the president's speeches. Newt Gingrich appeared on *This Week with George Stephanopolous* and said, "There clearly are people in America who believe in establishing euthanasia, including selective standards." Other Republican leaders took up the cause, and it was not until Obama flatly rejected death panels as "a lie, plain and simple" in his health care speech on September 9 that the public anxiety over them began to subside.

As this book goes to press, health care reform has yet to pass Congress, and it is unclear what effect the death panel uproar will have on the ultimate legislative outcome. But

Palin's "death panel" crusade has already provided a chilling lesson: that a minority armed with conspiracy theories is capable of occupying the national political discourse as long as they have conviction and a mouthpiece. This brand of politics—hostile to reform in Washington, despite its own reformist posture; unconstrained by any sense of obligation to be truthful and decent when confronting one's ideological foes—was not invented by Palin, but she has demonstrated a special knack for it ever since she landed on the national scene. During the election, it was Palin who trafficked in guilt by association, dredging up Obama's reed-thin connection to former Weatherman Bill Ayers and pushing McCain to make the Reverend Jeremiah Wright an issue, despite his pledge to leave Wright out of it. It was Palin who, addressing the surging, angry crowds at her campaign rallies, accused Obama of "palling around with terrorists," gratifying those who suspected him of being a secret Muslim born outside the country. It was Palin who, while campaigning in North Carolina, praised small towns as "the real America" and the "pro-America areas of this great nation," fanning racialized fears of urban America and stoking the notion that Obama and his supporters intended a hostile takeover of the U.S. government. And more recently, it was Palin who was among the first to suggest that Obama, in his attempt to alleviate some of the pain caused by the recession, has launched the country on the path to "socialism." Of course, Sarah Palin does not espouse the entirety of the paranoid right's propaganda. She does not ask to see Barack Obama's birth certificate, and she does not show up at town halls toting a rifle and a knife. But she doesn't have to; suggestion and innuendo are her game, and in the swirl of resentments and phobias that fuel the American right, she is never far from the center.

That Sarah Palin occupies such a vital place in the
Republican Party's zeitgeist—rivaled perhaps only by fellow
"outsiders" Glenn Beck and Rush Limbaugh—is even more
surprising when one considers the obscurity from which
she was plucked by McCain on August 29, 2008. Palin had
been mayor of a city of approximately 7,000 and was just
twenty months into her first term as governor of Alaska, the
forty-seventh-most-populous state in the nation. This was
hardly the resume with which to attack Obama for his lack
of experience, the McCain campaign's then going strategy.
But a unique set of circumstances convinced McCain's
advisers that choosing Palin was the "game-changing"
move they desperately needed to make. The Palin pick
was an arrow aimed not only at Obama but at the heart of
the fragile Democratic coalition. With the soul-wrenching
primary still a raw memory for Democrats torn between a
charismatic, visionary black man and a feisty, competent
female candidate, McCain's choice seemed at first to reflect
an almost demonic genius. From where progressives stood
at that time, Palin appeared to be the latest GOP rabbit-out-
of-a-hat, conjured up in some steel-plated war room the likes
of which we could scarcely imagine. All those passionate,
fresh-faced Obama volunteers with their Facebook pages
and house parties that we'd been celebrating as the new
transformative force in American politics suddenly seemed
pathetic, even tragic, next to the glowing apparition of Sarah
Palin on our TV screens.

The spectacle of a woman being elevated to such
a lofty place in the Republican Party hierarchy was
certainly something to behold. Before her there had been
Condoleezza Rice, secretary of state under Bush, and Liddy
Dole's truncated run for the Republican nomination in
2000, among others, but GOP women had been cast either

as bit players or members of the team, and now a woman was potentially entrusted with the presidency itself. What's more, Palin was clearly selected in part because of her womanly appeal. Her nomination was, to be sure, a milestone—finally, a working mother was being celebrated rather than guilt-tripped by family-values traditionalists. But it was also profoundly cynical. Well before McCain's advisers settled on the choice, Palin's fortunes were avidly being promoted by besotted male conservatives like the *Weekly Standard*'s Bill Kristol and Fred Barnes, Bush speechwriter Michael Gerson, and consultant Dick Morris, as Jane Mayer reports in her contribution here. The party that congratulated itself for anointing a woman simultaneously embraced a platform advocating draconian restrictions on women's reproductive freedom (supporting a ban on abortion even in cases of rape, incest, and when the life of the mother is at stake), and its leaders stood against the Lilly Ledbetter act for pay equity, along with every other agenda item for the women's movement. As pieces in this volume by Katha Pollitt and Gloria Steinem show, feminists were quick to expose the fraudulent nature of the GOP's gambit. As Steinem put it, "This isn't the first time a boss has picked an unqualified woman just because she agrees with him and opposes everything most other women want and need." The small matter of Palin's utter lack of qualifications for the job would become painfully more apparent as the campaign unfolded. For feminists—who had long heard complaints that affirmative action promotes mediocrity from the same quarters that now extolled Palin's virtues—the hypocrisy of the pick was too much to bear.

But there she was, the shining star of the Republican National Convention, and indisputably feminine. It was not only Palin herself but the sight of her brood of five children—

including baby Trig, and Bristol, 17 and pregnant—along with the ruggedly handsome "first dude" Todd, that riveted the nation. As JoAnn Wypijewski points out in her contribution, Palin and her family are exemplars of the new Christian sexual politics. Married, fertile, God-fearing, and hot: Palin's sex appeal was a major factor in her bolt to stardom. Finally, conservatives had found a fashionable and sexy icon—why let Hollywood liberals have all the fun?—and if Palin's looks led some to instantly dismiss her as a pretty airhead, then many others hung on her every wink and word.

This double-edged effect of her gender and her beauty was on our minds when we selected the title *Going Rouge* for this book. (Appearances aside, it had nothing to do with the fact that Sarah Palin's forthcoming memoir is called *Going Rogue*; any similarities are purely coincidental.) While we could never be participants in the "Sarah Palin Pity Party" (in Rebecca Traister's memorable phrase), we are not without sympathy for the bind she has found herself in. In all fairness to Palin, the media attention devoted to her $150,000 shopping spree to glam up her wardrobe— inappropriate though it may have been to use Republican National Committee cash for such a purpose, when the campaign was busy selling her as an Everywoman—was disproportionate. It was not only a frivolous focus at a moment when the financial system was imploding and the U.S. military was waging wars on multiple fronts, but it revealed that Palin was subject to a sort of scrutiny that male candidates are generally spared (yes, John Edwards took flak for his $400 haircuts, but even that had sexist overtones—he was labeled the "Breck Girl" for his excesses). On the other hand, Palin and, by extension, the overwhelmingly white and male Republican Party leadership, having made the decision to "go rouge"—that is, to use her gender and sex appeal to advance their campaign to capture the White House—can't have expected this remarkable image transformation to pass without criticism, especially when what they stood for was antithetical to most women's needs and desires.

Looking back, progressives and feminists did an admirable job in picking apart the GOP's first female vice presidential nominee. When they attacked, they did so largely for the right reasons. In this book, we have assembled highlights from the reporting and commentary on her rise. Chapter One focuses on her selection by John McCain— both the symbolic and the political reasons for the pick. Chapter Two examines her record in Alaska, as small-town mayor and then governor, with special attention to her links to the far right and her anti-environmental policies. Chapter Three, "Palintology," features an assortment of vintage Selected Palinisms and a cross section of her lies and misrepresentations. In Chapters Four and Five— "Lipstick on a Faux Feminist: Palin and Women" and "The Palin Pageant: Sex, God, and Country First"—the cultural implications of her ascension are explored. Chapter Six takes stock of the ideology of Palinism; Chapter Seven chronicles her missteps and ultimate electoral defeat; and Chapter Eight illuminates her legacy and future in the Republican Party.

As it turned out, at the ballot box, most Americans proved they were able to see through the glossy packaging and peg Palin for what she was: a Christian fundamentalist opposed to the teaching of honest sex education in schools and in favor of teaching creationism alongside evolution, a climate-change-denier and government-basher alarmingly ignorant of the world and totally unprepared to be president. Women voted overwhelmingly for Obama—56 percent to 43 percent for McCain/Palin—while men were about evenly split. Exit surveys showed that Palin was a drag on the Republican ticket.

But as we've seen, this is a woman with at least nine lives. By our count, having crashed and burned in Election 2008 and resigned ignominiously as governor, she's still got seven left.

1/ PICKING PALIN
The GOP's Gift to America

Beauty and the Beast

JoAnn Wypijewski

A man fiddling with his wedding ring in the presence of another woman usually has something on his mind. At his introduction of Sarah Palin to the world on August 29, John McCain appeared a man possessed, playing with his ring, fastening his gaze on her breasts, her backside, his right fingers sliding up from that dratted gold band to the finger tip, pinching it as if to control the volcano stirring within him. "Boxed up," the young McCain once said in a near-frenzy, describing to a confidante the state of his emotions under the Naval Academy's discipline; the expression suited his performance that Friday in Dayton, when he finally regained composure by assuming the rigid posture of attention that the academy had taught so well.

Here was McCain, the angry old warrior, deploying sex as a central political weapon to recharge his potency, his party's fortunes, and the cultural oomph of the right. Not gender. The Republicans didn't need just any woman to compete with Obama for the Wow factor, the Mmm factor, the stable, loving family factor. It is a calculated bonus that adherents can now speak loftily of making history, but for different reasons, drawing deep from the well of their identities, and not for the first time, both McCain and the right needed a sexual icon.

McCain's first wife, Carol, airbrushed from his "compelling story" even when her three children trooped onstage to complete the convention's family tableau, was a swimsuit model. Tall and slender when she saw John off to Vietnam, she was five inches shorter when he returned, broken grievously from a car accident, using a catheter and a wheelchair. "I don't look so good myself," he told her;

privately he told friends the sight of her "appalled" him. He began looking for a more alluring replacement almost immediately. Carol says she has "no bitterness," according to a story by Sharon Churcher in the London *Daily Mail*. John just "wanted to be 25 again."

At forty-two McNasty, as he was called in high school, took up with twenty-four-year-old Cindy, a former junior rodeo queen, and, having boosted his image and his net worth via a marriage vow, soon reverted to the pattern of insults and macho egotism that has typified most of his life. He denigrated her education at U.S.C. as a tour through "the University of Spoiled Children." For all but one of several miscarriages, he left her on her own. When she was popping ten to fifteen pills a day to mask her pain and "do everything he wanted," he never noticed. In 1992, in a rage over her gentle teasing about his thinning hair, he exploded, "At least I don't plaster on the makeup like a trollop, you cunt," a one-two punch hurled in front of three journalists and two aides but unreported until recently, by Cliff Schecter in *The Real McCain*. On the campaign trail in June he joked about "beating my wife" and took umbrage when others failed to grasp the simple good fun in the remark. In early August he said he'd encouraged Cindy to enter the Miss Buffalo Chip beauty pageant at the high-revving, flesh-swinging biker rally in Sturgis, South Dakota. It might have been a fine quip except that up on the stage with her daughter Meghan, staring out toward the throng where a sign urged, "Show Ur Tits 4 McCain," Cindy had the thin, fixed smile of endurance, not joy. Just before the Palin pick, Mrs. McCain was so brittle that a supporter's energetic handshake put her in a cast. With the press and vast swaths of the country swooning over the Obama family, John needed a new queen.

Like King Ahasuerus in the Book of Esther, who asserted his mastery by decreeing male headship and then held a kind of beauty pageant to replace Vashti as queen, McCain found his new "partner and soulmate" in Miss Wasilla 1984. Even Cindy, who suddenly let her hair down in bed-head style, perhaps at last relieved of the burdens of wifely duties, calls it "a perfect match." If only by association, John McCain may now fancy himself in the image of his deepest desire, top gun.

There may be a trap for him in the Book of Esther, which Sarah Palin, a biblical literalist, has used as a guide since becoming governor of Alaska, but more on that in a moment. For in her immediate ascendancy, Palin has fortified the Christian leadership that saw its first major organizing successes in the 1970s using sex as a weapon behind the banner of Miss Oklahoma 1958 (Anita Bryant) and her antigay crusade. With her husband, Todd, "quite a package," Palin has fired up the Christian rank and file, who, also since the 1970s, have been on the losing end of the economy but have drawn a diverting strength from simultaneously attacking the heralds of sexual liberation (feminists and gays) and appropriating their message: holding out mind-blowing sex as God's special gift to his truest heterosexual married believers; spawning a multimillion-dollar industry in Christian sex guides, aids, toys, soft-core porn (gussied up as novels or advice); and promoting a particular image of married womanhood as sex machine, urged, as Dagmar Herzog notes in an interesting new book, *Sex in Crisis*, to "keep their legs shaved and vaginas douched at all times. Just in case."

For the party's cynical power elite, who simply want to make gobs of money and have fun doing it, and never tire of a little culture war that helps them achieve both, Palin is the sex symbol they've been waiting for, better looking and more real than the ghastly gasbags Ann Coulter and Laura Ingraham. Rush Limbaugh, who began a push for Palin as V.P. in February, can hardly contain himself: "Sarah Palin: babies, guns, Jesus, hot damn!" he crowed. "We're the ones that have the babe on the ticket!" Never before has a political woman been pictured so often in a T-shirt, armed—Rambette. Never before in a major political figure has the image of Mother been merged so readily with fantasies from porno. "You Go, GILF," proclaim buttons on Republican chests, that is, Governor (or Grandmother) I'd Like to Fuck, a turn on the hungry married mom, or MILF, who has tapped the sex muscles and credit cards of porn lovers for years. While older working-class men talk of "Little Sarah" and her children, other men, including some on the left, have been rapturous in expressing their librarian fetish. "I was trying to be as frumpy as I could by wearing my hair on top of my head and these schoolmarm glasses," Palin told *Vogue*, as if insensible to that venerable erotic figure, the tigress unleashed once the glasses are removed and the tresses fall. Why, Mrs. Palin, you're, you're b-b-beautiful... Exactly right, sonny, and no fool either.

In Sarah Palin the right has its perfect emblem: moral avatar and commodity, uniting the put-upon woman who gushes, "She's just like me!" and the chest thumper who brays, "I'd do her, and her daughter" with those who have long exploited the fear and sorry machismo of both, with the help of another durable reactionary weapon. Now that it's official, as McCain's campaign manager said, that "this election is not about issues; this election is about a composite view of what people take away from these candidates," McCain's only live tag appears to be, Republicans Do It Better. Translation: small-town, gun-toting, rough-and-ready, all-American Sarah and Todd versus Barack and Michelle. White Power. (Or, close enough, White-ish.) Palin Power.

And there's the rub for McCain. It looks like Palin's party now, and whatever she does for his virility, she's not the hockey mom, or the babe, or the third wife he can stomp on. If her acceptance speech was indicative, she can match the "sneering, condescending attitude" that former Republican Senator Bob Smith says is fundamental to McCain, but with a smile and a dagger's turn. Her role model Esther doesn't just win favor from the king and a reprieve for herself and her people; she enables her people to engage in bloody slaughter against the king's other subjects, maneuvers for the public execution of his closest adviser and the man's sons, sees her de facto father become the de facto king; in sum, sabotages and unmans Ahasuerus. Palin has been too cagey to identify exactly who her people are, but in playing off cronies and oilmen in Alaska and even Christians to get where she is, she does seem to have grasped the art, so vital to politics, of the exquisitely timed double cross.

The Insiders: How John McCain Came to Pick Sarah Palin

Jane Mayer

"Here's a little news flash," Sarah Palin, the governor of Alaska and the Republican candidate for vice president, announced in September, during her debut at the party's convention, in St. Paul. "I'm not a member of the permanent political establishment. And I've learned quickly these past few days that if you're not a member in good standing of the Washington elite then some in the media consider a candidate unqualified for that reason alone." But, she added, "I'm not going to Washington to seek their good opinion."

In subsequent speeches, Palin has cast herself as an antidote to the elitist culture inside the Beltway. "I'm certainly a Washington outsider, and I'm proud of that, because I think that that is what we need," she recently told Fox News. During her first interview as John McCain's running mate, with ABC's Charles Gibson, Palin was asked about her lack of experience in foreign policy. She replied, "We've got to remember what the desire is in this nation at this time. It is for no more politics as usual, and somebody's big fat résumé, maybe, that shows decades and decades in the Washington establishment.... Americans are getting sick and tired of that self-dealing, and kind of that closed-door, good-ol'-boy network that has been the Washington elite."

Palin's sudden rise to prominence, however, owes more to members of the Washington elite than her rhetoric has suggested. Paulette Simpson, the head of the Alaska Federation of Republican Women, who has known Palin since 2002, said, "From the beginning, she's been underestimated. She's very smart. She's ambitious." John Bitney, a top policy adviser on Palin's 2006 gubernatorial campaign, said, "Sarah's very conscientious about crafting the story of Sarah. She's all about the hockey mom and Mrs. Palin Goes to Washington—the anti-politician politician." Bitney is from Wasilla, Palin's hometown, and has known her since junior high school, where they both played in the band. He considers Palin a friend, even though after becoming governor, in December, 2006, she dismissed him. He is now the chief of staff to the speaker of the Alaska house.

Upon being elected governor, Palin began developing relationships with Washington insiders, who later championed the idea of putting her on the 2008 ticket. "There's some political opportunism on her part," Bitney said. For years, "she's had D.C. in mind." He added, "She's not interested in being on the junior-varsity team."

During her gubernatorial campaign, Bitney said, he began predicting to Palin that she would make the short list of Republican vice presidential prospects. "She had the biography, I told her, to be a contender," he recalled. At first, Palin only laughed. But within a few months of being sworn in she and others in her circle noticed that a blogger named Adam Brickley had started a movement to draft her as vice president. Palin also learned that a number of prominent conservative pundits would soon be passing through Juneau, on cruises sponsored by right-leaning political magazines. She invited these insiders to the governor's mansion, and even led some of them on a helicopter tour.

Throughout the campaign, Palin has mocked what she calls "the mainstream media." Yet her administration made a concerted effort to attract the attention of East Coast publications. In late 2007, the state hired a public relations firm with strong East Coast connections, which began promoting Palin and a natural gas pipeline that she was backing in Alaska. The contract was for $37,000. The publicist on the project, Marcia Brier, the head of MCB Communications, in Needham, Massachusetts, was asked to approach media outlets in Washington and New York, according to the *Washington Post*. "I believe Alaska has a very small press organization," Brier told me. "They hired an outside consultant in order to get that East Coast press." Brier crafted a campaign depicting Palin as bravely taking on powerful oil interests by choosing a Canadian firm, TransCanada, rather than an American conglomerate such as ExxonMobil, to build the pipeline. ("Big Oil Under Siege" was the title of a typical press release.) Brier pitched Palin to publications such as the *New York Times*, the *Washington Post*, and *Fortune*.

From the start of her political career, Palin has positioned herself as an insurgent intent on dislodging entrenched interests. In 1996, a campaign pamphlet for her first mayoral run—recently obtained by the *New Republic*—strikes the same note of populist resentment that Palin did at the convention: "I'm tired of 'business as usual' in this town, and of the 'good ol' boys' network that runs the show here." Yet Palin has routinely turned to members of Washington's old guard for help. After she became the mayor of Wasilla, Palin oversaw the hiring of a law firm to represent the town's interests in Washington, D.C. The Wasilla account was handled by Steven Silver, a Washington-area lobbyist who had been the chief of staff to Alaska's long-serving Republican senator Ted Stevens, who was indicted in July on charges of accepting illegal gifts and is now standing trial. (Silver declined to discuss his ties to Palin.) As the *Washington Post* reported, Silver's efforts in the capital helped Wasilla, a town of 6,700 residents, secure $27 million in federal earmarks. During this election season, however, Palin has presented herself as more abstemious, saying, "I've championed reform to end the abuses of earmark spending by Congress."

In February 2007, Adam Brickley gave himself a mission: he began searching for a running mate for McCain who could halt the momentum of the Democrats. Brickley, a self-described "obsessive" political junkie who recently graduated from the University of Colorado at Colorado Springs, told me that he began by "randomly searching Wikipedia and election sites for Republican women." Though he generally opposes affirmative action, gender drove his choice. "People were talking about Hillary at the time," he recalled. Brickley said that he "puzzled over every Republican female politician I knew." Senator Kay Bailey Hutchison, of Texas, "waffled on social issues"; Senator Olympia Snowe, of Maine, was too moderate. He was running out of options, he recalled, when he said to himself, "What about that lady who just got elected in Alaska?" Online research revealed that she had a strong grassroots following; as Brickley put it, "I hate to use the words 'cult of personality,' but she reminded me of Obama."

Brickley registered a Web site—palinforvp.blogspot.com—which began getting attention in the conservative blogosphere. In the month before Palin was picked by McCain, Brickley said, his Web site was receiving about three thousand hits a day. Support for Palin had spread from one right-of-center Internet site to the next. First, the popular conservative blogger InstaPundit mentioned Brickley's campaign. Then a site called the American Scene said that Palin was "very appealing"; another, Stop the ACLU, described her as "a great choice." The traditional conservative media soon got in on the act: The *American Spectator* embraced Palin, and Rush Limbaugh, the radio host, praised her as "a babe."

Brickley's family, once evangelical Christians, now practice what he calls "Messianic Judaism." They believe that Jesus is the Messiah, but they also observe the Jewish holidays and attend synagogue; as Brickley puts it, "Jesus was Jewish, so to be like Him you need to be Jewish, too." Brickley said that "the hand of God" played a role in choosing Palin: "The longer I worked on it the less I felt I was driving it. Something else was at work."

Brickley is an authentic heartland voice, but he is also the product of an effort by wealthy conservative organizations in Washington to train activists. He has attended several workshops sponsored by the Leadership Institute, a group based in the Washington area and founded in 1979 by the Christian conservative activist Morton Blackwell. "I'm building a movement," Blackwell told me. Brickley also participated in a leadership summit held by Young America's Foundation (motto: "The Conservative Movement Starts Here") and was an intern at the Heritage Foundation. He currently lives in a dormitory, on Capitol Hill, run by the Heritage Foundation, and is an intern with townhall.com, a top conservative Web site.

While Brickley and others were spreading the word about Palin on the Internet, Palin was wooing a number of well-connected Washington conservative thinkers. In a stroke of luck, Palin did not have to go to the capital to meet these members of "the permanent political establishment"; they came to Alaska. Shortly after taking office, Palin received two memos from Paulette Simpson, the Alaska Federation of Republican Women leader, noting that two prominent conservative magazines—the *Weekly Standard*, owned by Rupert Murdoch's News Corporation, and *National Review*, founded by William F. Buckley Jr.—were planning luxury cruises to Alaska in the summer of 2007, which would make stops in Juneau. Writers and editors from these publications had been enlisted to deliver lectures to politically minded vacationers. "The governor was more than happy to meet these guys," Joe Balash, a special staff assistant to Palin, recalled.

On June 18, 2007, the first group disembarked in Juneau from the Holland America Line's MS *Oosterdam*, and went to the governor's mansion, a white wooden Colonial house with six two-story columns, for lunch. The contingent featured three of the *Weekly Standard*'s top writers: William Kristol, the magazine's Washington-based editor, who is also an op-ed columnist for the *New York Times* and a regular commentator on *Fox News Sunday*; Fred Barnes, the magazine's executive editor and the co-host of *The Beltway Boys*, a political talk show on Fox News; and Michael Gerson, the former chief speechwriter for President Bush and a *Washington Post* columnist.

By all accounts, the luncheon was a high-spirited, informal occasion. Kristol brought his wife and daughter; Gerson brought his wife and two children. Barnes, who brought his sister and his wife, sat on one side of Governor Palin, who presided at the head of the long table in the mansion's formal dining room; the Kristols sat on the other. Gerson was at the opposite end, as was Palin's chief of staff at the time, Mike Tibbles, who is now working for Senator Stevens's reelection campaign. The menu featured halibut cheeks—the choicest part of the fish. Before the meal, Palin delivered a lengthy grace. Simpson, who was at the luncheon, said, "I told a girlfriend afterwards, 'That was some grace!' It really set the tone." Joe Balash, Palin's assistant, who was also present, said, "There are not many politicians who will say grace with the conviction of faith she has. It's a daily part of her life."

Palin was joined by her lieutenant governor and by Alaska's attorney general. Also present was a local woman involved in upholding the Juneau school system's right to suspend a student who had displayed a satirical banner—"Bong Hits 4 Jesus"—across the street from his school. The student had sued the school district, on First Amendment grounds, and, at the time of the lunch, the case was before the Supreme Court. (The school district won.)

During the lunch, everyone was charmed when the governor's small daughter Piper popped in to inquire about dessert. Fred Barnes recalled being "struck by how smart Palin was, and how unusually confident. Maybe because she had been a beauty queen, and a star athlete, and succeeded at almost everything she had done." It didn't escape his notice, too, that she was "exceptionally pretty."

According to a former Alaska official who attended the lunch, the visitors wanted to do something "touristy," so a "flight-seeing" trip was arranged. Their destination was a gold mine in Berners Bay, some forty-five miles north of Juneau. For Palin and several staff members, the state leased two helicopters from a private company, Coastal, for two and a half hours, at a cost of $4,000. (The pundits paid for their own aircraft.) Palin explained that environmentalists had invoked the Clean Water Act to oppose a plan by a mining company, Coeur Alaska, to dump waste from the extraction of gold into a pristine lake in the Tongass National Forest. Palin rejected the environmentalists' claims. (The Ninth Circuit Court of Appeals ruled against Coeur Alaska, and the dispute is now before the Supreme Court.) Barnes was dazzled by Palin's handling of the hundred or so mineworkers who gathered to meet the group. "She clearly was not intimidated by crowds—or men!" he said. "She's got real star quality."

By the time the *Weekly Standard* pundits returned to the cruise ship, Paulette Simpson said, "they were very enamored of her." In July 2007, Barnes wrote the first major national article spotlighting Palin, titled "The Most Popular Governor," for the *Weekly Standard*. Simpson said, "That first article was the result of having lunch." Bitney agreed: "I don't think she realized the significance until after it was all over. It got the ball rolling."

The other journalists who met Palin offered similarly effusive praise: Michael Gerson called her "a mix between Annie Oakley and Joan of Arc." The most ardent promoter, however, was Kristol, and his enthusiasm became the talk of Alaska's political circles. According to Simpson, Senator Stevens told her that "Kristol was really pushing Palin" in Washington before McCain picked her. Indeed, as early as June 29, two months before McCain chose her, Kristol predicted on *Fox News Sunday* that "McCain's going to put Sarah Palin, the governor of Alaska, on the ticket." He described her as "fantastic," saying that she could go one-on-one against Obama in basketball, and possibly siphon off Hillary Clinton's supporters. He pointed out that she was a "mother of five" and a reformer. "Go for the gold here with Sarah Palin," he said. The moderator, Chris Wallace, finally had to ask Kristol, "Can we please get off Sarah Palin?"

The next day, however, Kristol was still talking about Palin on Fox. "She could be both an effective vice presidential candidate and an effective president," he said. "She's young, energetic." On a subsequent *Fox News Sunday*, Kristol again pushed Palin when asked whom McCain should pick: "Sarah Palin, whom I've only met once but I was awfully impressed by—a genuine reformer, defeated the establishment up there. It would be pretty wild to pick a young female Alaska governor, and I think, you know, McCain might as well go for it." On July 22, again on Fox, Kristol referred to Palin as "my heartthrob." He declared, "I don't know if I can make it through the next three months without her on the ticket." Reached last week, Kristol pointed out that just before McCain picked Palin he had ratcheted back his campaign a little; though he continued to tout her, he also wrote a *New York Times* column promoting Senator Joe Lieberman, of Connecticut.

On October 6, in another *Times* column, Kristol cryptically acknowledged having been entertained by the governor. He mentioned meeting Palin "in far more relaxed circumstances, in Alaska over a year ago." The column featured one of the few interviews that Palin has granted to the national media since becoming McCain's running mate. Kristol quoted Palin saying that the debate had been a "liberating" experience, then wrote, "Shouldn't the public get the benefit of another Biden-Palin debate, or even two? If there's difficulty finding a moderator, I'll be glad to volunteer."

On August 1, 2007, a few weeks after the *Weekly Standard* cruise departed from Juneau, Palin hosted a second boatload of pundits, this time from a cruise featuring associates of *National Review*. Her guests, arriving on the MS *Noordam*, included Rich Lowry, the magazine's editor and a syndicated columnist; Robert Bork, the conservative legal scholar and former federal judge; John Bolton, who served as the Bush administration's ambassador to the United Nations from 2004 to 2006; Victor Davis Hanson, a conservative historian who is reportedly a favorite of Vice President Dick Cheney; and Dick Morris, the ideologically ambidextrous political consultant, who writes a column for *The Hill* and appears regularly on Fox News.

As Jack Fowler, *National Review*'s publisher, recalled it, when the guest speakers were invited to come to a special reception at the governor's mansion, "We said, 'Sure!' There's only so much you can do in Juneau." The mansion itself, he said, was modest—"not exactly Newport." But the food was great, and included an impressive spread of salmon. Palin, who circulated nimbly through the room, and spoke admiringly of *National Review*, made a good impression. Fowler said, "This lady is something special. She connects. She's genuine. She doesn't look like what you'd expect. My thought was, Too bad she's way up there in Alaska, because she has potential, but to make things happen you have to know people."

Hanson, the historian, recalled Palin in high heels, "walking around this big Victorian house with rough Alaska floors, saying, 'Hi, I'm Sarah.' " She was "striking," he said. "She has that aura that Clinton, Reagan, and Jack Kennedy had—magnetism that comes through much more strongly when you're in the same room." He was delighted that Palin described herself as a fan of history, and as a reader of *National Review*'s Web site, for which he writes regularly. She spoke about the need to drill for oil in Alaska's protected wilderness areas, arguing that her husband had worked in nearby oil fields and knew firsthand that it wasn't environmentally hazardous. Hanson, a farm owner, found it appealing that she was married to an oil worker, rather than to an executive. Bolton, for his part, was pleased that Palin, a hunting enthusiast, was familiar with his efforts to stave off international controls on the global flow of small weapons. She spoke knowledgeably about missile defense, too, he said, and discussed his role, in 2001, in guiding the Bush administration's withdrawal from the Anti-Ballistic Missile Treaty. Jay Nordlinger, a senior editor at *National Review*, had a more elemental response. In an online column, he described Palin as "a former beauty-pageant contestant, and a real honey, too. Am I allowed to say that? Probably not, but too bad."

According to several accounts, however, no connection made that day was more meaningful than the one struck between Palin and Dick Morris. "He had this very long conversation with her," Fowler recalled. Lowry laughed in remembering it: "The joke going around was that he was going to take credit for making her." (Nordlinger's column went on to say, "Her political career will probably take her beyond Alaska. Dick Morris is only one who thinks so.")

In fact, in an admiring column published in the *Washington Post* two days after Palin was chosen, Morris wrote, "I will always remember taking her aside and telling her that she might one day be tapped to be vice president, given her record and the shortage of female political talent in the Republican Party. She will make one hell of a candidate, and hats off to McCain for picking her."

Morris offered Palin some advice during their encounter in Juneau, several of those present recollected, which he shared with the rest of the gathering in a short speech. As Lowry recalled it, Morris had warned her that a reformer, in order to be successful, needed to maintain her "outsider cred." In a similar vein, Simpson recalled that Morris "gave a little speech" in which he warned that "what happens to most people is that they campaign as outsiders, but when they get into power they turn into insiders. If you want to be successful, you have to stay an outsider."

Clearly, Palin has taken this advice to heart. Still, when the moment came for Morris and other guests to depart, Palin was sad to see the Washington insiders go. Hanson recalled, "She said, 'Hey—does anyone want to stay for dinner? We're going to eat right now.' She also invited everyone to come back the next day. 'If any of you are in the area, all you have to do is knock. Yell upstairs, I'll be right down.' "

By the end of February 2008, the chorus of conservative pundits for Palin was loud enough for the mainstream media to take note. Chris Cillizza, reporting for the Web site of the *Washington Post*, interviewed Palin and asked her if she'd accept an offer to be McCain's running mate. Though she dismissed the notion as a virtual "impossibility this go-round," Palin, who had been in office for only fourteen months, said, "Is it generally something that I would want to consider? Yes."

By the spring, the McCain campaign had reportedly sent scouts to Alaska to start vetting Palin as a possible running mate. A week or so before McCain named her, however, sources close to the campaign say, McCain was intent on naming his fellow senator Joe Lieberman, an independent, who left the Democratic Party in 2006. David Keene, the chairman of the American Conservative Union, who is close to a number of McCain's top aides, told me that "McCain and Lindsey Graham"—the South Carolina senator, who has been McCain's closest campaign companion—"really wanted Joe." But Keene believed that "McCain was scared off" in the final days, after warnings from his advisers that choosing Lieberman would ignite a contentious floor fight at the convention, as social conservatives revolted against Lieberman for being, among other things, pro-choice.

"They took it away from him," a longtime friend of McCain—who asked not to be identified, since the campaign has declined to discuss its selection process—said of the advisers. "He was furious. He was pissed. It wasn't what he wanted." Another friend disputed this, characterizing McCain's mood as one of "understanding resignation."

With just days to go before the convention, the choices were slim. Karl Rove favored McCain's former rival Mitt Romney, but enough animus lingered from the primaries that McCain rejected the pairing. "I told Romney not to wait by the phone, because 'he doesn't like you,' " Keene, who favored the choice, said. "With John McCain, all politics is personal." Other possible choices—such as former Representative Rob Portman, of Ohio, or Governor Tim Pawlenty, of Minnesota—seemed too conventional. They did not transmit McCain's core message that he was a "maverick." Finally, McCain's top aides, including Steve Schmidt and Rick Davis, converged on Palin. Ed Rogers, the chairman of BGR, a well-connected, largely Republican lobbying firm, said, "Her criteria kept popping out. She was a governor—that's good. The shorter the Washington résumé the better. A female is better still. And then there was her story." He admitted, "There was concern that she was a novice." In addition to Schmidt and Davis, Charles R. Black Jr., the lobbyist and political operative who is McCain's chief campaign adviser, reportedly favored Palin. Keene said, "I'm told that Charlie Black told McCain, 'If you pick anyone else, you're going to lose. But if you pick Palin you may win.' "(Black did not return calls for comment.) Meanwhile, McCain's longtime friend said, "Kristol was out there shaking the pom-poms."

McCain had met Palin once, but their conversation— at a reception during a meeting of the National Governors Association, six months earlier—had lasted only fifteen minutes. "It wasn't a real conversation," said the longtime friend, who called the choice of Palin "the fucking most ridiculous thing I've ever heard." Aides arranged a phone call between McCain and Palin, and scrutinized her answers to some seventy items on a questionnaire that she had filled out. But McCain didn't talk with Palin in person again until the morning of Thursday, August 28. Palin was flown down to his retreat in Sedona, Arizona, and they spoke for an hour or two. By the time he announced her as his choice, the next day, he had spent less than three hours in her company.

"It certainly was a risk—a risk a lot of people wouldn't take," Dan Coats, a former Indiana senator and now a volunteer with the McCain campaign, said. "But that's what I like about John. There's a boldness there."

The thoroughness of the campaign's vetting process, overseen by the Washington lawyer and former White House counsel Arthur B. Culvahouse Jr., remains in dispute. The campaign insists that Palin's record and personal history were carefully examined. (Culvahouse declined to comment for this story.) The *Los Angeles Times*, however, reported that the campaign never contacted several obvious sources of information on Palin, including Lyda Green—a Republican state senator in Alaska, and a former ally turned opponent. Also in dispute is whether Palin disclosed to the campaign, as she and officials have said, that her unwed teenage daughter was pregnant. "I am a hundred percent sure they didn't know," McCain's longtime friend said. Another campaign source, however, insisted that McCain's team knew about the pregnancy.

The selection of Palin thrilled the Republican base, and the pundits who met with her in Juneau have remained unflagging in their support. But a surprising number of conservative thinkers have declared her unfit for the vice presidency. Peggy Noonan, the *Wall Street Journal* columnist, recently wrote, "The Palin candidacy is a symptom and expression of a new vulgarization in American politics. It's no good, not for conservatism and not for the country. And yes, it is a mark against John McCain." David Brooks, the *New York Times* columnist, has called Palin "a fatal cancer to the Republican Party." Christopher Buckley, the son of *National Review*'s late founder, defected to the Obama camp two weeks ago, in part because of his dismay over Palin. Matthew Dowd, the former Bush campaign strategist turned critic of the president, said recently that McCain "knows in his gut" that Palin isn't qualified for the job, "and when this race is over, that is something he will have to live with.... He put the country at risk."

Palin initially provided the McCain campaign with a boost, but polls now suggest that she has become a liability. A top Republican close to the campaign said that McCain's aides have largely kept faith with Palin. They have been impressed by her work ethic, and by what a quick study she is. According to the Republican close to the campaign, she has sometimes discomfited advisers by travelling with a big family entourage. "It kind of changes the dynamic of a meeting to have them all in the room," he told me. John McCain's comfort level with Palin is harder to gauge. In the view of the longtime McCain friend, "John's personal comfort level is low with everyone right now. He's angry. But it was his choice."

Palin: Wrong Woman, Wrong Message

Gloria Steinem

Here's the good news: Women have become so politically
powerful that even the antifeminist right wing—the folks
with a headlock on the Republican Party—are trying
to appease the gender gap with a first-ever female vice
president. We owe this to women—and to many men too—
who have picketed, gone on hunger strikes, or confronted
violence at the polls so women can vote. We owe it to Shirley
Chisholm, who first took the "white-male-only" sign off the
White House, and to Hillary Rodham Clinton, who hung in
there through ridicule and misogyny to win 18 million votes.

But here is even better news: It won't work. This isn't
the first time a boss has picked an unqualified woman just
because she agrees with him and opposes everything most
other women want and need. Feminism has never been
about getting a job for one woman. It's about making life
more fair for women everywhere. It's not about a piece of
the existing pie; there are too many of us for that. It's about
baking a new pie.

Selecting Sarah Palin, who was touted all summer by
Rush Limbaugh, is no way to attract most women, including
die-hard Clinton supporters. Palin shares nothing but a
chromosome with Clinton. Her down-home, divisive, and
deceptive speech did nothing to cosmeticize a Republican
convention that has more than twice as many male delegates
as female, a presidential candidate who is owned and
operated by the right wing, and a platform that opposes
pretty much everything Clinton's candidacy stood for—and
that Barack Obama's still does. To vote in protest for McCain/
Palin would be like saying, "Somebody stole my shoes, so I'll
amputate my legs."

This is not to beat up on Palin. I defend her right to be wrong, even on issues that matter most to me. I regret that people say she can't do the job because she has children in need of care, especially if they wouldn't say the same about a father. I get no pleasure from imagining her in the spotlight on national and foreign policy issues about which she has zero background, with one month to learn to compete with Senator Joe Biden's thirty-seven years' experience.

Palin has been honest about what she doesn't know. When asked last month about the vice presidency, she said, "I still can't answer that question until someone answers for me: What is it exactly that the VP does every day?" When asked about Iraq, she said, "I haven't really focused much on the war in Iraq."

She was elected governor largely because the incumbent was unpopular, and she's won over Alaskans mostly by using unprecedented oil wealth to give a $1,200 rebate to every resident. Now she is being praised by McCain's campaign as a tax cutter, despite the fact that Alaska has no state income or sales tax. Perhaps McCain has opposed affirmative action for so long that he doesn't know it's about inviting more people to meet standards, not lowering them. Or perhaps McCain is following the Bush administration habit, as in the Justice Department, of putting a job candidate's views on "God, guns, and gays" ahead of competence. The difference is that McCain is filling a job one seventy-two-year-old heartbeat away from the presidency.

So let's be clear: The culprit is John McCain. He may have chosen Palin out of change-envy, or a belief that women can't tell the difference between form and content, but the main motive was to please right-wing ideologues; the same ones who nixed anyone who is now or ever has been a supporter of reproductive freedom. If that were not the case,

McCain could have chosen a woman who knows what a vice president does and who has thought about Iraq; someone like Texas senator Kay Bailey Hutchison or Senator Olympia Snowe of Maine. McCain could have taken a baby step away from right-wing patriarchs who determine his actions, right down to opposing the Violence Against Women Act.

Palin's value to those patriarchs is clear: She opposes just about every issue that women support by a majority or plurality. She believes that creationism should be taught in public schools but disbelieves global warming; she opposes gun control but supports government control of women's wombs; she opposes stem cell research but approves "abstinence-only" programs, which increase unwanted births, sexually transmitted diseases, and abortions; she tried to use taxpayers' millions for a state program to shoot wolves from the air but didn't spend enough money to fix a state school system with the lowest high-school graduation rate in the nation; she runs with a candidate who opposes the Fair Pay Act but supports $500 million in subsidies for a natural gas pipeline across Alaska; she supports drilling in the Arctic National Wildlife Reserve, though even McCain has opted for the lesser evil of offshore drilling. She is Phyllis Schlafly, only younger.

I don't doubt her sincerity. As a lifetime member of the National Rifle Association, she doesn't just support killing animals from helicopters, she does it herself. She doesn't just talk about increasing the use of fossil fuels but puts a coal-burning power plant in her own small town. She doesn't just echo McCain's pledge to criminalize abortion by overturning *Roe v. Wade*, she says that if one of her daughters were impregnated by rape or incest, she should bear the child. She not only opposes reproductive freedom as a human right but implies that it dictates abortion, without saying that it also protects the right to have a child.

So far, the major new McCain supporter that Palin has attracted is James Dobson of Focus on the Family. Of course, for Dobson, "women are merely waiting for their husbands to assume leadership," so he may be voting for Palin's husband.

Being a hope-aholic, however, I can see two long-term bipartisan gains from this contest.

Republicans may learn they can't appeal to right-wing patriarchs and most women at the same time. A loss in November could cause the centrist majority of Republicans to take back their party, which was the first to support the Equal Rights Amendment and should be the last to want to invite government into the wombs of women.

And American women, who suffer more because of having two full-time jobs than from any other single injustice, finally have support on a national stage from male leaders who know that women can't be equal outside the home until men are equal in it. Barack Obama and Joe Biden are campaigning on their belief that men should be, can be, and want to be at home for their children.

This could be huge.

2/ HALF-BAKED ALASKA
Palin's Real Record

Meet Sarah Palin's Radical Right-Wing Pals
Max Blumenthal and David Neiwert

On the afternoon of September 24 in downtown Palmer, Alaska, as the sun began to sink behind the snowcapped mountains that flank the picturesque Mat-Su Valley, fifty-one-year-old Mark Chryson sat for an hour on a park bench, reveling in tales of his days as chairman of the Alaskan Independence Party. The stocky, gray-haired computer technician waxed nostalgic about quixotic battles to eliminate taxes, support the "traditional family," and secede from the United States.

So long as Alaska remained under the boot of the federal government, said Chryson, the AIP had to stand on guard to stymie a New World Order. He invited a Salon reporter to see a few items inside his pickup truck that were intended for his personal protection. "This here is my attack dog," he said with a chuckle, handing the reporter an exuberant eight-pound papillon from his passenger seat. "Her name is Suzy." Then he pulled a nine-millimeter Makarov PM pistol—once the standard-issue sidearm for Soviet cops—out of his glove compartment. "I've got enough weaponry to raise a small army in my basement," he said, clutching the gun in his palm. "Then again, so do most Alaskans." But Chryson added a message of reassurance to residents of that faraway place some Alaskans call "the 48." "We want to go our separate ways," he said, "but we are not going to kill you."

Though Chryson belongs to a fringe political party, one that advocates the secession of Alaska from the Union, and that organizes with other like-minded secessionist movements from Canada to the Deep South, he is not without peculiar influence in state politics, especially the rise of Sarah Palin. An obscure figure outside of Alaska, Chryson has been a political fixture in the hometown of the Republican vice presidential nominee for over a decade. During the 1990s, when Chryson directed the AIP, he and another radical right-winger, Steve Stoll, played a quiet but pivotal role in electing Palin as mayor of Wasilla and shaping her political agenda afterward. Both Stoll and Chryson not only contributed to Palin's campaign financially, they played major behind-the-scenes roles in the Palin camp before, during, and after her victory.

Palin backed Chryson as he successfully advanced a host of anti-tax, pro-gun initiatives, including one that altered the state constitution's language to better facilitate the formation of antigovernment militias. She joined in their vendetta against several local officials they disliked, and listened to their advice about hiring. She attempted to name Stoll, a John Birch Society activist known in the Mat-Su Valley as Black Helicopter Steve, to an empty Wasilla City Council seat. "Every time I showed up her door was open," said Chryson. "And that policy continued when she became governor."

When Chryson first met Sarah Palin, however, he didn't really trust her politically. It was the early 1990s, when he was a member of a local libertarian pressure group called SAGE, or Standing Against Government Excess. (SAGE's founder, Tammy McGraw, was Palin's birth coach.) Palin was a leader in a pro-sales-tax citizens' group called WOW, or Watch Over Wasilla, earning a political credential before her 1992 campaign for city council. Though he was impressed by her interpersonal skills, Chryson greeted Palin's election warily, thinking she was too close to the Democrats on the council and too pro-tax.

But soon, Palin and Chryson discovered they could be useful to each other. Palin would be running for mayor, while

Chryson was about to take over the chairmanship of the Alaskan Independence Party, which at its peak in 1990 had managed to elect a governor.

The AIP was born of the vision of "Old Joe" Vogler, a hard-bitten former gold miner who hated the government of the United States almost as much as he hated wolves and environmentalists. His resentment peaked during the early 1970s when the federal government began installing Alaska's oil and gas pipeline. Fueled by raw rage—"The United States has made a colony of Alaska," he told author John McPhee in 1977—Vogler declared a maverick candidacy for the governorship in 1982. Though he lost, Old Joe became a force to be reckoned with, as well as a constant source of amusement for Alaska's political class. During a gubernatorial debate in 1982, Vogler proposed using nuclear weapons to obliterate the glaciers blocking roadways to Juneau. "There's gold under there!" he exclaimed.

Vogler made another failed run for the governor's mansion in 1986. But the AIP's fortunes shifted suddenly four years later when Vogler convinced Richard Nixon's former interior secretary, Wally Hickel, to run for governor under his party's banner. Hickel coasted to victory, out-flanking a moderate Republican and a centrist Democrat. An archconservative Republican running under the AIP candidate, Jack Coghill, was elected lieutenant governor.

Hickel's subsequent failure as governor to press for a vote on Alaskan independence rankled Old Joe. With sponsorship from the Islamic Republic of Iran, Vogler was scheduled to present his case for Alaskan secession before the United Nations General Assembly in the late spring of 1993. But before he could, Old Joe's long, strange political career ended tragically that May when he was murdered by a fellow secessionist.

Hickel rejoined the Republican Party the year after Vogler's death and didn't run for reelection. Lieutenant Governor Coghill's campaign to succeed him as the AIP candidate for governor ended in disaster; he peeled away just enough votes from the Republican, Jim Campbell, to throw the gubernatorial election to Democrat Tony Knowles.

Despite the disaster, Coghill hung on as AIP chairman for three more years. When he was asked to resign in 1997, Mark Chryson replaced him. Chryson pursued a dual policy of cozying up to secessionist and right-wing groups in Alaska and elsewhere while also attempting to replicate the AIP's success with Hickel in infiltrating the mainstream.

Unlike some radical right-wingers, Chryson doesn't put forward his ideas freighted with anger or paranoia. And in a state where defense of gun and property rights often takes on a real religious fervor, Chryson was able to present himself as a typical Alaskan.

He rose through party ranks by reducing the AIP's platform to a single page that "90 percent of Alaskans could agree with." This meant scrubbing the old platform of what Chryson called "racist language" while accommodating the state's growing Christian right movement by emphasizing the AIP's commitment to the "traditional family."

"The AIP is very family-oriented," Chryson explained. "We're for the traditional family—daddy, mommy, kids— because we all know that it was Adam and Eve, not Adam and Steve. And we don't care if Heather has two mommies. That's not a traditional family."

Chryson further streamlined the AIP's platform by softening its secessionist language. Instead of calling for immediate separation from the United States, the platform now demands a vote on independence.

Yet Chryson maintains that his party remains committed to full independence. "The Alaskan Independence Party has got links to almost every independence-minded movement in the world," Chryson exclaimed. "And Alaska is not the only place that's about separation. There's at least thirty different states that are talking about some type of separation from the United States."

This has meant rubbing shoulders and forging alliances with outright white supremacists and far-right theocrats, particularly those who dominate the proceedings at such gatherings as the North American Secessionist conventions, which AIP delegates have attended in recent years. The AIP's affiliation with neo-Confederate organizations is motivated as much by ideological affinity as by organizational convenience. Indeed, Chryson makes no secret of his sympathy for the Lost Cause. "Should the Confederate states have been allowed to separate and go their peaceful ways?" Chryson asked rhetorically. "Yes. The War of Northern Aggression, or the Civil War, or the War between the States—however you want to refer to it—was not about slavery, it was about states' rights."

Another far-right organization with whom the AIP has long been aligned is Howard Phillips's militia-minded Constitution Party. The AIP has been listed as the Constitution Party's state affiliate since the late 1990s, and it has endorsed the Constitution Party's presidential candidates (Michael Peroutka and Chuck Baldwin) in the past two elections.

The Constitution Party boasts an openly theocratic platform that reads, "It is our goal to limit the federal government to its delegated, enumerated, Constitutional functions and to restore American jurisprudence to its original Biblical common-law foundations." In its 1990s incarnation as the U.S. Taxpayers Party, it was on the front lines in promoting the "militia" movement, and a significant portion of its membership comprises former and current militia members.

At its 1992 convention, the AIP hosted both Phillips—the USTP's presidential candidate—and militia-movement leader Colonel James "Bo" Gritz, who was campaigning for president under the banner of the far-right Populist Party. According to Chryson, AIP regulars heavily supported Gritz, but the party deferred to Phillips's presence and issued no official endorsements.

In Wasilla, the AIP became powerful by proxy—because of Chryson and Stoll's alliance with Sarah Palin. Chryson and Stoll had found themselves in constant opposition to policies of Wasilla's Democratic mayor, who started his three-term, nine-year tenure in 1987. By 1992, Chryson and Stoll had begun convening regular protests outside city council meetings. Their demonstrations invariably involved grievances against any and all forms of "socialist government," from city planning to public education. Stoll shared Chryson's conspiratorial views: "The rumor was that he had wrapped his guns in plastic and buried them in his yard so he could get them after the New World Order took over," Stein told a reporter.

Chryson did not trust Palin when she joined the city council in 1992. He claimed that she was handpicked by Democratic city council leaders and by Wasilla's Democratic mayor, John Stein, to rubber-stamp their tax-hike proposals. "When I first met her," he said, "I thought she was extremely left. But I've watched her slowly as she's become more pronounced in her conservative ideology."

Palin was well aware of Chryson's views. "She knew my beliefs," Chryson said. "The entire state knew my beliefs.

I wasn't afraid of being on the news, on camera speaking my views."

But Chryson believes she trusted his judgment because he accurately predicted what life on the city council would be like. "We were telling her, 'This is probably what's going to happen,' " he said. " 'The city is going to give this many people raises, they're going to pave everybody's roads, and they're going to pave the city council members' roads.' We couldn't have scripted it better because everything we predicted came true."

After intense evangelizing by Chryson and his allies, they claimed Palin as a convert. "When she started taking her job seriously," Chryson said, "the people who put her in as the rubber stamp found out the hard way that she was not going to go their way." In 1994, Sarah Palin attended the AIP's statewide convention. In 1995, her husband, Todd, changed his voter registration to AIP. Except for an interruption of a few months, he would remain registered was an AIP member until 2002, when he changed his registration to undeclared.

In 1996, Palin decided to run against John Stein as the Republican candidate for mayor of Wasilla. While Palin pushed back against Stein's policies, particularly those related to funding public works, Chryson said he and Steve Stoll prepared the groundwork for her mayoral campaign.

Chryson and Stoll viewed Palin's ascendancy as a vehicle for their own political ambitions. "She got support from these guys," Stein remarked. "I think smart politicians never utter those kind of radical things, but they let other people do it for them. I never recall Sarah saying she supported the militia or taking a public stand like that. But these guys were definitely behind Sarah, thinking she was the more conservative choice."

"They worked behind the scenes," said Stein. "I think they had a lot of influence in terms of helping with the backscatter negative campaigning."

Indeed, Chryson boasted that he and his allies urged Palin to focus her campaign on slashing, character-based attacks. For instance, Chryson advised Palin to paint Stein as a sexist who had told her "to just sit there and look pretty" while she served on Wasilla's city council. Though Palin never made this accusation, her 1996 campaign for mayor was the most negative Wasilla residents had ever witnessed.

While Palin played up her total opposition to the sales tax and gun control—the two hobgoblins of the AIP—mailers spread throughout the town portraying her as "the Christian candidate," a subtle suggestion that Stein, who is Lutheran, might be Jewish. "I watched that campaign unfold, bringing a level of slime our community hadn't seen until then," recalled Phil Munger, a local music teacher who counts himself as a close friend of Stein.

"This same group [Stoll and Chryson] also [publicly] challenged me on whether my wife and I were married because she had kept her maiden name," Stein bitterly recalled. "So we literally had to produce a marriage certificate. And as I recall, they said, 'Well, you could have forged that.' "

When Palin won the election, the men who had once shouted antigovernment slogans outside city hall now had a foothold inside the mayor's office. Palin attempted to pay back her newfound pals during her first city council meeting as mayor. In that meeting, on October 14, 1996, she appointed Stoll to one of the city council's two newly vacant seats. But Palin was blocked by the single vote of then-councilman Nick Carney, who had endured countless rancorous confrontations with Stoll and considered him a "violent" influence on local politics. Though Palin considered consulting attorneys about finding another means of placing Stoll on the council, she was ultimately forced to back down and accept a compromise candidate.

Emboldened by his nomination by Mayor Palin, Stoll later demanded she fire Wasilla's museum director, John Cooper, a personal enemy he longed to sabotage. Palin obliged, eliminating Cooper's position in short order. "Gotcha, Cooper!" Stoll told the deposed museum director after his termination, as Cooper told a reporter for the *New York Times*. "And it only cost me a campaign contribution." Stoll, who donated $1,000 to Palin's mayoral campaign, did not respond to numerous requests for an interview. Palin has blamed budget concerns for Cooper's departure.

The following year, when Carney proposed a local gun-control measure, Palin organized with Chryson to smother the nascent plan in its cradle. Carney's proposed ordinance would have prohibited residents from carrying guns into schools, bars, hospitals, government offices, and playgrounds. Infuriated by the proposal that Carney viewed as a common-sense public-safety measure, Chryson and seven allies stormed a July 1997 council meeting.

With the bill still in its formative stages, Carney was not even ready to present it to the council, let alone conduct public hearings on it. He and other council members objected to the ad hoc hearing as "a waste of time." But Palin—in plain violation of council rules and norms—insisted that Chryson testify, stating, according to the minutes, that "she invites the public to speak on any issue at any time."

When Carney tried later in the meeting to have the ordinance discussed officially at the following regular council meeting, he couldn't even get a second. His proposal died that night, thanks to Palin and her extremist allies.

"A lot of it was the ultraconservative far right that is against everything in government, including taxes," recalled Carney. "A lot of it was a personal attack on me as being anti-gun, and a personal attack on anybody who deigned to threaten their authority to carry a loaded firearm wherever they pleased. That was the tenor of it. And it was being choreographed by Steve Stoll and the mayor."

Asked if he thought it was Palin who had instigated the turnout, he replied: "I know it was."

By Chryson's account, he and Palin also worked hand-in-glove to slash property taxes and block a state proposal that would have taken money for public programs from the Permanent Fund Dividend, or the oil and gas fund that doles out annual payments to citizens of Alaska. Palin endorsed Chryson's unsuccessful initiative to move the state legislature from Juneau to Wasilla. She also lent her support to Chryson's crusade to alter the Alaska constitution's language on gun rights so cities and counties could not impose their own restrictions. "It took over ten years to get that language written in," Chryson said. "But Sarah [Palin] was there supporting it."

"With Sarah as a mayor," said Chryson, "there were a number of times when I just showed up at city hall and said, 'Hey, Sarah, we need help.' I think there was only one time when I wasn't able to talk to her, and that was because she was in a meeting."

Chryson says the door remains open now that Palin is governor. (Palin's office did not respond to Salon's request for an interview.) While Palin has been more circumspect in her dealings with groups like the AIP as she has risen through the political ranks, she has stayed in touch.

When Palin ran for governor in 2006, marketing herself as a fresh-faced reformer determined to crush the GOP's ossified power structure, she made certain to appear at the AIP's state convention. To burnish her maverick image, she also tapped one-time AIP member and born-again Republican Walter Hickel as her campaign co-chair. Hickel barnstormed the state for Palin, hailing her support for an "all-Alaska" liquefied gas pipeline, a project first promoted in 2002 by an AIP gubernatorial candidate named Nels Anderson. When Palin delivered her victory speech on election night, Hickel stood beaming by her side. "I made her governor," he boasted afterward. Two years later, Hickel has endorsed Palin's bid for vice president.

Just months before Palin burst onto the national stage as McCain's vice presidential nominee, she delivered a videotaped address to the AIP's annual convention. Her message was scrupulously free of secessionist rhetoric, but complimentary nonetheless. "I share your party's vision of upholding the constitution of our great state," Palin told the assembly of AIP delegates. "My administration remains focused on reining in government growth so individual liberty can expand. I know you agree with that…. Keep up the good work and God bless you."

When Palin became the Republican vice presidential nominee, her attendance at the 1994 and 2006 AIP conventions and her husband's membership in the party (as well as Palin's videotaped welcome to the AIP's 2008 convention) generated a minor controversy. Chryson claimed, however, that Sarah and Todd Palin never even played a minor role in his party's internal affairs. "Sarah's never been a member of the Alaskan Independence Party," Chryson insisted. "Todd has, but most of rural Alaska has too. I never saw him at a meeting. They were at one meeting I was at. Sarah said hello, but I didn't pay attention because I was taking care of business."

But whether the Palins participated directly in shaping the AIP's program is less relevant than the extent to which they will implement that program. Chryson and his allies have demonstrated just as much interest in grooming major party candidates as they have in putting forward their own people. At a national convention of secessionist groups in 2007, AIP vice chairman Dexter Clark announced that his party would seek to "infiltrate" the Democratic and Republican parties with candidates sympathetic to its hard-right, secessionist agenda. "You should use that tactic. You should infiltrate," Clark told his audience of neo-Confederates, theocrats, and libertarians. "Whichever party you think in that area you can get something done, get into that party. Even though that party has its problems, right now that is the only avenue."

Clark pointed to Palin's political career as the model of a successful infiltration. "There's a lot of talk of her moving up," Clark said of Palin. "She was a member [of the AIP] when she was mayor of a small town, that was a nonpartisan job. But to get along and to go along she switched to the Republican Party.... She is pretty well sympathetic because of her membership."

Clark's assertion that Palin was once a card-carrying AIP member was swiftly discredited by the McCain campaign, which produced records showing she had been a registered Republican since 1988. But then why would Clark make such a statement? Why did he seem confident that Palin was a true-blue AIP activist burrowing within the Republican Party? The most salient answer is that Palin was once so thoroughly embedded with AIP figures like Chryson and Stoll and seemed so enthusiastic about their agenda, Clark may have simply assumed she belonged to his party.

Now, Palin is a household name and her every move is scrutinized by the Washington press corps. She can no longer afford to kibitz with secessionists, however instrumental they may have been to her meteoric ascendancy. This does not trouble her old AIP allies. Indeed, Chryson is hopeful that Palin's inauguration will also represent the start of a new infiltration.

"I've had my issues, but she's still staying true to her core values," Chryson concluded. "Sarah's friends don't all agree with her, but do they respect her? Do they respect her ideology and her values? Definitely."

Palin's Party: Her Religious Right Roots
Michelle Goldberg

Wasilla, Alaska

Pat O'Hara, a journalist who served on the Wasilla school board for twelve years, remembers how the religious right made her feel like a stranger in her own community. The Mat-Su Valley, which includes the neighboring towns of Wasilla and Palmer, had once been a libertarian sort of place, full of blue-collar individualists who didn't fit in elsewhere. "I had the dog team in the woods, the cabin in the woods. My friends were teachers, farmers, construction workers," she said as she stood with about 1,500 demonstrators at a September 13, 2008, anti–Sarah Palin rally in Anchorage. "It was kind of a working, very much Democratic community. And then it changed."

The Valley, Alaska's fastest-growing region, is a spectacular area of lakes and birch and spruce forests, surrounded by granite-colored snowcapped mountains that poke through the clouds. Palmer has a community core, a walkable few blocks with a lively coffee shop, Vagabond Blues. Wasilla, though, has developed as a sprawl of strip malls containing a mix of pawnshops, gun shops, and chain stores—and, incongruously, a decent sushi place, with a Korean chef from California. It is a little piece of the American South near the North Pole, rough-hewn but slowly upscaling.

It wasn't until the 1990s that local churches like the Wasilla Assembly of God, which Palin grew up attending, became aggressively political. A few years before Palin became mayor, a group of preachers confronted the school board with questions about social issues that had never before surfaced in local politics, according to O'Hara, who wrote first for the *Mat-Su Valley Frontiersman* and then for the *Anchorage Daily News.* "They started asking me, 'Would you allow a homosexual to teach in schools?' and 'Do you favor abortion?' " she said. "At the time, I didn't know what was coming. I said, 'This is not a school board issue. We have overcrowding. We have funding problems.' " The last time O'Hara ran, conservative pastors mounted an effort to defeat her, saying she favored hiring homosexuals, but they failed. Nevertheless, in 1996, feeling increasingly alienated in a place she'd lived for twenty-five years, she quit the school board and moved to more liberal Anchorage.

"The whole community changed," she said. "It became extremely rigid and intolerant, and you can see that in every election since." Palin, said O'Hara, "represents the worst of those values. She feels that because she's a member of the right church, she's chosen by God to inflict her values on everyone."

With her vice presidential nomination, Sarah Palin has become the ultimate religious-right success story. Ever since the Christian Coalition was formed using the infrastructure of Pat Robertson's 1988 presidential run, the movement has focused on building power from the ground up, turning conservative churches into little political machines. "I would rather have a thousand school board members than one president and no school board members," Christian Coalition head Ralph Reed said in 1996. Palin, who got her start in a local church-backed political struggle, is very much the product of Reed's strategy.

She has not always governed as a zealot; in fact, she's a bit of a cipher, with scant record of speeches or writings on social issues or foreign policy. Nevertheless, several people who've dealt with her say that those concerned about church-state separation should be chilled by the idea of a Palin presidency. "To understand Sarah Palin, you have to realize that she is a religious fundamentalist," said Howard Bess, a retired liberal Baptist minister living in Palmer. "The structure of her understanding of life is no different from a Muslim fundamentalist."

Palin's nomination, and the energy she has injected into the GOP, show that, once again, reports of the death of the Christian right have been greatly exaggerated. Not long ago, pundits and journalists were lining up to explain how the religious right, long the largest and best-organized faction in the Republican Party, was deteriorating. Last year the liberal evangelical Jim Wallis published a piece in *Time* headlined "The Religious Right's Era Is Over." Several months later the *New York Times Magazine* followed with a cover story titled "The Evangelical Crackup." Liberal columnist E. J. Dionne argued, in his book *Souled Out: Reclaiming Faith and Politics after the Religious Right,* that the movement was collapsing.

Obviously the religious right has endured many setbacks in recent years. Ted Haggard, former head of the National Association of Evangelicals, slunk away in disgrace following a scandal involving a gay prostitute and crystal meth. Ralph Reed was tainted by his association with the extravagantly corrupt lobbyist Jack Abramoff. Jerry Falwell died, as did the influential Florida televangelist D. James Kennedy. Tom DeLay, one of the movement's fiercest allies, left Congress after being indicted on charges of criminal conspiracy. Nonetheless, the Republican Party is actually more dependent on religious conservatives than ever.
In the 2006 midterms, the most significant GOP defeats were among moderate Republicans from the Northeast, where the party lost almost a third of its House seats, and from the Midwest, where it lost 15 percent. As moderates and independents abandoned the party, its center of gravity moved rightward. In order to maintain the support of the

party that reluctantly nominated him, John McCain had to choose a vice president who represented the base. Indeed, never before has someone with such deep roots in the movement been on a major party ticket.

It's a familiar pattern: The Christian right often has its greatest triumphs just after it's been pronounced moribund. In 1999, just as the Christian right was about to achieve unprecedented power in the Bush administration, *The Economist* wrote, "The armies of righteousness, which once threatened to overwhelm the Republican Party, are downcast and despondent." One could have written the same thing last month. Now, as then, the movement has been resurrected. At the recent Values Voter Summit, a religious-right gathering in Washington, D.C., sponsored by the Family Research Council, attendees were ebullient. "The surge of energy is unbelievable," said Emily Buchanan, executive director of the Susan B. Anthony List, a PAC that supports antiabortion candidates and aims to mobilize antiabortion women. "Sarah Palin is going to be our poster woman," she said. "She represents exactly what we've been trying to do since we were founded in 1992."

Palin—who opposes gay rights, believes abortion should be banned even in cases of rape and incest, and supports the teaching of creationism—wasn't known as a leader in Alaska's religious right, but she clearly had ties to it, and to some of the more extreme fundamentalists in the United States. As has been widely reported, her husband, Todd, was a member of the separatist Alaskan Independence Party. She reportedly attended the party's 1994 convention, and as governor she gave a video address to the group's gathering this year in Fairbanks. Less well-known are the Alaskan Independence Party's ties to the theocratic Constitution Party—a vice chair of the former is the state representative for the latter. According to its platform, the Constitution Party aims "to restore American jurisprudence to its Biblical foundations" and advocates criminalizing gay sex and abolishing Social Security.

When Palin ran for mayor in 1996, she leveraged the support of the religious conservatives. Wasilla mayoral races are nonpartisan and in the past had been focused on local issues like taxes and policing. In her challenge to Republican mayor John Stein, Palin changed that, touting her opposition to abortion, her religion, and her support for gun rights. "She got a lot of help from the Christian groups," said Curt Menard, mayor of Mat-Su Borough (which includes Wasilla). "They came out and did telephone polling and things like that."

Menard and his wife, Republican state senate candidate Linda Menard—the former director of the Miss Wasilla pageant—have known Palin since she was in third grade. She was a classmate and close friend of their late son, who, before he died in a 2001 plane crash, was the godfather of Palin's son Track. Their families attend the same church—Wasilla Bible Church, which Palin joined in 2002—and the Menards are caring for Palin's dog, Agia, named after Palin's proudest legislative accomplishment, the Alaska Gasline Inducement Act, while she is on the campaign trail. They clearly adore Palin, and when Curt Menard describes her connections to the religious right, he doesn't intend to be critical.

Echoing Pat O'Hara's account, Menard recalled that the area had been solidly Democratic until the rise of politicized right-wing religion. "Pat Robertson, when he organized the Christian right... that's when this area really changed," he said. "To my knowledge, I would say [Palin] was supportive of the movement," he added, though he said she wasn't at the forefront of it.

Nevertheless, the movement was at the forefront of her mayoral campaign. According to Stein, a national anti-abortion organization sent out postcards to Wasilla voters on Palin's behalf. There was a whisper campaign that Stein, a Lutheran, was actually Jewish. Some Palin supporters suggested that Stein and his wife, Karen Marie, weren't really married because they didn't have the same last name. "We had to produce a marriage certificate just to demonstrate that," said Stein. "I believe that was Sarah's campaign committee who brought that up."

Much has been made of Palin's gestures toward book-banning as mayor. To understand what happened, it's useful to realize that the Mat-Su Valley was in the middle of a roiling controversy over a book by Bess, the retired minister, titled *Pastor, I Am Gay*. Bess, 80, is deeply respected by the Valley's small progressive community. Educated at Northwestern's Garrett Biblical Institute—now called the Garrett Evangelical Theological Seminary—he comes from a Baptist tradition committed to church-state separation. In 1980 he left his church in Santa Barbara, California, to become pastor of Anchorage First American Baptist. Over the years Bess developed an intense concern about gay rights, and he went out of his way to welcome gay people into his Anchorage church. After he had served seven years at First Baptist, the board of the church asked him to lower his profile on the issue. Unwilling to do so, he resigned, took early retirement and ended up moving to Palmer to pastor a tiny liberal congregation, the Church of the Covenant, which he did without pay.

Bess published *Pastor, I Am Gay* in 1995. It recounts his experiences ministering to gay men and lesbians, calls for the church to take a stand against discrimination, and even draws parallels between the experience of gay people and that of Jesus. "They are despised and rejected," he wrote. "They suffer and are acquainted with infirmity. They are rejected by a perversion of justice.... Is it possible that the will of the Lord will prosper through them?"

Local conservatives, including at Wasilla Assembly of God, mobilized against the book. Christian bookstores as well as secular retailers refused to sell it. Bess donated two copies to the Wasilla Public Library, but they vanished from the shelves, so he donated more. The atmosphere toward Bess was toxic; a 1997 cartoon in the *Frontiersman* showed a slobbering, doll-clutching pedophile approaching his church, whose sign said, "Wasilla Church of the Covenant. Howard Bess, Pastor. All Sinners Welcome! Bible Interpretations to Suit Your 'Lifestyle.'"

Most reports have said that, when asking about banning books, Palin never mentioned any specific titles, but the presence of *Pastor, I Am Gay* in the library was, at the time, a matter of fierce contention. "I'm as sure that that book was at issue with Sarah Palin as I am that I'm talking to you right now," said Bess.

When Palin ran for governor in 2006, Christian conservatives mobilized to help elect her—the Alaska Family Council, a group that formed that year and is loosely affiliated with Focus on the Family, distributed a voter guide showing Palin's alignment with its ideology. During her nineteen months as governor, it's important to note, she has mostly ignored divisive social issues, instead focusing on getting a gas pipeline built. If she hasn't governed as a fire-breather, though, her record nevertheless offers some evidence that in Washington she would likely continue George W. Bush's injection of religious dogmatism into government appointments and policy-making. Opposition to abortion is, for her, a litmus test. When Sarah Palin ran for mayor of

Wasilla, Faye Palin, Todd's stepmother, supported her, but when Faye Palin ran for mayor in 2002, Sarah supported her opponent. The reason, said Menard, was that Faye Palin is pro-choice. "To my knowledge, that was the big issue," he said.

Last year, when Vic Kohring, a Republican state representative from Wasilla, left office after being indicted for bribery and extortion, Sarah Palin appointed Wes Keller, an elder in her church, to replace him. He introduced a bill to make the performance of intact dilation and extraction abortions—so-called "partial-birth abortions"—a felony, and according to a McClatchy Newspapers report, he plans to introduce legislation mandating the teaching of intelligent design in public schools.

Like McCain, Palin appears to believe that the United States is a Christian nation. As governor, she signed a resolution declaring October 21–27 Christian Heritage Week in Alaska, in order to remind Alaskans of "the role Christianity has played in our rich heritage." Written in the mode of some right-wing revisionist historians, it describes the nation's founders—including George Washington and Thomas Jefferson—as "Christians of caliber and integrity who did not hesitate to express their faith."

The conviction that America is a Christian nation could be especially worrisome when coupled with the kind of apocalyptic beliefs espoused by the Wasilla Assembly of God, since the combination suggests a profoundly messianic foreign policy. In a widely seen video taken just months before she received the vice presidential nomination, Palin stood onstage in her old church with pastor Ed Kalnins as he explained how, in the last days, Alaska would be a refuge for Christians fleeing the Lower 48. "Hundreds of thousands of people are going to come to this state to seek refuge, and the church has to be ready to minister to them." Palin's current religious home, Wasilla Bible Church, is rather more moderate and low-key, but it, too, subscribes to a theology that includes a literal belief in a biblical End Times scenario. In August, it hosted David Brickner, executive director of Jews for Jesus, who told the congregation, "But what we see in Israel, the conflict that is spilled out throughout the Middle East, really which is all about Jerusalem, is an ongoing reflection of the fact that there is judgment…. There's a reality to the judgment of unbelief."

Brickner's beliefs, said Menard, are shared by many at Wasilla Bible Church, though he said he couldn't speak to the particulars of Palin's faith. Whatever her original convictions about the Middle East—or anything else—they have likely stayed intact throughout her tutorials by the McCain campaign team. "Once she makes her mind up on an issue, it takes a ninety-mile-an-hour Alaska north wind to move her off course," said Menard. Of course, he meant it as a compliment, not a warning.

Our Polar Bears, Ourselves

Mark Hertsgaard

It wasn't much noticed at the time, but three weeks before she was chosen as John McCain's vice presidential running mate, Alaska Governor Sarah Palin played a key supporting role in the latest episode of the Bush administration's eight-year war on the Endangered Species Act, one of the cornerstones of American environmental law. On August 4, 2008, Alaska sued the government for listing the polar bear as a "threatened" species, an action, the lawsuit asserted, that would harm "oil and gas...development" in the state. In an accompanying statement, Palin complained that the listing "was not based on the best scientific and commercial data available" and should be rescinded.

The Bush administration had not wanted to designate the polar bear as threatened in the first place; now Palin's lawsuit provided cover to backtrack on the decision. The Interior Department had issued the listing only after environmental groups filed two lawsuits and the courts ordered compliance. While the polar bear population was currently stable, the plaintiffs argued, greenhouse gas emissions were melting the Arctic ice that polar bears rely on to hunt seals, their main food source. A study by the United States Geological Survey supported this argument, concluding that two-thirds of all polar bears could be gone by 2050 if Arctic ice continues to melt as scientists project. The listing was the first time global warming had been cited as the sole premise in an Endangered Species Act case, and Interior Secretary Dirk Kempthorne clearly wanted it to be the last. When Kempthorne an-nounced the polar bear listing on May 14, 2008, he emphasized that it would not affect federal policy on global warming or block development of "our natural resources in the Arctic."

A week after Palin's lawsuit, Kempthorne delivered on that pledge. On August 11 he proposed new rules that could allow federal agencies to decide for themselves whether their actions will imperil a threatened or endangered species. The rule reverses precedent: Since passage of the Endangered Species Act in 1973, scientists from the Fish and Wildlife Service have made such determinations independent of the agency involved. Under the new rule, if the Army Corps of Engineers is building a dam, the corps can decide whether it is putting species at risk. To make sure no one missed the point, Kempthorne told reporters that the new rule, which he termed "a narrow regulatory change," would keep the Endangered Species Act from becoming "a back door" to making climate change policy.

Hated by the right wing as an infringement on property rights, the Endangered Species Act has been on Bush's hit list since the beginning of his presidency, when he chose Gale Norton as his first Interior secretary. A Republican woman of the West like Palin, Norton assailed the act and did all she could to undermine it. "The Bush administration has listed only sixty species as threatened or endangered, compared with 522 under Clinton and 231 under the first President Bush," says Noah Greenwald, science director of the Center for Biological Diversity, the lead plaintiff in the polar bear case. "And it took a court order to make each of those sixty listings happen."

Kempthorne's proposal nevertheless seems likely to go forward. An obligatory thirty-day period for public comment expires September 15, after which Interior can begin to implement the rule. Congress could block funding, but few expect that to happen. Lawsuits are certain to follow, but critics say the quickest solution would be for the next administration to withdraw the rule. Barack Obama seems likely to do that; he immediately condemned Kempthorne's proposal. John McCain was silent. But his choice of Palin—who does not believe global warming is caused by humans but does think it's acceptable for humans to gun down wolves from airplanes—suggests that Arctic creatures have much to fear from a McCain administration.

And not just Arctic creatures. What's missing from most discussions about endangered species is that preserving other species is not an act of charity; it is essential to our own survival. "Endangered species issues are usually seen as humans versus nature—we act in favor of one or the other—and that's just not the case," says Aaron Bernstein, a fellow at the Center for Health and the Global Environment at Harvard and an editor (with Eric Chivian) of *Sustaining Life: How Human Health Depends on Biodiversity.* "Polar bears hold tremendous value to medicine, for example," explains Bernstein. "There is something about the metabolism of female polar bears that allows them to put on tremendous amounts of fat before winter but not become type 2 diabetic. We don't understand how they do it yet, but this research is hugely important for the tens of millions of people who suffer from type 2 diabetes."

But human dependence on other species is even broader. "We need [ants] to survive, but they don't need us at all," notes naturalist E. O. Wilson in a quote Bernstein and Chivian include in *Sustaining Life.* Without ants (and countless other underground species that will never be the subject of impassioned environmental appeals) to ventilate the soil, the earth would rot, halting food production. Without trees and other elements of a healthy forest, water supplies would shrink. Take away coral reefs and you destroy the bottom of the marine food chain. Global warming is on track to make as much as one-quarter of all plant and animal species on earth extinct by 2040, threatening general ecosystem collapse. To study the natural world is to realize, in the words of the environmental axiom, that everything is connected. What we do to the polar bears, we do to ourselves.

Palin's Petropolitics
Michael T. Klare

In the clinical terminology of political science, Alaska is a
classic "petrostate." That is, its political system is geared
toward the maximization of oil "rents"—royalties and other
income derived from energy firms—to the neglect of all other
economic activities. Such polities have an inherent tendency
toward corruption because of the close ties that naturally
develop between government officials and energy executives
and because oil revenues replace taxation as a source of
revenue (Alaska has no state income tax), insulating officials
from the scrutiny of taxpayers. Ever since the discovery of
oil in the North Slope, Alaska's GOP leadership has largely
behaved in this fashion. And while Governor Sarah Palin has
made some commendable efforts to dilute her party's ties to
Big Oil, she is no less a practitioner of petrostate politics than
her predecessors.

To put things in perspective: In 2007 Alaska produced
approximately 719,000 barrels of oil per day. That puts it
in the same ballpark as Egypt (710,000), Oman (718,000),
and Malaysia (755,000). Of these, Oman is particularly
interesting as a parallel. According to the Energy
Department, "Oman's economy is heavily reliant on
oil revenues, which account for about 75 percent of the
country's export earnings"—an assessment that would
describe Alaska nicely if it were an independent nation.
Equally revealing, oil rents provide 42 percent of Alaska's
annual revenue, more than any other source. If lavish
federal contributions were discounted (Alaska has one of the
nation's highest per capita rates of federal subsidies), oil's
share of state revenue would jump to 53 percent—about the
same as in Venezuela.

Since taking office as governor in 2006, Palin has devoted herself to a single overarching objective: increasing Alaska's income from oil and gas. To this end, she has pushed through two signal pieces of legislation: the creation of Alaska's Clear and Equitable Share (ACES) tax on oil and natural gas production, and the Alaska Gasline Inducement Act (AGIA). The ACES tax replaced the Petroleum Profits Tax, which had been instituted by her now-disgraced Republican predecessor, Frank Murkowski, and which was widely viewed as being excessively favorable to the oil companies. Under ACES the companies are taxed at a higher rate, and a progressive surcharge of 0.4 percent is added for every dollar the net profit per barrel exceeds $30. But—and this is a big *but*—the companies receive an increased tax credit for some new investments in exploration and infrastructure improvements.

The AGIA proposal, which has received more national attention, is intended to facilitate construction of a natural gas pipeline from Alaska's North Slope to Canada and eventually the Lower 48. Under the bill, Alaska will provide incentives, including a $500 million handout, to any company willing to build the $40 billion–plus conduit. (The $500 million will be used to help defray the costs of gaining regulatory approval, clearing environmental hurdles and so forth.) In August the Alaska senate approved a state license for TransCanada Corporation of Calgary to pursue federal certification for construction of a 1,715-mile pipeline from the North Slope to Canada's Alberta Gas Hub. Palin said at the GOP convention that the pipeline will "help lead America to energy independence," but it's clear from her advocacy of the AGIA and TransCanada's application that her principal goal was to increase Alaska's income from gas production. (The fact that the proposed pipeline will end in Canada, not the United States, does not seem to have attracted any notice.)

The question thus arises: How does Palin's experience as a maestro of petropolitics bear on her candidacy for vice president? To begin with, it should be clear that she has nothing in common with the leaders of any other state. Although it is true that Texas produces more oil per day than Alaska, Texas is no longer a petrostate, since its economy has become so much more diversified. Alaska is virtually alone in possessing a large (oil-supplied) state budget surplus—now about $5 billion—at a time when most states and the federal government are facing massive deficits and citizen groups are rising up in fury at the prospect of budget cuts. Palin is simply unqualified to deal with the demanding economic realities of any nation that is not a petrostate.

Second, Palin's only real nitty-gritty legislative experience is in measures aimed at expanding oil and gas production, to the virtual exclusion of other factors, including the environment. Although critical of the cozy ties between her GOP predecessors and Big Oil, Palin, like them, views Alaska as an unlimited source of raw materials to be exploited for maximum economic benefit, much as the leaders of comparable petrostates (Kuwait, Nigeria, and Venezuela) do. She says she cares about the environment, but her support for drilling in the Arctic National Wildlife Refuge and her eagerness to push the AGIA pipeline through forests in Alaska and the Yukon suggest otherwise. We can only assume that, as veep, she would favor similar policies in the Lower 48, entailing more drilling, digging, and pipe-laying in environmentally sensitive areas.

Finally, much like the leaders of other petrostates that depend on oil sales to fill government coffers, Palin is leery of efforts to promote renewable sources of energy and other petroleum alternatives—the exact opposite of running mate John McCain's proclaimed objective and that of most members of Congress. At a meeting of the National Governors Association in February, Palin argued against providing subsidies for alternative energy sources, claiming that domestic sources of oil and gas—many located in Alaska—can satisfy the nation's needs for a long time to come. "The conventional resources we have can fill the gap between now and when new technologies become economically competitive and don't require subsidies," she asserted. When pressed by a reporter for *Oil & Gas Journal* she went further, denouncing government support for renewable energy. "I just don't want things to get out of hand with incentives for renewables, particularly since they imply subsidies, while ignoring fuels we already have on hand." Surely, at this moment in history—with global oil output facing imminent decline and global warming an inescapable reality—anyone opposed to government support of renewable energy should be considered stupendously ill equipped for national office.

Northern Exposure: Sarah Palin's Toxic Paradise

Sheila Kaplan and Marilyn Berlin Snell

There's no reason to doubt Sarah Palin's sincerity when she talks about her commitment to family and—more specifically—special-needs kids. When she introduced her son, who has Down syndrome, to the audience at the Republican convention, the family tableau drew cheers. And she issued a promise. "To the families of special-needs children all across this country, I have a message for you," she told the crowd. "For years, you've sought to make America a more welcoming place for your sons and daughters, and I pledge to you that, if we are elected, you will have a friend and advocate in the White House."

Unfortunately, as governor of a state with a birth-defect rate that's twice the national average, and which has the gloomy status as repository of toxic chemicals from around the world, Palin has pursued environmental policies that seem perfectly crafted to swell the ranks of special-needs kids. It's true that Alaska's top leaders have placed industry wishes over environmental protection for years. But instead of correcting this problem, she's compounded it. Peer into her environmental record, and Palin ends up looking a lot like George W. Bush.

In the past twenty years, research has shown that exposure to some metals and to chemicals such as pesticides, flame retardants, and polychlorinated biphenyls (PCBs) can cause birth defects and permanent developmental disorders both prenatally and in the first years of childhood. And Alaska is vulnerable to some of the worst environmental pollutants out there. In a state whose wealth depends on the exploitation of its natural resources, the toxic byproducts of mining and energy development, such as arsenic, mercury, and lead, are particular problems. Alaska Natives, such as the Inuit people, eat a diet that is heavy in fish, seals, and whales—animals that are high on the food chain and therefore more likely to be contaminated with high doses of PCBs and mercury. And the state is vulnerable not only to homegrown pollution, but also to industrial pollution: Trace gases and tiny airborne particles are contaminating the polar regions, carried there on atmospheric and oceanic currents, according to the National Oceanic and Atmospheric Administration.

The mess of pollutants in Alaska has clearly taken its toll. In general, the state has double the national average of birth defects. While the causes are unknown, environmentalists point to the region that includes the North Slope, an area slightly larger than Minnesota, where most of Alaska's oil is produced. The byproducts of oil production can cause serious nervous system disorders, and the North Slope and its environs, home to Alaska Natives and itinerant oil workers, has the highest prevalence of birth defects in the state—11 percent—compared with 6 percent statewide and 3 percent nationwide.

Palin, however, has not addressed these concerns. Her administration irked environmentalists in February 2008, when it opposed legislation that would have given parents at least forty-eight hours' notice before schools were to be sprayed with pesticides and other toxic chemicals. Currently, parents get twenty-four hours, which the bill's proponents say is not sufficient for parents who want to arrange to keep kids out of school for a few days after the chemicals are applied. Palin's administration argued that the bill was too restrictive and would force schools to notify parents before cleaning toilets with disinfectant—which, supporters say, is not true. In the same month, members of Palin's administration testified against language in legislation that would have banned polybrominated diphenyl ethers—flame retardants that, studies show, harm the developing brain. Then, in the summer of 2007, Palin allowed oil companies to move forward with a toxic-dumping plan in Alaska's Cook Inlet, the only coastal fishery in the nation where toxic dumping is permitted. The Bush administration initially OK'd the companies' request to increase toxic releases, but the permits could not be issued without Alaska's certification that the discharges met the state's water-quality standards, says Bob Shavelson, executive director of Cook Inletkeeper, an organization founded to protect the area's watershed. Palin complied. "Palin's Department of Environmental Conservation issued that certification [based on] the long-discounted notion that 'dilution is the solution to pollution'—turning the federal Clean Water Act on its head and actually increasing toxic pollution," Shavelson says.

Palin next took on the Clean Water Initiative, also known as Proposition 4, which appeared on the Alaska ballot on August 26, 2008. The measure would have limited the runoff of toxic metals—known to cause developmental and birth defects, according to the Centers for Disease Control and Prevention—from all mining operations, but it was aimed at stopping the proposed Pebble Mine, a huge mining proposal that was controversial for its potential impact on Bristol Bay, the world's largest commercial wild salmon fishery (for which Palin's oldest daughter was named). The project had been in the works for years, and, when she ran for governor in 2006, Palin told the *Alaska Journal of Commerce* that, if the mine was green-lighted, "there will be remediation from now to eternity." Once in office, though, environmental concerns took a backseat. In a TV interview six days before the vote, Palin said, "Let me take my governor's hat off for just a minute, and tell you personally, Prop 4—I vote no on that." Alaska's mining industry parlayed Palin's face and words into an advertising blitz—and came from behind to defeat it.

Palin's next antienvironmental effort also came in August, when she attempted to block California's plan to curb its air pollution. The Golden State is trying to reduce its toxic emissions with a port fee that would pay for pollution-reduction projects around the state. Arguing that it would hurt Alaska's economy, Palin asked California Governor Arnold Schwarzenegger to veto the proposed legislation.

Finally, Palin was pushed by environmental activists and Alaska Natives to pressure the military in its cleanup of one of the most contaminated sites in Alaska—but the state didn't act. This was on the old Northeast Cape Air Force Base on remote St. Lawrence Island in the Bering Sea—one of the state's closest spots to Russia. When the military closed its operations in the 1970s, it left thousands of barrels of toxic waste, containing solvents, fuels, heavy metals, pesticides, and PCBs, a group of toxic organic chemicals that have persisted in the environment. For the past few years, the Army Corps of Engineers has been slowly cleaning up parts of the site and claims it will leave it safe. (One federally funded study still in progress by the state's premier watchdog on chemical pollutants, Alaska Community Action on Toxics (ACAT), tested the local water and got a reading that was more than one thousand times the level that the EPA considers safe. "If the Corps of Engineers want to fill up their canteens in there, they are welcome to it," says Kathrine Springman, the toxicologist who did that study. "Actually, I wouldn't want them to drink it... any more than I would ask them to drink Drano.")

But critics say the army is taking too long, and that its plan will leave too many untreated chemicals, PCBs in particular, at the site. According to Pamela Miller, ACAT's executive director, Palin should have used her powers as governor to forge a better cleanup plan. "Certainly this was also a pattern in the Murkowski administration, but, under Palin, it's gotten worse," she said. "Her administration has done nothing to work with the military to avoid possible contamination." Scientists have also opposed the army's plan, saying it will leave the area dangerous.

Supporters note that Palin did boost school spending for children with the most severe disabilities, but, in general, the Alaskan government under Palin has done nothing to protect those children and future generations from the toxic stew that the state has become. "She doesn't have a good understanding of the science," says Ruth Etzel, who until recently was research director at the Alaska Native Medical Program in Anchorage. "What she tends to do is talk about personal responsibility as the key to good health."

Andrea Doll, a Democratic state representative from Juneau, says she tried to get Palin interested in her bill on flame retardants early on: "I told her about the bill. She totally was not interested in any way, shape, or form. It was that look on her face—that 'don't even go there' look."

Why Troopergate Matters

John Nichols

Anchorage

On day one of the Republican National Convention, NBC News correspondent Andrea Mitchell breathlessly reported from the floor of the session that "there are Republican lawyers right now up in Alaska doing a deeper vet on Sarah Palin." Mitchell was both right and wrong. A "jump team" of top lawyers and communications operatives had indeed decamped to Anchorage. But the dozen McCain campaign fixers—led by a veteran of the *Bush v. Gore* Florida recount fight of 2000—did not head north to perform a post-selection vetting of vice presidential pick Palin. The hired guns were on the Last Frontier to manage a mess: the prospect that the state-sanctioned investigation of an abuse-of-power scandal involving Palin would destroy the governor's credibility as a reformer—and with it the argument that their new No. 2's relative inexperience was mitigated by her able leadership.

Palin had other issues—a record of demanding earmarks while claiming to reject them, extreme religious views, an underutilized passport, and a Cheneyesque penchant for official secrecy and executive excess that put the lie to her presumed commitment to openness. But it was the Troopergate scandal that really had the McCain camp spooked. With its intimations that the governor dismissed Alaska's top cop because he refused to fire Palin's former brother-in-law—a state trooper with whom she and her husband were feuding—the controversy threatened Palin's carefully manufactured image. Weeks before she joined the ticket, her ethics counselor, Wevley Shea, a former U.S. Attorney for Alaska, had warned her with regard to

Troopergate that "the situation is now grave." Despite statements to the contrary, the decision by top McCain campaign adviser Steve Schmidt to send a strike force, and the relentless focus on Troopergate by its members, like former Justice Department prosecutor Ed O'Callaghan, leaves no doubt that the McCain camp shared Shea's assessment.

"The fight is over how [Palin] is going to be defined in the eyes of the American public," admitted former McCain campaign manager Terry Nelson. "All the information about her has not been introduced, and once that information comes to light people are going to draw conclusions about her, and the campaigns are fighting to shape the conclusions."

The most politically volatile conclusion—an election-season determination that Palin had abused her authority in a manner that could lead to official sanctions, perhaps even impeachment—was not something the McCain camp was willing to leave to chance. Top aides parachuted into Anchorage on a two-tier mission. On the ground in Alaska, they initiated a series of stalling schemes designed to prevent a damaging report from being released before the November 4 election. At the same time, McCain acolytes, led by former New York mayor and presidential hopeful Rudy Giuliani, appeared on national television to spin the story that the bipartisan inquiry was a partisan witch hunt. In so doing, McCain's aides provided vivid illustration of precisely what can happen when a determined presidential campaign is willing to do anything to maintain the carefully crafted image of a running mate who has become essential to its electoral prospects.

"The McCain campaign decided it could come into a small state and stop a legitimate investigation," explained Democratic State Representative Les Gara, a former Alaska assistant attorney general. "They knew they had a problem with Troopergate, but they decided they could roll over everyone in Alaska. They've unleashed what for Alaska is an unprecedented amount of spin. They've attacked a bipartisan investigation and a nonpartisan investigator as somehow partisan. It's all about muddying things up rather than providing the transparency that Sarah Palin says she's all about." Alaska House Judiciary Committee chair Jay Ramras, a Republican, was blunter. "I remain a McCain supporter, but certainly not on this issue," said Ramras, who charged that McCain's operatives were attempting to "rewrite history" by seeking to derail the Palin investigation.

The rewrite proceeded rapidly. By the time the GOP national convention opened—three days after Palin's selection—the McCain team, led by veteran Bush/Cheney aide Taylor Griffin and reporting directly to campaign adviser Schmidt, had established a command center in Anchorage and conducted conference calls with Alaska GOP legislators, conservative leaders, and associates of Palin to instruct them on how to say "supportive things," according to an Alaska Republican who was in on the calls but spoke to media on condition of anonymity. "All I keep hearing is, 'Why don't you toe the line?' " said Rick Rydell, a conservative Anchorage radio host. Many Republicans did just that; former Alaska house speaker Gail Phillips, who initially complained to reporters about McCain's failure to vet Palin, suddenly stopped giving interviews. Calls to Palin's office by national reporters started being routed to McCain campaign operatives. And Anchorage news cycles came to be dominated by denunciations of the probe from top GOP officials, announcements that Palin aides would not cooperate with the investigation, the filing of lawsuits, and press conferences where O'Callaghan—who six weeks before had been working in the U.S. Attorney's office in New York—commented, with seeming authority, about how the Troopergate inquiry was "tainted."

While national news reports lumped Palin's personal and political conflicts into a muddy file of Alaskana, serious political observers in the state understood that the primary concern of McCain aides was Troopergate, a controversy that exploded with Palin's July 2008 dismissal of Public Safety Commissioner Walt Monegan, allegedly after he refused to fire Palin's former brother-in-law, a state trooper who had been involved in an ugly divorce fight with the governor's sister. Arthur Culvahouse Jr., the lawyer who conducted the pre-selection review of Palin for McCain, admits he "spent a lot of time with her lawyer" discussing the scandal. But it soon became evident that the McCain camp was uninterested in hearing that Palin had problems that might disqualify her. "They had to handle Troopergate. So they hijacked the investigation," complained Camille Conte, a popular progressive radio host in Anchorage.

Essential to the McCain team's initiative was a claim that the investigation, which had begun a month before Palin was tapped for vice president, was a partisan project cooked up by Barack Obama's campaign. This spin was primarily for national consumption; Alaskans knew Monegan as the respected former Anchorage police chief and were aware that the probe of his firing had been unanimously authorized by the state's Republican-controlled legislative council.

McCain's operatives did not let facts get in their way. Within hours of his arrival in Alaska, Taylor Griffin—who was the GOP "media coordinator" during the 2000 *Bush v. Gore* fight before joining the White House Office of Media Affairs— was peddling the line that the investigation "has become a political circus and has gotten out of control." Palin, who initially greeted the inquiry with a call for the legislature to "hold me accountable," underwent an extreme political makeover. Suddenly the governor and her "first dude" husband, Todd—who reportedly had joined the governor in pressuring Monegan—had private counsel. And their lawyer said the governor wouldn't cooperate until the legislature shut down its inquiry and turned over responsibility to the state personnel board, whose members are appointed by the governor (unlike the legislative council, due to finish its inquiry before election day, the personnel board was unlikely to get anything done until after the November voting).

On the first day of the GOP convention, when party leaders were supposedly fretting about Hurricane Gustav, Palin found time to file the equivalent of an ethics complaint against herself, prompting the personnel board probe. The notoriously secretive governor dispensed with the "open and transparent" ruse she had employed to challenge Alaska's good-ol'-boy politics in her 2006 statewide campaign—and that the McCain campaign was celebrating in its ads. What reemerged was the calculating politician with a history of avoiding accountability that recalled her controversial days as mayor of Wasilla. She was accused of removing Wasilla employees who questioned her authority and using city offices and equipment for political purposes. Palin—who, it was revealed in September, uses two BlackBerrys in order to keep certain communications out of the official record—may be running as an outsider. But Alaska's Conte sees the governor as a smooth fit with the vice president she seeks to replace. "She had to make a choice between sticking with what she said she would do—cooperating with the inquiry—and doing what the McCain people told her to do," said Conte. "They came in with their Karl Rove/Dick Cheney tactics and she said, Count me in."

McCain's camp caught a break when some liberal bloggers and the national media got excited about Palin's family matters—especially the pregnancy of her seventeen-year-old daughter—rather than the political record that would have been the first focus for a male nominee and that would have turned national attention to Troopergate. This gave Palin insulation—she and McCain aides could complain about "cheap shots" from "the liberal media"— and precious time to reframe the investigation as Democratic victimization.

Palin had always denied wrongdoing in the firing of Monegan. The governor, who as Wasilla's mayor had fired a police chief who tried to crack down on local taverns that encouraged late-night drinking, claimed she dismissed Monegan for failing to address alcohol abuse in rural Alaska. Palin's story evolved until her lawyer accused Monegan of "outright insubordination." Monegan insisted that "she's not telling the truth to the media about her reasons for firing me." From the start, a number of prominent Republicans and Alaska conservatives expressed their faith in Monegan. Former GOP legislator Andrew Halcro, who pushed for the inquiry, argued, "Walt Monegan got fired for all of the wrong reasons. Walt Monegan got fired because he had the audacity to tell Governor Palin no, when apparently nobody is allowed to say no to Governor Palin.... Monegan said no to firing a state trooper who had divorced Governor Palin's sister because the guy was being maliciously hounded by Palin's family."

Legislators shared the suspicion. The Legislative Council's eight Republicans and four Democrats decided unanimously to hire a retired prosecutor, Steve Branchflower, to run the inquiry. Declaring its intent "that the investigation be professional, unbiased, independent, objective and conducted at arm's length from the political process," the council selected state senate Judiciary Committee chair Hollis French II, an Anchorage Democrat who had been elected to the legislature after a career as a criminal prosecutor, to manage the probe. Palin, who welcomed the inquiry, had reason to feel lucky: Far from being a bitter partisan, French had recently crossed party lines to work closely with her to establish more responsible tax policies regarding the state's oil companies.

As late as mid-August, French—whose Anchorage office is lined with history and law books and who retains the cool, measured style of a prosecutor—was assuring reporters that the Palin administration was cooperating with the inquiry. It was unlikely that subpoenas would need to be issued, said French, who predicted Palin would volunteer to be deposed.

Like legislators of both parties, French said he was shocked that the McCain campaign made no effort to contact senators involved in the probe during what McCain claimed was a "completely thorough" vetting of Palin. "If they had done their job, they never would have picked her. Now they may have to deal with an October surprise," French told reporters, noting that the Troopergate report had been set for a late October release (the timetable was later sped up, with an eye toward dialing down partisan rancor, and was set for October 10).

McCain operatives leapt on the "October surprise" line to smear French as an Obama operative out to discredit the governor. GOP state representative John Coghill—who says he called McCain's campaign after Palin's selection to say, "Hey, I'm your boy now"—demanded, after consulting with McCain lieutenants, that French quit as manager of the investigation, charging that he was "steering the direction of the investigation, its conclusion, and its timing in a manner that will have maximum partisan political impact on the national and state elections."

Coghill was wrong, and he knew it: The date for the release of the report had been set long before Palin joined McCain's ticket, and it was French who had said early on that in order to avoid partisanship, "We need to hand this off to someone." That someone, veteran prosecutor Branchflower, is conducting the investigation and preparing the report.

The state's largest paper, the *Anchorage Daily News*— which has a mixed record of praising and pillorying Palin— dismissed Coghill's attack as "a partisan overreaction." Legislators in both parties agreed, and after Palin aides started refusing to assist the probe, the senate Judiciary Committee decided in a bipartisan vote taken September 12 to issue subpoenas to thirteen people—including Todd Palin—to compel their cooperation. The state attorney general, a Palin appointee, objected, as did Todd Palin's lawyer, and prospects that the probe would follow its original timeline dimmed. Meanwhile, the McCain camp was busy discrediting a legitimate investigation with big lies that reverberated in the national media echo chamber, as the facts were dismissed or forgotten. It wasn't just Rush Limbaugh or Sean Hannity or even the right-wing blogs that attacked Hollis French as "a made man in the Obama mafia" and an "Obamabot." Ed O'Callaghan was on CNN from Alaska, telling anchor Rick Sanchez that French and other Democratic legislators were doing Obama's bidding, failing to note that key Alaska Republicans, like Senate President Lyda Green, continued to support the investigation. Rudy Giuliani appeared on *Meet the Press* saying, "That whole investigation in, in Alaska...that's being run by Obama supporters."

By mid-September national media were reporting Palin's refusal to cooperate. The Obama campaign, meanwhile, was doing everything it could to keep the discussion on McCain and the economy, offering little if any push-back. In Alaska, however, even conservatives were griping. "I want McCain and Palin to win too," argued Dan Fagan, a popular right-wing Anchorage radio host. "But with Palin's refusal to cooperate with the independent investigator and her transparent delay tactics, Americans deserve to know what Palin is trying to hide before we vote her a heartbeat away from the leader of the free world."

Jay Ramras, the GOP Judiciary Committee chair, was frustrated. "It's a shame for anybody who buys this bag of oats that the McCain camp is peddling," Ramras said. His Democratic colleague Les Gara said, "Usually, the spin wins. We caught them on it here. But they're still spinning. It doesn't seem to matter, even when they're confronted with the truth."

Gara's right. So the question is no longer merely, How did Sarah Palin abuse her authority? Or even, What did she know and when did she know it? The fundamental political question of the moment is whether the McCain camp will succeed in spinning Palin's nasty home-state scandal into something just convoluted enough to get the fickle national media to give the Alaska governor a soft pass. If that happens, it will be because a crack campaign team, made up of veteran Bush/Cheney operatives and reporting directly to McCain campaign adviser Schmidt, stirred up sufficient confusion and partisan rancor to obscure what's really happening in a small state that has never before been a prime battleground in a presidential race.

If spin wins, it will not just be the truth that takes a hit. As Troopergate and its fallout reveal, Sarah Palin is more than a hockey mom. She is a fiercely ambitious politician with a penchant for secrecy and a history of using positions of public trust to advance her personal and ideological agendas. It is no coincidence that Bush's vice president has lavished praise on Palin—saying he "loved" her "superb" convention speech. Dick Cheney is often portrayed as the ultimate insider, just as Palin is packaged as the ultimate outsider. But Cheney recognizes in Palin someone who meets his warped standard for "an effective vice president." That's the inconvenient truth the McCain campaign is working overtime to hide until after November 4.

Examining Palin's Record on Violence Against Women
Brentin Mock

Governor Sarah Palin of Alaska says that she's a champion for women, professing that, as the Republican vice presidential nominee, she is the breakthrough that authenticates the 18 million cracks in the proverbial glass ceiling opened by Senator Hillary Clinton. But before Palin can claim any authenticity as a fighter for gender issues, she needs to address some important questions: With Alaska having the highest rates of rape, sexual assault, and domestic violence in the United States, according to statistics from the U.S. Department of Justice and the Centers for Disease Control and Prevention, what did Palin do as a mayor, and as governor, to remedy these problems? And what would she do as vice president to address gender-based violence as a national issue?

Her previous and current governing acts signal that the protection of women's rights is not much of a priority for her. For all of Alaska's dismal statistics on violence against women, Palin took steps that worked against the interests of vulnerable women—especially Native Alaskan women. As mayor, Palin refused to have the City of Wasilla cover the costs of the forensic kits for women who said they had been raped. As governor, Palin stood in the way of efforts to expand legal-service resources to victims of sexual assault, and fired Walt Monegan, one man who had almost unanimous respect from police, urban Alaskans, and Native Alaskans alike for his dedication to this issue.

As mayor of Wasilla from 1996 to 2000, Palin decided she would defy a bill from then-governor Tony Knowles that said local law enforcements should foot the bill for "rape

kits"—the forensic analysis needed to trace the identity
of attackers—when victims filed complaints or sought
treatment in medical centers. The kits cost between $300
and $1,200, putting them out of the reach of low-income
women and adding a financial weight to an already
burdened accuser. But Mayor Palin thought instead
that the kits were too much of a financial drain on the
city government.

The Alaska that Palin inherited as governor had a rape
rate 2.5 times the national average. Its rates of sexual assault
against children are six times the national average. And its
per capita rate of women killed by men is the highest in the
nation. For Native Alaskan women, reality is even grimmer.
A major Amnesty International report on violence against
American Indian and Alaskan Indian women found that an
alarming one in three female Native Alaskans and American
Indians (two distinct groups) are raped in their lifetime, and
three in four have been sexually assaulted. Native Alaskan
women are ten times more likely to be sexually assaulted
than all other Alaskan women.

These women are often cut off from the avenues to
justice—literally. Since many Native Alaskan women live
in rural villages that have no connecting roads to the main
cities with police stations, they have a difficult time filing
complaints. The Alaska Network on Domestic Violence and
Sexual Assault reports that 30 percent of Alaskan women
have no access to victim services where they live. According
to the Amnesty International report, police are themselves
handicapped—often underfunded—in trying to get to the
villages when complaints arise. And in interviews Amnesty
International conducted with Native Alaskan sexual-assault
survivors, respondents said that police and medical
professionals often wrote them off as being drunk when they

complained. Doctors and police wouldn't follow up on investigations.

In what was hailed as a step in the right direction, Palin appointed Monegan, the former Anchorage police chief, as public-safety commissioner in 2006, just after she was elected governor. The first Native Alaskan to hold this position, Monegan was a well-respected public figure among both city- and village-dwelling Alaskans. He's a board member of the Alaska Native Justice Center, which advocates on behalf of Alaskan Natives. As commissioner, he established and supported measures to strengthen law enforcement in the native rural areas, and advocated for more protection of native women, who are the prime targets for assault, rape, and murder—mostly by non-native men. He also established a Citizens Police Academy, which empowered residents to report crimes as they surfaced. One program he hoped to put in place would have deputized villagers and eventually elevated them to official state troopers—a program which, if carried out, would have given sexual-assault victims a law enforcement service in their own front yards.

But Monegan bumped up against Palin's staunch position that she wouldn't support any programs that she felt would burden taxpayers. Monegan went to Washington, D.C., to request federal funds to combat sexual assault and domestic violence. It was this move that drew him into conflict with Palin and her way of governing. Palin reportedly had not "authorized" the program to expand the sexual-assault legal services that Monegan wanted to implement. According to her lawyer, Thomas Van Flein, Palin considered Monegan's trip to D.C. to request funding "the last straw."

Palin's spokeswoman Sharon Leighow said Monegan was fired because the governor wanted the public-safety department to move "in a new direction"—although this "new" strategy seemed remarkably similar to what Monegan was already doing. Palin's interim replacement for Monegan was Kenai police officer Charles Kopp, who at the time was facing accusations of sexually harassing a female employee—a "new direction," indeed.

All of this stands in stark contrast to Palin's counterpart on the Democratic ticket, Senator Barack Obama's running mate, Senator Joseph Biden, who has a strong congressional record on these issues—most notably his long battle in establishing, promoting, strengthening, and sustaining the Violence Against Women Act. (It was, in fact, this signature piece of legislation that made funds for Monegan's proposed programs possible.)

Palin's record of standing in the way of progress and justice for those women suffering from the most egregious of crimes undermines her claim that she represents a step forward for women. Her record in Alaska makes clear that her chosen style of governing often means choosing to save a dollar rather than save a woman's life.

Palin Enthusiastically Practices
Socialism, Alaska-Style
Elstun Lauesen

I make a motion that we change the name of our state. Henceforth we should be known as the State of Irony, thanks to Sarah Palin's sashay down the catwalk of national politics.

Todd and Sarah's Excellent Adventure during the fiftieth anniversary of statehood is actually a great vehicle for a meditation on one of the unique aspects of our state: socialism.

Candidate Palin, along with such formidable intellects as Samuel Joseph Wurzelbacher (aka Joe the Plumber), Elisabeth Hasselbeck, and Victoria Jackson, attacked Barack Obama during the campaign for being, variously, a Marxist, a communist, and a socialist. Ironically, as Keith Olbermann of MSNBC noted last week, Sarah Palin just presided over a huge redistribution of wealth when she signed an energy "rebate" of $1,200 for every man, woman, and child in Alaska. The money for that wealth redistribution comes from our collective wealth, which we have thanks to our state constitution. Article VIII, Section 2 holds that the resources of the state will be utilized, developed, and conserved for the "maximum benefit of its people." This precept of public management of benefit is precisely what makes Alaska today one of a handful of states that enjoy a budget surplus while other states are struggling with deficits. The framers of our constitution wisely didn't want state resources to be privatized as they are in Texas, for example, where the people are separated from their wealth by billionaires. Thanks to the framers of our state's constitution, our collective ownership of state resources guarantees low taxes and high revenues, not to mention a Permanent Fund dividend program, another socialist scheme that gave each Alaskan over $2,000 this year.

Alaskans like to boast that they are different, that they "don't give a damn how they do it in the Lower 48." Ironically, Sarah Palin and her handlers and many of her fans here in Alaska don't understand how different we Alaskans really are.

Truth be told, when Governor Palin redistributes the wealth held in common by the people of Alaska, she is fulfilling the socialist dream of many of Alaska's pioneers.

I'm from Fairbanks and each summer we celebrate "Golden Days," a celebration honoring the mining days of yore. Golden Days has morphed into a cowboy, Western-style show since the construction of the Trans-Alaska Pipeline; that's understandable, considering where many of the pipeline immigrants come from. Ironically, many of the early miners and pioneers of Alaska were from Europe, with corresponding accents and political views including European socialist views. The history of mining in Alaska in the late nineteenth and early twentieth centuries has a parallel history of socialist political organizing. Many of our forefathers and mothers here in Alaska were proud members of socialist parties or worker affiliates in Ketchikan, Nome, and Fairbanks.

A local blog, insurgent49.com, published a review of the early leftist history of Alaska. Regarding my hometown the review notes, "Lena Morrow Lewis started publishing the semimonthly *Alaska Socialist* newspaper in Fairbanks, which lasted for about three years. Two other left-wing Fairbanks publications from this period that were shorter-lived were the *Tanana Valley Socialist* and the *Socialist Press*. Around the same time, Gustave Sandberg served as secretary of the Alaska Socialist Educational Society, which did such activities as lecturing in mining camps. At least several times, a young writer named Jack London was one of the lecturers."

In 1914 the Alaska Socialist Party was formed and the platform advocated typical socialist ideas like federal funding of railroads and highways in Alaska.

When Alaskans sing about the "gold of the early sourdough's dreams" in the Alaska Flag Song, we should also remember an associated dream held by many of those pioneer Alaskans honored in that song: a world where all people would get a fair day's pay for a fair day's work, and where the prejudices and inequalities among people disappear as the fruits of prosperity are shared by all.

Ironically, despite her posturing before adoring mobs in the Lower 48, Sarah Palin has so far been a pretty good socialist governor. I hope that when she returns, she continues her good work and stops worrying so much about how they do it Outside.

Letter from the Other Alaska

Shannyn Moore

Homer, Alaska

On the morning of John McCain's announcement that he had picked our governor, Sarah Palin, as his running mate, before she walked onto the national stage, Palin called in to the radio show I was on. "Today is a great day for Alaska and Alaskans," she proclaimed. "You accepted?" was my response. I couldn't believe it. There was an awkward silence. (Maybe she blinked.) But I would have said the same thing if she had been invited to do medical mission work repairing cleft palates in third world countries.

I have more in common in with Sarah Palin than most anyone I know. Raised in small-town Alaska; both parents public school teachers; local pageants, state pageant, second runner-up and Miss Congeniality, respectively; hunting; commercial fishing; and a great pride in the independence and strength in being an Alaskan woman. We both know the comfort of ExtraTuf Boots and fishing gear. Part of me was proud and part of me knew she'd traded for a whole different set of heels. Heels I'd never be comfortable in.

"I have nothin' to lose," Palin told Rush Limbaugh weeks after our radio conversation. Palin's statement was the most honest thing I'd heard her say. She had nothing to lose, and she didn't. John McCain lost. The Republican Party lost. Alaska lost. But Sarah Palin didn't lose.

Unlike Governors Clinton and Bush, Sarah wouldn't relinquish her position to Lieutenant Governor Sean Parnell. Alaska state business was taken over by Storm Trooper–like forces from the McCain campaign. To this day, political shrapnel is still surfacing.

More recently, Palin said about her upcoming and heavily discounted book, *Going Rogue*, "There have been so many things written and said through mainstream media that have not been accurate, and it will be nice through an unfiltered forum to get to speak truthfully about who we are and what we stand for and what Alaska is all about." Who is "we"? How could Sarah Palin possibly know what "Alaska is all about"? No one can sum this place up; that's what I love about it. We are too mavericky to have one voice define us.

But Sarah Palin stole Alaska's voice. During the campaign, "She Doesn't Speak For Me!" bumper stickers were seen more often than McCain/Palin stickers. Sarah Palin didn't speak for all Alaskans, yet our mountains, oceans, culture, and wild things became props in her campaign.

The weeks after the election/rejection of Palin were intense. Many of my friends—those who had become like family to me—had worked tirelessly, for no money, and managed to get the truth to the mainstream media about our governor. Yes, we declared victory on election night, but we knew she was coming home, and she wasn't happy about it. Neither were we.

As if that weren't bad enough, we'd been hearing loons talk about secession up here for years. In Alaska, the three top ballot spots—for president, Senate and House of Representatives—have candidates from the secessionist Alaskan Independence Party. In two of the three, the AIP holds at least 4 percent of the vote. Meanwhile, the felonious Ted Stevens had convinced over a hundred thousand Alaskans what he couldn't convince twelve jurors of a few weeks before the election—i.e., his innocence.

Talking heads had the temerity to ask if it's too late to sell Alaska back to the Russians. Repeatedly. America's liberal boy-wonder, Keith Olbermann, was breaking up with us. Chris Matthews, Rachel Maddow, Bill Maher, and various radio jocks suggested putting Alaska up on eBay. I could only handle one breakup at a time.

I'm like many Alaskans, just not the one America had been forced to get to know during the election. I knew what newspapers I read. I knew that Africa is *not* a country. I knew Stephen Harper is the Prime Minister of Canada, and I even knew which countries comprised NAFTA—which I thought was a crock when it passed. My favorite birthday present in 2008 was the return of habeas corpus in a 5–4 U.S. Supreme Court decision on June 12.

I was born in Alaska; Sarah Palin was not. I don't have a *Fargo* accent that sounds like I make casseroles with leftover tater tots and mushroom soup. Numerous brilliant, artistic, articulate and cultured citizens call Alaska home. On November 4, 2008, many in the Lower 49 got to shake their shoes of our Governor. They slept easier. Gone were the train-wreck fantasies that kept them up at night; the 3:00 a.m. phone call and she, a heartbeat away from the "nukular" codes.

But for Alaskans, she was back, and we didn't know what that would mean.

Progressive Alaskans had a target on our backs for speaking out about her archaic philosophies and faith-based policies. We waited for the January 2009 legislative session to include a bill allowing the aerial hunting of the exotic, endangered species, *Alaskan liberals.*

At the same time Palin was coming home, Alaska was in chaos over the Senate race between Ted Stevens and Mark Begich. Her ability to split her own party had left her with few Republican friends, and her campaign had alienated her from her allies among Democratic lawmakers.

The 2009 legislative session was one of the biggest wastes of time in Alaska history. Wars raged between the administration and legislators on both sides of the aisle. When word came of her book deal, there were constitutional questions about her dual role as governor and author as well as the resulting personal financial benefit. At the time, I thought, That's fantastic! Great! Get a laptop and a bottle of Adderall... you'll be fine. If you get stuck...well, make it up. It's worked so far.

But I knew she couldn't write a book that would capture why, to me, Alaska is one of the best things about America. We are the last frontier. What once was wild in America still is here. It takes my breath; the northern lights over Denali can trump a full moon; a phosphorescent glow in the wake of my row boat; bears fishing salmon out of Brooks Falls; glaciers bigger than cruise ships.

First Alaskans thrived in a frozen land for thousands of years and left no footprint. In 1867, Russia gave us a hell of a deal at 1.9 cents an acre. The Klondike Gold Rush was a quick payback, and it gave Charlie Chaplin some great material.

Homesteading pioneers farmed, fished, and flourished. In 1922, a Tlingit Chief, Charlie Jones was jailed for *voting*. His protest gave way to Native Alaskans getting the right to vote two years before Native Americans. In 1944, years before the Civil Rights movement in the States, Roberta Schenck, a Native woman, refused to budge from her seat in the "Whites Only" section of a movie theater in Nome. She was dragged out and jailed. Schenck was Alaska's Rosa Parks—before Rosa Parks. Because of her bravery and the moving testimony of Elizabeth Peratrovich, on February 16, 1945, territorial governor Ernest Gruening signed an antidiscrimination law. Against the argument that the law would not eliminate discrimination, Peratrovich said, "Do your laws against larceny and even murder eliminate those crimes?"

We decriminalized abortion before *Roe v. Wade*. Our privacy laws are the strongest in the country. A man told me he moved here after studying the Alaska Constitution at law school; it could have been Section 22, which allowed Alaskans the right to possess marijuana.

During World War II the Japanese occupied the Alaska islands of Kiska and Attu for almost two years. Because of the harsh conditions, frostbite became worthy of a Purple Heart. In 1958, the Inupiat village of Point Hope protested Project Chariot, a proposal to create an artificial port on the North Slope by detonating nuclear devices there. As a thank-you, the federal government transported the contamination from the 1962 Nevada Test Site to the Chariot location and buried it there. Cancer rates among villagers are staggering. Where's Erin Brockovich when we need her? In 1988 Homer, Alaska, voted to officially become a "Nuclear-Free Zone" in response to proposed nuclear subs. That same town—my hometown—twenty years later had the only known "spontaneous" Obama headquarters in the country.

It's wrong to be hard on anyone for not knowing that Alaskans aren't all Palinbots. After such a close Senate race, it would be fair to wonder if we suffer from Reality Deficit Disorder. Yet it's easy to want to knock sense into folks who have ignored our history; rich with strength, true with characters and patriotism that deserve to be called American.

Not to play the blame game, but in the spirit of transparency you only get in therapy, the colonization of the forty-ninth state by Global Enterprise has gone largely unnoticed. We could use some help fighting to ensure that the fragile wild salmon runs of Bristol Bay stay pristine against the looming threat of Pebble Mine. Your aid would be appreciated in keeping our wolves and bears safe from aerial "hunting." And were your voices lifted with ours in a message to Exxon, maybe our fishermen would have been able to maintain their industry despite an unprecedented environmental catastrophe, still wreaking havoc twenty years later.

Alaska will eventually recover from the damage of the Palin phenomenon. Will America take a lesson from us? I can only hope.

The Ugly Irony of *Going Rogue*
Jeanne Devon

Going Rogue. It's cute. It's sassy. It's mavericky. The title of
Sarah Palin's memoir is designed to sell books. If it had been
titled *Everything I Need to Know I Learned Playing Point Guard
for the Wasilla High School Girls Basketball Team*, it might not
have had quite the same zing. Perhaps the title was intended
to encapsulate the fierce, independent spirit that many had
learned to associate with the woman who came closer to the
vice presidency than any Republican woman in history. But
there are many back here in Alaska who heard *Going Rogue*
and were horrified, struck by the ugly irony of her book title.

When the Lower 48 was still asking "Sarah who?" the
GOP was relying on the talking point "She's the most popular
governor in the nation." And she was. While other governors
with approval ratings in the high fifties were feeling pretty
pleased with themselves, Sarah Palin was luxuriating in
approval ratings that at one point approached a stratospheric
90 percent. Without that number, she would likely never
have become the vice presidential nominee.

But as it was, that statistic played a significant role in the
magical attraction to this virtually unknown candidate, who
appeared to be the best kept secret in the country. If people
in her own state were so thrilled, then she obviously must be
doing something right, people reasoned. After all, how could
90 percent of Alaskans be wrong? That question has a two-
part answer.

1. She was not Frank Murkowski.
Frank Murkowski, the man who preceded Palin in the
governorship, was, to put it kindly, a disaster. He had been
Alaska's senator from 1981 to 2002, when he decided to run

for governor. It only took one term of Murkowski actually being present in the state, where everyone could watch him work up close, for Alaskans to conclude that they'd rather have anyone else. The pricey new executive jet he purchased for his own use became known as "The Bald Ego." Bumper stickers with the slogan "Anyone But Frank" appeared on vehicles across the state.

Murkowski was humiliated by Palin in the primary, garnering only 19 percent of the vote. The fact that Palin got the Republican nomination had little to do with any perceived mastery of policy, experience, or leadership ability. She got the nomination because she had a great story, and Alaskans needed a hero. Here she was, a relatively inexperienced politician from Alaska's Bible Belt, fresh-faced and full of family values, gun-toting and adventurous, spunky and energetic, a wife, a mother, and a no-nonsense politician who took on the oil companies and the good ol' boys, with some energy credentials to boot. She wowed Alaskans much like she did the rest of the country that fateful day in August 2008.

Many centrists and moderate progressives in Alaska liked her. They may have disagreed with her social conservatism, but it was quite amazing to watch this young woman step up to the plate out of nowhere, with her slingshot in hand, and conk Frank "Goliath" Murkowski on the noggin with a big fat rock. When he tipped over and landed on his back in a big dust cloud, the crowd went wild. The bumper stickers changed to "Go, Sarah, Go!" She was Everywoman. She was proof that a regular person could take on the system and win. She was Joan of Arc, Political Barbie, and *Mrs. Smith Goes to Juneau* all wrapped into one, with a dash of *Charlie's Angels* thrown in for good measure. And she was most definitely *not* Frank Murkowski.

When the gubernatorial race was won, just like after a great football game, we all left smiling and exhausted. We slapped each other on the back and went back to our regular lives...which brings us to reason number two.

2. We weren't paying attention.

Just as we weren't paying much attention to issues during the gubernatorial primary and general election, we *kept* not paying attention to Palin after she took office.

A developing ethics scandal was in the news, and we watched as a string of Alaska legislators, known as the Corrupt Bastards Club, were indicted and convicted on corruption charges. Votes were bought and sold for a few thousand dollars; Alaskan politicians went cheap. Video of money changing hands in a hotel suite in Juneau and incriminating audio of drunken officials using crude language and talking skulduggery surfaced. Alaskans *needed* their patron saint of clean government and reform. In the cesspool of political corruption surrounding us, she was proof that somebody had integrity. Alaskans had Sarah, and they trusted her. If there was something amiss, they didn't want to know.

And then there was Troopergate. This pre-nomination scandal was a wake-up call for many Alaskans. Troopergate had all the ingredients of a trashy political novel. Trooper meets girl, trooper marries girl, trooper is a cad, trooper and girl divorce. Custody hearing gets ugly. All the bad stuff trooper did for years, and a bunch of stuff he didn't do as well, suddenly comes out. And the girl's sister just happens to be the governor. That's where it got messy. The divorce was elevated to state business, and the considerable power of the governor's office was turned to thoughts of revenge.

During the custody investigation, the Palins leveled all kinds of accusations at state trooper Mike Wooten. He was investigated on dozens of complaints, disciplined on two counts, and allowed to keep his position with the troopers. Case closed, or so he thought. Enter Walt Monegan, Palin's new commissioner of the Department of Public Safety and head of the troopers. Monegan was well respected by those who served under him; he did a bang-up job with minimal funding; but somehow he suddenly got axed. Palin was out of town, and Monegan was "offered another job." There was no explanation to Alaskans, and a critical department was left with no leadership. Rumors started to swirl that the highly respected Monegan was dismissed because he had refused to fire the ne'er-do-well ex-brother-in-law, who had already been investigated and disciplined.

Palin vehemently denied that she or anyone on her staff had ever talked to Monegan or pressured him in any way to fire Wooten. It came out before her nomination for vice president, however, that there were literally dozens of conversations in which exactly such pressure was applied. One of the instances took the form of a recorded phone call from a Palin aide to the Alaska state troopers. Todd Palin himself even talked about it to Monegan in the governor's office while she was away.

It was a difficult journey of discovery for many of us; we had to come to terms with the Sarah Palin that really was. Like the painful revelation that there is no tooth fairy or Easter bunny, we had to learn that the Sarah Palin that we thought we knew, the one that we wanted and needed desperately, existed only in our imaginations. We had been told a beautiful story, which we chose to believe, about the *idea* of a politician. Most Alaskans chose to remain in denial.

Nobody paid much attention to the rumors that Sarah Palin was on the short list of McCain's potential running mates. Those who followed the news closely felt that surely no campaign in their right mind would choose a politician in the middle of an ethics scandal, especially one with so few credentials and from a state with so few electoral college votes.

So when Sarah Palin stepped onto the stage at the Republican National Convention in Minneapolis, it was surreal. Many Alaskans watched both dumbfounded and elated as the girl next door stood in front of the nation and made Alaska legitimate. No longer would people think we were backwards and backwoods, unworthy of attention. No longer were we simply three sad little frozen electoral votes somewhere off in the middle of nowhere. We would become more than just salmon and mountains and oil. We felt like we were part of the country. We had been invited to the dance, and we said yes.

While much of Alaska was simply enjoying their newfound relevance, it's important to remember that others—who had been paying closer attention and had questioned Palin's qualifications—were horrified. The realization dawned: The McCain campaign had no idea who they chose. They didn't vet her, or they didn't care. They were either incompetent or irresponsible. It was obvious from the very beginning. We knew we had ringside seats to the biggest political disaster imaginable—Sarah Palin a heartbeat away from being the leader of the free world. It was like watching a political horror movie.

One thing became very clear to the McCain campaign after Palin's nomination: Troopergate needed to be managed and managed quickly. All of a sudden it wasn't just the understaffed *Anchorage Daily News* looking at the scandal. It wasn't just an audience who wanted to believe the best about Sarah Palin. All spotlights shone on Alaska, and the mass migration of mainstream media began. Enter the *Wall Street Journal*, the *New York Times*, the *Washington Post*, *Newsweek*, and a host of others from around the world, all poking around, talking to locals, questioning, and researching. Something needed to be done.

And so the "rogues" were born. First, it was Wooten. Palin was quick to defend herself by labeling him a "rogue" trooper and saying that he was a danger not only to her family, whom she claimed he had threatened, but to the public at large. This was serious business. Wooten's less-than-sympathetic story made the character assassination all that much easier. When the Alaska state legislature looked into the Troopergate affair, a bipartisan legislative council appointed an independent investigator to examine these claims.

That investigator, Stephen Branchflower, wrote in his report: "I conclude that such claims of fear were not bona fide and were offered to provide cover for the Palins' real motivation: to get Trooper Wooten fired for personal family reasons." But despite this finding, Wooten ended up with a desk job. Palin's accusations that he was a "rogue" and a danger to the public had brought about threats that made it impossible for him to work out in the open as a trooper. Nobody likes a rogue cop.

While Wooten was sometimes difficult to defend, Walt Monegan was another matter. The commissioner of public safety was a former marine, a former Anchorage chief of police, very well liked and respected. Palin's spokeswoman Meghan Stapleton once again used the word "rogue," but this time to attack Monegan. In a stinging press conference, Stapleton said that Monegan had displayed "egregious rogue behavior." He had a "rogue mentality." What had Monegan done to earn this smear? According to Palin's office, he had resisted the governor's budget policies. He wanted to travel to Washington, D.C., to seek funding to help combat sexual assault in a state that leads the nation in that category. Stapleton, who had been a respected news anchor before her association with Palin, suffered withering criticism from Alaskans across the political spectrum. The venom she used while eviscerating Monegan laid bare just how desperate the McCain/Palin campaign was to discredit anyone who might act as a roadblock to victory. Alaska is a small town. Monegan was no "rogue"; everyone knew it, and many felt the use of the term was quite simply disgraceful.

In September 2008, a rally was held in downtown Anchorage. A crowd of well over a thousand Alaskans showed up to protest the administration's handling of "Troopergate," the insinuation of the McCain campaign's attorneys into Alaska's Department of Law, and the outrageous behavior of Meghan Stapleton, Attorney General Talis Colberg, and Governor Palin herself. One of the speakers at the rally was Betty Monegan, who carried a sign saying, "I am the Mother of the 'rogue' Walt Monegan, and I love him." This tiny, soft-spoken woman stood behind the microphone and spoke her piece. She was choked with emotion, and the crowd soon was too. They cheered for Betty Monegan and for her son. In a state where a street-corner political gathering of twenty-five people is generally considered a success, the demonstration made a resounding statement: This was not OK.

The Branchflower report found Palin guilty of abusing her power as governor under the Alaska Executive Branch Ethics Act. The attorney general would ultimately resign his position amid legislative pressure, and Todd Palin and several administration officials would be found guilty of contempt for ignoring legislative subpoenas. Walt Monegan requested a due process hearing before the Alaska Personnel Board to address reputational harm from the administration's labeling him a "rogue." In a rather astounding strategic move,

Palin had earlier filed an ethics complaint against herself before that very same board, hoping to negate the findings of the legislative investigation. The three-person board, appointed by the governor, not only found Palin innocent of wrongdoing on November 3, the day before the election, it also refused to give Monegan his hearing.

When she returned home to Alaska after the election, licking her wounds, the mood in Alaska was icy. Suddenly, there was no McCain campaign. The national media was gone. All that was left was the governor having to live and work with the Democrats she had thrown under the bus and the Republicans who never liked her in the first place. Things began to fall apart. A series of back-and-forth power struggles to fill an empty state senate seat left her defeated. Her selection for attorney general to replace Colberg proved to be so controversial and exhibited such poor judgment, that for the first time in the history of the state a gubernatorial cabinet appointment was rejected by the legislature.

The not-so-glamorous return to work, her unwillingness and inability to use diplomacy to solve problems and heal campaign-inflicted wounds, and the lure of a lucrative book deal were among the factors that led to her shocking announcement on the Friday of Fourth of July weekend. She stood in front of her house, on the shore of Lake Lucille, in front of the media and a raft of honking waterfowl, and she quit. She stepped down from the governorship of the state, leaving in her wake a long list of people who were on the receiving end of blame, vitriol, and accusation—not just the two "rogue" cops but citizens who had filed ethics complaints against her administration, Democratic legislators who had helped her in the past, the father of her grandchild, political bloggers on both sides of the aisle who had written about her unfavorably, Republican critics, and of course the media in general. And finally, after months of watching her approval ratings sink and her disapproval ratings rise, the lines crossed. Once the most popular governor in America, she was now viewed unfavorably by the majority of people in her own state.

But that was then, and this is now. A new day is dawning for ex-governor Palin. She is reinventing herself, and her career in the national political sphere is just beginning. Outfitted with handlers, writers, and editors, she's ready to take on the world. And by titling her new book *Going Rogue*, she hopes to transform the term. Now it's reframed and repackaged to be impish and endearing. But it wasn't endearing when it was used as a finely sharpened tool to malign those who stood in the way of her power scramble to become the vice president of the United States.

Her ghostwriter, her book publisher, and those in the Lower 48 who buy and read her book may never learn her full story. But the very fact that the title of the book made it past Palin herself is illustrative of her own gaping disconnect with how she is perceived, the consequences of her actions, and the indifference with which she regards those who have been ground up in the gears of her political aspirations. And those qualities are the very ones that lost her the title of America's Most Popular Governor. *Rogue* has gone from a lie of desperation to a slab of red meat tossed out to a pack of starving, starry-eyed Republican lions.

3/ PALINTOLOGY

Selected Palinisms
Compiled by Sebastian Jones

PIT BULLS AND HOCKEY MOMS
From Sarah Palin's September 3, 2008, Republican National Convention speech

Sarah Palin I had the privilege of living most of my life in a small town. I was just your average hockey mom and signed up for the PTA.

Audience Hockey moms! Hockey moms! Hockey moms!

SP: I love those hockey moms. You know, they say the difference between a hockey mom and a pit bull: lipstick.... Before I became governor of the great state of Alaska I was mayor of my hometown. And since our opponents in this presidential election seem to look down on that experience, let me explain to them what the job involves. I guess a small-town mayor is sort of like a community organizer, except that you have actual responsibilities.

GOD AND THE IRAQ WAR—THE GRAND PLAN

From ABC News transcript of Palin's interview with World News Tonight *anchor Charles Gibson, September 11, 2008*

Charles Gibson You said recently, in your old church, "Our national leaders are sending U.S. soldiers on a task that is from God." Are we fighting a holy war?

SP: You know, I don't know if that was my exact quote.

CG: Exact words.

SP: But the reference there is a repeat of Abraham Lincoln's words.... I would never presume to know God's will or to speak God's words.... I do believe, though, that this war against extreme Islamic terrorists is the right thing. It's an unfortunate thing, because war is hell and I hate war, and, Charlie, today is the day that I send my first born, my son, my teenage son overseas with his Stryker brigade, 4,000 other wonderful American men and women, to fight for our country, for democracy, for our freedoms...

CG: I take your point about Lincoln's words, but you went on and said, "There is a plan and it is God's plan."

SP: I believe that there is a plan for this world and that plan for this world is for good. I believe that there is great hope and great potential for every country to be able to live and be protected with inalienable rights that I believe are God-given, Charlie, and I believe that those are the rights to life and liberty and the pursuit of happiness.

That, in my world view, is a grand—the grand plan.

CRISIS MODE—PALIN'S ECONOMIC SOLUTION

From CBS News transcript of Palin's interview with
Evening News *anchor Katie Couric, September 24, 2008*

Katie Couric If [the $700 billion government bailout] doesn't pass, do you think there's a risk of another Great Depression?

Sarah Palin Unfortunately, that is the road that America may find itself on. Not necessarily this, as it's been proposed, has to pass or we're going to find ourselves in another Great Depression. But, there has got to be action—bipartisan effort—Congress not pointing fingers at one another but finding the solution to this, taking action, and being serious about the reforms on Wall Street that are needed.

KC: Would you support a moratorium on foreclosures to help average Americans keep their homes?

SP: That's something that John McCain and I have both been discussing—whether that... is part of the solution or not. You know, it's going to be a multifaceted solution that has to be found here.

KC: So you haven't decided whether you'll support it or not?

SP: I have not.

KC: What are the pros and cons of it, do you think?

SP: Oh, well, some decisions that have been made poorly should not be rewarded, of course.

KC: By consumers, you're saying?

SP: Consumers—and those who were predator lenders also. That's, you know, that has to be considered also. But again, it's got to be a comprehensive, long-term solution found... for this problem that America is facing today. As I say, we are getting into crisis mode here.

PUTIN REARS HIS HEAD

From CBS News transcript of Palin's interview with
Evening News *anchor Katie Couric, September 25, 2008*

KC: You've cited Alaska's proximity to Russia as part of your foreign policy experience. What did you mean by that?

SP: That Alaska has a very narrow maritime border between a foreign country, Russia, and, on our other side, the land boundary that we have with Canada. It's funny that a comment like that was kinda made to... I don't know, you know... reporters.

KC: Mocked?

SP: Yeah, mocked, I guess that's the word, yeah.

KC: Well, explain to me why that enhances your foreign-policy credentials.

SP: Well, it certainly does, because our, our next-door neighbors are foreign countries, there in the state that I am the executive of. And there...

KC: Have you ever been involved in any negotiations, for example, with the Russians?

SP: We have trade missions back and forth, we do. It's very important when you consider even national security issues with Russia. As Putin rears his head and comes into the air space of the United States of America, where do they go? It's Alaska. It's just right over the border. It is from Alaska that we send those out to make sure that an eye is being kept on this very powerful nation, Russia, because they are right there, they are right next to our state.

WHERE DO YOU GET YOUR NEWS?

From CBS News transcript of Palin's interview with Evening News anchor Katie Couric, September 30, 2008

KC: And when it comes to establishing your worldview, I was curious, what newspapers and magazines did you regularly read before you were tapped for this to stay informed and to understand the world?

SP: I've read most of them, again with a great appreciation for the press, for the media.

KC: What, specifically?

SP: Um, all of them, any of them that have been in front of me all these years.

KC: Can you name a few?

SP: I have a vast variety of sources where we get our news, too. Alaska isn't a foreign country, where it's kind of suggested, "Wow, how could you keep in touch with what the rest of Washington, D.C., may be thinking when you live up there in Alaska?" Believe me, Alaska is like a microcosm of America.

ON ABORTION AND CONTRACEPTION

From CBS News *transcript of Palin's interview with* Evening News *anchor Katie Couric, September 30, 2008*

KC: If a 15-year-old is raped by her father, do you believe it should be illegal for her to get an abortion, and why?

SP: I am pro-life. And I'm unapologetic in my position that I am pro-life. And I understand there are good people on both sides of the abortion debate. In fact, good people in my own family have differing views on abortion, and when it should be allowed. [I do] respect people's opinions on this. Now, I would counsel to choose life. I would also like to see a culture of life in this country. But I would also like to take it one step further. Not just saying I am pro-life and I want fewer and fewer abortions in this country, but I want them, those women who find themselves in circumstances that are absolutely less than ideal, for them to be supported, and adoptions made easier.

KC: But ideally, you think it should be illegal for a girl who was raped or the victim of incest to get an abortion?

SP: I'm saying that, personally, I would counsel the person to choose life, despite horrific, horrific circumstances that this person would find themselves in. And, um, if you're asking, though, kind of foundationally here, should anyone end up in jail for having an... abortion, absolutely not. That's nothing I would ever support.

KC: Some people have credited the morning-after pill for decreasing the number of abortions. How do you feel about the morning-after pill?

SP: Well, I am all for contraception. And I am all for preventative measures that are legal and safe, and should be taken, but Katie, again, I am one to believe that life starts at the moment of conception. And I would like to see...

KC: And so you don't believe in the morning-after pill?

SP: ... I would like to see fewer and fewer abortions in this world. And again, I haven't spoken with anyone who disagrees with my position on that.

KC: I'm sorry, I just want to ask you again. Do you not support or do you condone or condemn the morning-after pill?

SP: Personally, and this isn't McCain/Palin policy ...

KC: No, that's OK, I'm just asking you.

SP: But personally, I would not choose to participate in that kind of contraception.

DRED SCOTT V. SANDFORD, ANYONE?

From CBS News *transcript of Palin's interview with* Evening News *anchor Katie Couric, October 1, 2008*

KC: What other Supreme Court decisions do you disagree with?

SP: Well, let's see. There's, of course in the great history of America there have been rulings, that's never going to be absolute consensus by every American. And there are those issues, again, like *Roe v. Wade,* where I believe are best held on a state level and addressed there. So you know, going through the history of America, there would be others, but ...

KC: Can you think of any?

SP: Well, I could think of... any, again, that could be best dealt with on a more local level, maybe I would take issue with. But, you know, as mayor, and then as governor and even as a vice president, if I'm so privileged to serve, [I] wouldn't be in a position of changing those things but in supporting the law of the land as it reads today.

CANDIDATE'S PREROGATIVE
From the vice presidential debate, October 2, 2008

I may not answer the questions that either the moderator or you want to hear, but I'm going to talk straight to the American people and let them know my track record also.

PALIN AROUND WITH TERRORISTS

Palin on the stump, as quoted by the New York Times, *October 4, 2008*

There is a lot of interest, I guess, in what I read and what I've read lately. Well, I was reading my copy of today's New York Times and I was interested to read about Barack's friends from Chicago.

I get to bring this up not to pick a fight, but it was there in the *New York Times*, so we are gonna talk about it. Turns out one of Barack's earliest supporters is a man who, according to the *New York Times*, and they are hardly ever wrong, was a domestic terrorist and part of a group that, quote, launched a campaign of bombings that would target the Pentagon and U.S. Capitol. Wow. These are the same guys who think patriotism is paying higher taxes.

This is not a man who sees America as you see it and how I see America. We see America as the greatest force for good in this world. If we can be that beacon of light and hope for others who seek freedom and democracy and can live in a country that would allow intolerance in the equal rights that again our military men and women fight for and die for all of us. Our opponent though, is someone who sees America, it seems, as being so imperfect that he's palling around with terrorists who would target their own country.

WRONG ON WRIGHT

Palin in an interview with Bill Kristol, published October 5, 2008 in the New York Times

To tell you the truth, Bill, I don't know why that association [between Obama and Jeremiah Wright] isn't discussed more, because those were appalling things that that pastor had said about our great country, and to have sat in the pews for twenty years and listened to that—with, I don't know, a sense of condoning it, I guess, because he didn't get up and leave— to me, that does say something about character. But, you know, I guess that would be a John McCain call on whether he wants to bring that up.

INTERNAL TROUBLE OVER TODD AND THE ALASKAN INDEPENDENCE PARTY

A chain of e-mails between Sarah Palin and Steve Schmidt on October 15, 2008, focusing on the Alaskan Independence Party and Todd's involvement with it, which had just been the subject of an article by Max Blumenthal and David Neiwert in Salon (reprinted in this book). Here is the exchange as reported by CBS News on July 1, 2009:

Palin's first e-mail "Pls get in front of that ridiculous issue that's cropped up all day today—two reporters, a protestor's sign, and many shout-outs all claiming Todd's involvement in an anti-American political party. It's bull, and I don't want to have to keep reacting to it.... Pls have statement given on this so it's put to bed."

Schmidt's first reply "Ignore it.... He was a member of the aip? My understanding is yes. That is part of their platform. Do not engage the protestors. If a reporter asks say it is ridiculous. Todd loves america."

Palin's second e-mail "That's not part of their platform and he was only a 'member' bc independent alaskans too often check that 'Alaska Independent' box on voter registrations thinking it just means non partisan.... He caught his error when changing our address and checked the right box. I still want it fixed."

Schmidt's second reply "Secession.... It is their entire reason for existence. A cursory examination of the website shows that the party exists for the purpose of seceding from the union. That is the stated goal on the front page of the web site. Our records indicate that todd was a member for seven years. If this is incorrect then we need to understand the discrepancy. The statement you are suggesting be released would be innaccurate. The innaccuracy would bring greater media attention to this matter and be a distraction. According to your staff there have been no media inquiries into this and you received no questions about it during your interviews. If you are asked about it you should smile and say many alaskans who love their country join the party because it speeks to a tradition of political independence. Todd loves his country ...We will not put out a statement and inflame this and create a situation where john has to adress this."

PRO-AMERICA AMERICA

Palin at an October 17, 2008, fundraiser in North Carolina

"We believe that the best of America is not all in Washington, D.C. We believe... that the best of America is in these small towns that we get to visit, and in these wonderful little pockets of what I call the real America, being here with all of you hardworking, very patriotic, um, very, um, pro-America areas of this great nation. This is where we find the kindness and the goodness and the courage of everyday Americans. Those who are running our factories and teaching our kids and growing our food and are fighting our wars for us. Those who are protecting us in uniform. Those who are protecting the virtues of freedom."

FREEDOM OF THE PRESS (TO LEAVE ME ALONE!)

From an October 31, 2008, interview with Washington, D.C.'s WMAL-AM

"If [the media] convince enough voters that that is negative campaigning, for me to call Barack Obama out on his associations, then I don't know what the future of our country would be in terms of First Amendment rights and our ability to ask questions without fear of attacks by the mainstream media."

SO MANY WARS TO FIGHT

From a November 1, 2008, interview with Fox News

We realize that more and more Americans are starting to see the light there and understand the contrast. And we talk a lot about, OK, we're confident that we're going to win on Tuesday, so from there, the first hundred days, how are we going to kick in the plan that will get this economy back on the right track and really shore up the strategies that we need over in Iraq and Iran to win these wars?

MY WIFE WROTE A SONG FOR YOU
From a prank call to Palin made by the Masked Avengers,
a Canadian Comedy Duo, who were impersonating French
president Nicolas Sarkozy

Avengers You know my wife is a popular singer and a former top model, and she's so hot in bed. She even wrote a song for you.

Sarah Palin Oh my goodness, I didn't know that.

A: Yes, in French it's called "Du rouge à lèvre sur un cochon" [translation: "Lipstick on a Pig"], or if you prefer in English, "Joe the Plumber"... it's his life, Joe the Plumber.

SP: Maybe she understands some of the unfair criticism, but I bet you she is such a hard worker, too, and she realizes you just plow through that criticism.

A: I just want to be sure. That phenomenon Joe the Plumber. That's not your husband, right?

SP: That's not my husband, but he's a normal American who just works hard and doesn't want government to take his money.

A: Yes, yes, I understand. We have the equivalent of Joe the Plumber in France. It's called Marcel, the guy with bread under his armpit.

SP: Right, that's what it's all about, the middle class and government needing to work for them. You're a very good example for us here....

CULTURE WARRIOR

From Palin's Facebook page, a note over the controversy surrounding Carrie Prejean, a contestant in the 2009 Miss USA pageant, and her remarks on gay marriage. Posted May 13, 2009

The liberal onslaught of malicious attacks against Carrie Prejean for expressing her opinion is despicable.

Carrie and I spoke soon after the attacks started; I can relate as a liberal target myself. What I find so remarkable is that these politically-motivated attacks fail to show that what Carrie and I believe is also what President Obama and Secretary Clinton believe—marriage is between a man and a woman.

I applaud Donald Trump for standing with Carrie during this time. And I respect Carrie for standing strong and staying true to herself, and for not letting those who disagree with her deny her protection under the nation's First Amendment Rights.

Our Constitution protects us all—not just those who agree with the far left.

ONLY DEAD FISH...

From the transcript of Palin's resignation announcement, as posted to her Facebook account, July 3, 2009 (emphasis, in all caps, is Palin's)

Some say things changed for me on August 29th last year—the day John McCain tapped me to be his running-mate—I say others changed.

Let me speak to that for a minute.

Political operatives descended on Alaska last August, digging for dirt. The ethics law I championed became their weapon of choice. Over the past nine months I've been accused of all sorts of frivolous ethics violations—such as holding a fish in a photograph, wearing a jacket with a logo on it, and answering reporters' questions.

Every one—all 15 of the ethics complaints have been dismissed. We've won! But it hasn't been cheap—the State has wasted THOUSANDS of hours of YOUR time and shelled out some two million of YOUR dollars to respond to "opposition research"—that's money NOT going to fund teachers or troopers—or safer roads. And this political absurdity, the "politics of personal destruction"... Todd and I are looking at more than half a million dollars in legal bills in order to set the record straight. And what about the people who offer up these silly accusations? It doesn't cost them a dime so they're not going to stop draining public resources—spending other peoples' money in their game.

It's pretty insane—my staff and I spend most of our day dealing with THIS instead of progressing our state now. I know I promised no more "politics as usual," but THIS isn't what anyone had in mind for ALASKA.

If I have learned one thing: LIFE is about choices!

And one chooses how to react to circumstances. You

can choose to engage in things that tear down, or build up. I choose to work very hard on a path for fruitfulness and productivity. I choose NOT to tear down and waste precious time; but to build UP this state and our country, and her industrious, generous, patriotic, free people!

Life is too short to compromise time and resources.... it may be tempting and more comfortable to just keep your head down, plod along, and appease those who demand: "Sit down and shut up," but that's the worthless, easy path; that's a quitter's way out. And a problem in our country today is apathy. It would be apathetic to just hunker down and "go with the flow".

Nah, only dead fish "go with the flow."

THE LONG GOOD BYE

From Palin's farewell speech as governor, July 27, 2009

And getting up here I say it is the best road trip in America soaring through nature's finest show. Denali, the great one, soaring under the midnight sun. And then the extremes. In the wintertime it's the frozen road that is competing with the view of ice-fogged frigid beauty, the cold though, doesn't it split the Cheechakos from the Sourdoughs? And then in the summertime, such extreme summertime, about a hundred and fifty degrees hotter than just some months ago, than just some months from now, with fireweed blooming along the frost heaves and merciless rivers that are rushing and carving and reminding us that here, Mother Nature wins. It is as throughout all Alaska, that big, wild, good life teeming along the road that is north to the future. That is what we get to see every day. Now what the rest of America gets to see along with us is in this last frontier there is hope and opportunity, and there is country pride. And it is our men and women in uniform securing it....

Together we do stand with gratitude for our troops who protect all of our cherished freedoms, including our freedom of speech which, par for the course, I'm going to exercise. And first, some straight talk for some, just some in the media because another right protected for all of us is freedom of the press, and you all have such important jobs reporting facts and informing the electorate, and exerting power to influence. You represent what could and should be a respected, honest profession that could and should be the cornerstone of our democracy. Democracy depends on you, and that is why, that's why our troops are willing to die for you. So, how 'bout, in honor of the American soldier, ya quit makin' things up. And don't underestimate the wisdom of the people....

TV TIME

From Palin's Facebook page, in a note titled "An Invitation," posted August 26, 2009

FOX News' Glenn Beck is doing an extraordinary job this week walking America behind the scenes of 1600 Pennsylvania Avenue and outlining who is actually running the White House.

Monday night he asked us to invite one friend to watch; tonight I invite all my friends to watch.

PALINOMICS 101

From Palin's remarks to Hong Kong investors on September 23, 2009 (as reported by the Wall Street Journal)

While we might be in the wilderness, conservatives need to defend the free market system and explain what really caused last year's collapse. According to one version of the story, America's economic woes were caused by a lack of government intervention and regulation and therefore the only way to fix the problem, because, of course, every problem can be fixed by a politician, is for more bureaucracy to impose itself further, deeper, forcing itself deeper into the private sector.

I think that's simply wrong. We got into this mess because of government interference in the first place. The mortgage crisis that led to the collapse of the financial market, it was rooted in a good-natured, but wrongheaded, desire to increase home ownership among those who couldn't yet afford to own a home. In so many cases, politicians on the right and the left, they wanted to take credit for an increase in home ownership among those with lower incomes. But the rules of the marketplace are not adaptable to the mere whims of politicians.

... Lack of government wasn't the problem. Government policies were the problem. The marketplace didn't fail. It became exactly as common sense [as one] would expect it to. The government ordered the loosening of lending standards. The Federal Reserve kept interest rates low. The government forced lending institutions to give loans to people who, as I say, couldn't afford them. Speculators spotted new investment vehicles, jumped on board, and rating agencies underestimated risks.

Palin's Prevarications
Compiled by Sebastian Jones

Note: Throughout the 2008 campaign, blogger Andrew Sullivan (andrewsullivan.theatlantic.com) ran an extremely useful recurring segment called "The Odd Lies of Sarah Palin," chronicling the former governor's various inconsistencies, exaggerations, and outright lies. Many of those assembled here come from Sullivan's blog, though we've added a few of our own.

ON HER AND TODD'S ACTIONS IN THE TROOPERGATE SCANDAL

Fiction

To allege that I, or any member of my family, requested, received or released confidential personnel information on an Alaska State Trooper, or directed disciplinary action be taken against any employee of the Department of Public Safety, is, quite simply, outrageous.

Palin press release, July 17, 2008

Fact

Governor Palin knowingly permitted a situation to continue where impermissible pressure was placed on several subordinates in order to advance a personal agenda, to wit: to get Trooper Michael Wooten fired...[and] permitted Todd Palin to use the Governor's office ...to continue to contact subordinate state employees in an effort to find some way to get Trooper Wooten fired.

Branchflower report to the Alaska legislature, October 10, 2008

Analysis

See John Nichols's "Why Troopergate Matters" for more on the scandal involving efforts by Sarah and Todd Palin to fire former brother-in-law Michael Wooten from his job as an Alaska state trooper and the dismissal of Alaska public safety commissioner Walter Monegan.

ON EARMARKS, GENERALLY

Fiction

We...championed reform to end the abuses of earmark spending by Congress.

Palin speech at the Republican convention, September 3, 2008

Fact

Representative Don Young, especially, God bless him, with transportation—Alaska did so well under the very basic provisions of the transportation act that he wrote just a couple of years ago. We had a nice bump there. We're very, very fortunate to receive the largesse that Don Young was able to put together for Alaska.

Palin at a gubernatorial forum, October, 2006

Analysis

During the 2008 campaign, Palin broadly condemned Congressional earmarking. However, back in 2006, she praised the work of one of Congress's most notorious earmarkers, Don Young, and the "largesse" he brought to Alaska.

ON THE GRAVINA ISLAND CROSSING
PROJECT (AKA THE BRIDGE TO NOWHERE)

Fiction
I told the Congress 'thanks but no thanks' for that Bridge to Nowhere.

Palin convention speech, September 3, 2008

Fact
She cited the widespread negative attention focused on the Gravina Island crossing project.

"We need to come to the defense of Southeast Alaska when proposals are on the table like the bridge and not allow the spinmeisters to turn this project or any other into something that's so negative."

Interview with the *Ketchikan Daily News*, October 2, 2006

Analysis
During the 2008 campaign, Palin repeatedly claimed to have been against the Gravina Island Bridge, more commonly known as the Bridge to Nowhere, but during the 2006 gubernatorial campaign, Palin supported the project.

ON POLAR BEARS GAINING ENDANGERED
SPECIES STATUS

Fiction

I strongly believe that adding [polar bears] to the list is the wrong move at this time. My decision is based on a comprehensive review by state wildlife officials of scientific information from a broad range of climate, ice and polar bear experts. In fact, there is insufficient evidence that polar bears are in danger of becoming extinct within the foreseeable future—the trigger for protection under the Endangered Species Act.

Sarah Palin op-ed in the *New York Times*,
January 5, 2008

Fact

Rick Steiner, a University of Alaska professor, sought the e-mail messages of state scientists who had examined the effect of global warming on polar bears.... An administration official told Mr. Steiner that his request would cost $468,784 to process.

When Mr. Steiner finally obtained the e-mail messages—through a federal records request—he discovered that state scientists had in fact agreed that the bears were in danger, records show.

New York Times report, September 14, 2009

Analysis

For more on Palin and the polar bears, see Mark Hertsgaard's "Our Polar Bears, Ourselves."

ON WHETHER HUMANS ARE RESPONSIBLE FOR GLOBAL WARMING

Fiction

I think you are a cynic because show me where I have ever said that there's absolute proof that nothing that man has ever conducted or engaged in has had any effect, or no effect, on climate change.

Palin in an interview with ABC News anchor Charles Gibson, September 11, 2008

Fact

I'm not a doom and gloom environmentalist like Al Gore blaming the changes in our climate on human activity.

Palin in the *Fairbanks Daily News-Miner*, December 4, 2007

Analysis

Despite her claims otherwise during the 2008 campaign, Palin had expressed doubt about the causes of global warming on several previous occasions. For more on her environmental record as governor, see Sheila Kaplan and Marilyn Berlin Snell's "Northern Exposure."

ON ALASKA'S SHARE OF U.S. DOMESTIC ENERGY SUPPLY

Fiction

Let me speak specifically about a credential that I do bring to this table, Charlie, and that's with the energy independence that I've been working on for these years as the governor of this state that produces nearly 20 percent of the U.S. domestic supply of energy, that I worked on as chairman of the Alaska Oil and Gas Conservation Commission, overseeing the oil and gas development in our state to produce more for the United States.

Palin in an interview with ABC News anchor Charles Gibson, September 11, 2008

Fact

According to EIA [the Energy Information Administration], Alaska actually produced 2,417.1 trillion BTUs [British Thermal Units] of energy in 2005, the last year for which full state numbers are available. That's equal to just 3.5 percent of the country's domestic energy production.

And according to EIA analyst Paul Hess, that would calculate to only "2.4 percent of the 100,368.6 trillion BTUs the U.S. consumes."

Factcheck.org analysis, September 12, 2008

Analysis

During an interview with Charles Gibson, Palin wildly exaggerated the share of the domestic energy supply Alaska provides. During the campaign, John McCain said Palin "knows more about energy than probably anyone else in the United States of America."

For more on Alaska's energy politics see Michael T. Klare's "Palin's Petropolitics."

ON WHETHER SHE HAD TO "WING" HER CONVENTION SPEECH WITHOUT A TELEPROMPTER

Fiction

"There Ohio was right out in front, right in front of me," Palin said. "The teleprompter got messed up, I couldn't follow it, and I just decided I'd just talk to the people in front of me. It was Ohio."

Palin remarks at a Canton, Ohio fundraiser, September 15, 2008

Fact

Sarah Palin delivered a powerful speech last night, but she did not "wing it."...I frequently looked up at the machine, and there was no serious malfunction. A top convention planner confirms this morning that there were no major problems.

Politico report, September 4, 2008

Analysis

Palin helped promote a post-convention myth widely discussed on conservative blogs: namely that her teleprompter had broken mid-speech, forcing her to improvise her remarks. Reporters at the convention claimed otherwise.

ON "LIVING BY EXAMPLE" VIA TAKING A PAY CUT WHILE MAYOR

Fiction
As mayor I took a voluntary pay cut, which didn't thrill my husband...

Palin in Bloomberg News, September 15, 2008

Fact
"As a Council member she voted against hiking the mayor's salary from $64,000 to $68,000, but it passed anyway. When she came in as mayor, she passed the ordinance which brought her salary down to $61,200. But that may not actually have taken effect, and Council-mandated raises brought her actual salary up to $68,000."

TalkingPointsMemo.com, September 18, 2008

Analysis
Palin often presented herself as living a "frugal" life, despite reports of frequent and expensive in-state travel as Governor and the $150,000 spent by the Republican National Committee on her campaign wardrobe revealed by *Politico*.

ON DIVESTMENT FROM SUDAN

Fiction

When I and others in the legislature found out that we had some millions of dollars [of Permanent Fund investments] in Sudan, we called for divestment through legislation of those dollars.

Palin in the vice presidential debate, October 2, 2009

Fact

"The legislation is well intended, and the desire to make a difference is noble, but mixing moral and political agendas at the expense of our citizens' financial security is not a good combination," testified Brian Andrews, Palin's deputy treasury commissioner.

ABC News report, October 3, 2009

Analysis

While claiming during a debate with Joe Biden to have supported Alaskan divestment from Sudan, supporters of divestment informed ABC News that the Palin administration had publicly opposed their efforts.

ON "TURKEYGATE"

Fiction
*"The [Alaska] governor did not know it was going on behind her,"
Palin's spokesperson tells ET of the reportedly grisly scene at
Triple D Farm & Hatchery outside Wasilla.*

Entertainment Tonight, November 21, 2008

Fact
*Scott Jensen is the one who filmed the scene. He's local station
KTUU's award-winning chief photographer. He told...KUDO
radio yesterday that Sarah Palin, who was standing next to her
personal assistant throughout the entire interview, chose the
spot on which she stood for the "turkey slaughter interview."...
The turkey slaughter was already underway when the governor
chose the spot. The photographer pointed out what was going on
and asked her if she wanted to move. She said, "No worries."*

Mudflats blog, November 22, 2008

Analysis
Weeks after the election, Palin held a press conference in
Wasilla, using an in-progress turkey slaughter as a backdrop.
After much ridicule in the press, Palin claimed to have
not known what was happening behind her. Much like
the convention teleprompter incident, those at the scene
contradicted her claims.

ON STIMULUS FUNDING

Fiction

Palin announced last week she was not accepting $288 million of the $930.7 million that the state is due in the federal stimulus.

Anchorage Daily News, March 24, 2009

Fact

"The governor has not rejected any funds—that I think was perhaps the interpretation and I know certainly in some of the coverage of the press event last week," Karen Rehfeld, the governor's budget director, told the House Finance Committee on Tuesday.

Anchorage Daily News, March 24, 2009

Analysis

Palin publicly opposed President Obama's stimulus plan that passed Congress in February 2009. However, as Louisiana did under fellow conservative governor Bobby Jindal, Alaska ended up accepting the vast majority of its stimulus funds.

ON "DEATH PANELS"

Fiction

And who will suffer the most when they ration care? The sick, the elderly, and the disabled, of course. The America I know and love is not one in which my parents or my baby with Down Syndrome will have to stand in front of Obama's "death panel" so his bureaucrats can decide, based on a subjective judgment of their "level of productivity in society," whether they are worthy of health care. Such a system is downright evil.

Sarah Palin's Facebook page, August 7, 2009

Fact

Palin's statement sounds more like a science fiction movie (Soylent Green, anyone?) than part of an actual bill before Congress. We rate her statement Pants on Fire!

PolitiFact analysis of Palin's remarks, August 10, 2009

Analysis

This summer, Palin contributed to the health care debate by claiming the old and infirm will have to submit to "death panels," launching a meme that spread widely in conservative circles and, eventually, was cited as a reason to oppose health care reform by prominent Republican politicians. Ironically, the end-of-life counseling provision in the health care reform bill that served as inspiration for Palin's notion of death panels was something she supported at the state level while governor.

ON THE COST OF ETHICS INVESTIGATIONS

Fiction

We keep proving [our innocence] every time we win an ethics violation lawsuit, and we've won every one of them. But it has been costing our state millions of dollars. It's cost Todd and me.

Palin in an ABC News interview, July 7, 2009

Fact

In fact, the Anchorage Daily News *reports that the complaints cost the state $286,000, and the most costly set (there were several) had to do with Troopergate, which had exploded before Palin was tapped by...McCain. The most costly Troopergate complaint apparently involved one Palin herself made, hoping the investigation would exonerate her.*

Salon, July 9, 2009

Analysis

Palin consistently inflated and exaggerated the costs and burdens associated with ethics investigations of her actions as governor of Alaska. In addition to reporting that the costs of the investigations were in the hundreds of thousands of dollars, as opposed to millions, the *Anchorage Daily News* also revealed that much of that money would have been spent retaining lawyers, with or without ethics complaints being filed.

ON THE "DEPARTMENT OF LAW"

Fiction

Palin said there is a difference between the White House and what she has experienced in Alaska. If she were in the White House the "department of law" would protect her from baseless ethical allegations.

"I think on a national level your department of law there in the White House would look at some of the things that we've been charged with and automatically throw them out," she said.

ABC News report, July 7, 2009

Fact

There is no "Department of Law" at the White House.

ABC News report, July 7, 2009

Analysis

Throughout the 2008 campaign and after, Palin demonstrated some confusion as to what the vice president actually does and how the First Amendment functions. In this case, she created an entire governmental department out of thin air.

Palin's Top 25 Tweets
Compiled by Sebastian Jones

The Hills Are Alive
Riding 2 Kenai; writing last Govs speech on way; country music streaming & countryside screaming inspiration 4 pro-developmnt + pro-enviro msg *12:52 PM Jul 21st*

Inspiration
Couple of thoughts for the day on beautiful bright AK morn: "You have to sacrifice to win. That's my philosophy in 6 words."— George Allen. & *8:03 AM Jul 8th*

Today, try this: "Act in accordance to your conscience -risk- by pursuing larger vision in opposition to popular, powerful pressure"—unknown *8:12 AM Jul 8th*

More talk of #2 "Stimulus" Pkg? Please no- for so many reasons- incl the 1st one hasn't done what's promised, & debt forced on AKn kids is.. *10:54 PM Jul 11th*

selfish & immoral bc it robs their future opportunities! "If there is trouble, let it be in my day, that my child may have peace" Thomas Paine *11:02 PM Jul 11th*

"Criticism is something easily avoided by saying nothing, doing nothing, being nothing." Aristotle Don't fear it; it means u make a difference *12:29 AM Jul 14th*

Campbell's fiscally conserv. position on this = M. Levin's "Conservatism is antidote to tyranny bc its principles ARE our founding principles" *8:52 AM Jul 21st*

Awesome AK night sensing summer already winding down w/fireweed near full bloom; finally sitting down to pen; listening to Big & Rich "Shuttin 9:53 PM Jul 22nd

Detroit Down" & "Rollin": "Aint gonna shut my mouth/I know there's got to be a few hundred million more like me/ just trying to keep it free" 9:58 PM Jul 22nd

For the Children

I join Auto Dealers today for kids' safety seat law/promo. NOTHING more important than safety of our babies: Life's most precious ingredient 9:51 AM Jun 17th

Kids: be more concerned w/your character vs reputation bc character is what you are, reputation is merely what others think you are. J Wooden 10:44 PM Jul 13th

No time to waste: teach US youth to avoid idleness; they can lead new American Industrial Revolution w/WORK & embrace "Buy American" mission 12:08 PM Jul 19th

Mama Bear

Great day w/bear management wildlife biologists; much to see in wild territory incl amazing creatures w/mama bears' gutteral raw instinct to 10:34 PM Jul 15th

protect & provide for her young; She sees danger? She brazenly rises up on strong hind legs, growls Don't Touch My Cubs & the species survives 10:38 PM Jul 15th

& mama bear doesn't look 2 anyone else 2 hand her anything; biologists say she works harder than males, is provider/ protector for the future 10:40 PM Jul 15th

High Stakes

AK Aces vs SC Stingrays tonight. 1st Family & I will be on hand for win—anticipate winning friendly bet w/SC Gov. Sanford, too. Go, Aces! *12:55 PM May 22nd*

Keepin' the dream alive! Thank you AK Aces! OT win last night brings Kelly Cup game 6 home Thurs. Bet w/SC Gov is alive too. Save Our Salmon *9:26 AM May 31st*

The Hacking Paradox

Unfortunately fake "Gov Sarah Palin" twitter sites r doing their thing today: unscrupulous, untrue- so sorry if u recv false info @ fake site *3:12 PM Jul 4th*

Funny! In the words of my sis: Aren't the same ones w/fake twitter sites & blogs crying "she's 'abandoning' us" the same ones wishing u gone? *3:49 PM Jul 4th*

Best Broken Promise

elected is replaceable; Ak WILL progress! + side benefit=10 dys til less politically correct twitters fly frm my fingertps outside State site *12:39 AM Jul 17th*

The Palin Doctrine

Learn how Wild AK Seafood can help combat world hunger. Pure, healthy, abundant protein; exciting initiative rolled out in NY this week. *9:57 AM May 3rd*

More N Korea nuke tests: why consider US missile program cuts now? AK military program helps secure US. Now is NOT time to cut our defense. *9:48 AM May 25th*

W/deadly Iranian protests let us be thankful for, & supportive of, U.S. Military defending OUR democracy & freedom. God protect the innocent *12:46 PM Jun 20th*

Why U.S. peace missions for freedom? "America is still the abiding alternative to tyranny. That is our purpose in the world." Ronald R... *6:23 AM Jun 26th*

Seeking a Solution
Announced the "stay of execution", orphaned moose calves to be protected @ this time by Dept of Fish & Game. Long-term solution still needed *6:28 PM Jun 4th*

Buyer's Remorse
Compiled by Sebastian Jones

Some of the sharpest barbs tossed at Palin have come not from liberals but from conservatives. While a few die-hards, like William Kristol, have steadfastly defended her, many other establishment conservatives either found themselves quickly disenchanted or never warmed to her in the first place. Statements like the following indicate where the party's fault lines lie as Palin surveys the 2012 landscape:

Rod Dreher, conservative columnist, September 25, 2008, on his Beliefnet blog, responding to the Couric interview:
Couric's questions are straightforward and responsible. Palin is mediocre, again, regurgitating talking points mechanically, not thinking. Palin's just babbling. She makes George W. Bush sound like Cicero.

Kathleen Parker, September 26, 2008, writing in *National Review*:
If BS were currency, Palin could bail out Wall Street herself.

David Frum, September 29, 2008, in an interview with the *New York Times*:
I think [Palin] has pretty thoroughly—and probably irretrievably—proven that she is not up to the job of being president of the United States.

Anonymous McCain Adviser, October 26, 2008, in an interview with CNN:
She is a diva. She takes no advice from anyone.... She does not have any relationships of trust with any of us, her family or

anyone else. Also she is playing for her own future and sees
herself as the next leader of the party. Remember: Divas trust
only unto themselves, as they see themselves as the beginning
and end of all wisdom.

Steve Schmidt, October 2, 2009, speaking at the *Atlantic*'s "First Draft of History" event; Schmidt would, only days later, reassert that Palin was the correct choice in 2008:

I think she has talents, but my honest view is that she would not be a winning candidate for the Republican Party in 2012.... Were she to be the nominee, we could have a catastrophic election result.

David Brooks, October 8, 2009, at the *Atlantic*'s "First Draft of History" event:

[Sarah Palin] represents a fatal cancer to the Republican Party.... There has been a counter, more populist tradition, which is not only to scorn liberal ideas but to scorn ideas entirely. And I'm afraid that Sarah Palin has those prejudices.

Peggy Noonan, July 10, 2009, in the *Wall Street Journal*:

Mrs. Palin's supporters have been ordering her to spend the next two years reflecting and pondering. But she is a ponder-free zone. She can memorize the names of the presidents of Pakistan, but she is not going to be able to know how to think about Pakistan. Why do her supporters not see this? Maybe they think "not thoughtful" is a working-class trope!

The Poetry of Sarah Palin
Recent works by the Republican vice presidential candidate
Hart Seely

It's been barely six weeks since the arctic-fresh voice of
Alaskan poet Sarah Heath Palin burst upon the Lower 48. In
campaign interviews, the governor, mother, and maverick
GOP vice presidential candidate has chosen to bypass the
media filter and speak directly to fans through her intensely
personal verses, spoken poems that drill into the vagaries of
modern life as if they were oil deposits beneath
a government-protected tundra.

The poems collected here were compiled verbatim from
only three brief interviews. So just imagine the work Sarah
Palin could produce over the next four (or eight) years.

On Good and Evil
It is obvious to me
Who the good guys are in this one
And who the bad guys are.
The bad guys are the ones
Who say Israel is a stinking corpse,
And should be wiped off
The face of the earth.

That's not a good guy.

To Katie Couric, CBS News, September 25, 2008

You Can't Blink

You can't blink.
You have to be wired
In a way of being
So committed to the mission,

The mission that we're on,
Reform of this country,
And victory in the war,
You can't blink.

So I didn't blink.

To Charles Gibson, ABC News, September 11, 2008

Haiku

These corporations.
Today it was AIG,
Important call, there.

To Sean Hannity, Fox News, September 18, 2008

Befoulers of the Verbiage

It was an unfair attack on the verbiage
That Senator McCain chose to use,
Because the fundamentals,
As he was having to explain afterwards,
He means our workforce.
He means the ingenuity of the American.
And of course that is strong,
And that is the foundation of our economy.
So that was an unfair attack there,
Again based on verbiage.

To Sean Hannity, Fox News, September 18, 2008

Secret Conversation

I asked President Karzai:
"Is that what you are seeking, also?
That strategy that has worked in Iraq?
That John McCain had pushed for?
More troops?
A counterinsurgency strategy?"
And he said, "Yes."

To Katie Couric, CBS News, September 25, 2008

Outside

I am a Washington outsider.
I mean,
Look at where you are.
I'm a Washington outsider.
I do not have those allegiances
To the power brokers,
To the lobbyists.
We need someone like that.

To Charles Gibson, ABC News, September 11, 2008

On the Bailout

Ultimately,
What the bailout does
Is help those who are concerned
About the health care reform
That is needed
To help shore up our economy,
Helping the—
It's got to be all about job creation, too.

Shoring up our economy
And putting it back on the right track.
So health care reform
And reducing taxes
And reining in spending
Has got to accompany tax reductions
And tax relief for Americans.
And trade.

We've got to see trade
As opportunity
Not as a competitive, scary thing.
But one in five jobs
Being created in the trade sector today,
We've got to look at that
As more opportunity.
All those things.

To Katie Couric, CBS News, September 25, 2008

Challenge to a Cynic
You are a cynic.
Because show me where
I have ever said
That there's absolute proof
That nothing that man
Has ever conducted
Or engaged in,
Has had any effect,
Or no effect,
On climate change.

To Charles Gibson, ABC News, September 11, 2008

On Reporters
It's funny that
A comment like that
Was kinda made to,
I don't know,
You know...
Reporters.

To Katie Couric, CBS News, September 25, 2008

Small Mayors
You know,
Small mayors,
Mayors of small towns—
Quote, unquote—
They're on the front lines.

To Sean Hannity, Fox News, September 19, 2008

4/ LIPSTICK ON A FAUX FEMINIST
Palin and Women

Sarah Palin, Affirmative Action Babe
Katha Pollitt

Ah, meritocracy! Not so long ago, conservatives had a lock on it: no affirmative action, no A's for effort, no competitions where everyone gets a prize. People who complained that racism or sexism or any other *ism* was holding them back were whiners looking for excuses. They either didn't want to work hard or, as Charles Murray claimed in *The Bell Curve*, they weren't smart enough to make the grade.

Well, never mind. Sarah Palin has done for meritocracy what she's done for those other conservative obsessions: working mothers (you go, girl!), teen pregnancy (a challenge!), masculine authority (the first dude?)—to say nothing of gravitas, statesmanship, wisdom, and all those other weighty abstract nouns George Will likes to talk about. "I'm in love. Truly and deeply in love," Murray told the *New York Times*'s Deborah Solomon. "The last thing we need are more pointy-headed intellectuals running the government." Palin is new, young, attractive, charismatic, a natural speaker. She's a fascinating combination of opposites—relatable (horrible word) and down to earth but also intense and weirdly thrilling—half Rachael Ray, half Boudicca, a warrior mom. Feminist triumph or feminist nightmare? Maybe both! She's hot in all senses of the word. If she wasn't a big reactionary, she'd make a fantastic community organizer.

But let's be real: There is just no way Sarah Palin is equipped to be vice president, much less president. She doesn't know enough; she lacks the necessary grasp of, and curiosity about, our complex world; her political philosophy could fit on a bumper sticker: Us versus Them. The lack of stamps in her recently acquired passport has been much noted (yes, I know, Bill Kristol, Lincoln was not a big traveler, either); it isn't even clear she's well acquainted with the Lower 48. She's prepping for her debate with Joe Biden like a student jock cramming for a test. The McCain campaign, tacitly acknowledging how out of her depth she'll be no matter how many all-nighters she pulls, demanded—and, shockingly, got—special modifications to the veep debate format so that there would be no follow-up questions. After all, it wouldn't be right to expect Palin to compete on normal terms with Joe Biden, who has the totally unfair advantage of being deeply versed in domestic and foreign policy and knowing how the world's business is done. Lower standards for potential leaders of the world's most powerful country, in the name of diversity: That's what Republicans stand for now.

Hillary Clinton said her campaign put 18 million cracks in the glass ceiling; Sarah Palin, adding that "the women of America aren't finished yet"—as if women had stormed the barricades to nominate her—claimed her election would "shatter the glass ceiling once and for all." That's ridiculous. The glass ceiling is the invisible barrier of gender prejudice that prevents women, as a class, from rising to the level that their qualifications and abilities merit—the level they would reach if they were men. Like her or not, Hillary Clinton was more than equipped to run the United States; her nomination would have been a true glass-ceiling breakthrough. But Palin's only qualification for the second or, God forbid, the first job in the land is that John McCain thought she'd lend his sagging campaign a shot of estrogen and some right-wing Christian fairy dust.

Whether or not the gambit succeeds, it has nothing to do with recognizing accomplishment, experience or even steady old boring competence. Just ask McCain's gaffe-prone economic adviser Carly Fiorina, ushered off the stage after she pointed out that Sarah Palin couldn't run a major corporation; Fiorina, who was fired as CEO of Hewlett Packard after a fairly disastrous tenure, ought to know. Or ask Olympia Snowe, Susan Collins, Condoleezza Rice, Hawaii governor Linda Lingle, or the many other Republican women McCain could have chosen had he cared about governing. As has been known to happen in less exalted workplaces, Palin got the promotion because the boss just liked her. She will do no more to shatter the glass ceiling for other women as a group than such women usually do.

There's an upside, in that the old attack on Obama as a lightweight who is inexperienced and overreaching has all but vanished. Plus, there's the fun of watching conservative pundits scramble to deny the obvious. "There are Republicans who are unhappy about John McCain's selection of Sarah Palin," acknowledged William Kristol in his September 1 column. "Many are insiders who highly value—who overly value—'experience.'" Ah yes, experience. What is that, anyway? My people choose their leaders by inspecting the entrails of chickens, and the gods have always multiplied our herds! Besides, as Rush Limbaugh said recently, "She'll be surrounded by a sea of advisers." Hmmm, where did I hear that before? Was it not in 2000, when doubts were raised about whether George W. Bush could handle the job?

The stress on high-end conservative pundits is beginning to show. These are people, after all, who belong to the Ivy-educated, latte-drinking, Tuscan-vacationing urban elite they love to ridicule and who see themselves, however deludedly, as policy intellectuals and grown-ups. They've written endlessly about "excellence" and "standards." McCain's erratic flounderings, and Palin's patent absurdity, have driven David Brooks and George Will to write columns so anguished I'd feel sorry for them had they not made their bed by spending the past eight years rationalizing the obvious inadequacies of George W. Bush.

I want the people running the country to be smarter and wiser and more judicious and more knowledgeable than I am. If that's elitism, count me in.

The F-Card Won't Wash: Sarah Palin Is Disastrous for Women's Rights

Jessica Valenti

The *New York Post* calls her "a feminist dream." National
Public Radio asks if she's the "new face of feminism."
And the *Wall Street Journal*, ever subtle, calls it "Sarah
Palin Feminism." I call it well-spun garbage. (Yes, I'd even
call it a pig in lipstick.) It seems you can't open a newspaper or turn on the television without running across
a piece about how the Republican vice presidential candidate,
Sarah Palin, is not just a feminist, but *the* feminist—a
sign that all is right in the United States when it comes to
gender equality. (Turn in those Birkenstocks and picket
signs, gals!)

Palin's conservative cohorts are claiming her candidacy
as a win for women and proof that it's Republicans who
are the real agents of change. After all, what more could
American women want in a vice presidential candidate
than a well-coiffed "hockey mom"?

Never mind that Palin talks about her teen daughter's
decision to keep her child while awaiting the chance to
take that choice away from American women. Don't worry
about how Palin cut funding for a transitional home for
teenage mothers. And forget that, under Palin's mayoralty,
women in Wasilla, Alaska, were forced to pay for their
own rape kits to the tune of up to $1,200.

We're not supposed to care about these issues because,
say Republicans, we should just be happy that there's a
woman on the ticket. The McCain campaign is cynically
trying to re-create the excitement that surrounded Hillary
Clinton's candidacy, believing that all women want is...
another woman.

Ann Friedman, deputy editor of the *American Prospect*, wrote: "In picking Palin, Republicans are lending credence to the sexist assumption that women voters are too stupid to investigate or care about the issues, and merely want to vote for someone who looks like them... McCain has turned the idea of the first woman in the White House from a true moment of change to an empty pander."

What's worse is conservatives can't understand why women aren't lining up to thank them. In fact, the same people who moaned that women—those darn feminists, especially—were only supporting Hillary because of her gender are now screaming to the rafters because they're not supporting Palin for the same reason. That's what makes Republicans pulling the feminist card that much more insulting—the stunning hypocrisy. The McCain touting himself as the person who will put a woman in the White House is the same man who joked that Chelsea Clinton is "so ugly" because "her father is Janet Reno."

And despite the talk about being the party of change, appropriating feminist symbols—at a Pennsylvania rally people held up signs of Rosie the Riveter with Palin's face—and propping up antifeminist women as trailblazers is typical of the Republicans.

Organizations such as the Independent Women's Forum and Concerned Women for America, who call themselves the "real" feminists while fighting against things such as equal pay and legislation to combat violence against women, have been around (and funded by conservatives) for years. Their brand of feminism means benefiting from the gains of the women's movement while striving to keep other women down, all for a patriarchal pat on the head. Sound familiar?

As the feminist writer Rebecca Traister says: "Palin's femininity is one that is recognizable to most women: She's the kind of broad who speaks on behalf of other broads but appears not to like them very much.... It's like some dystopian future,... feminism without any feminists."

The good news is, this twisted homage to feminism means conservatives must recognize it as a force in American politics—why spend so much time framing Palin as feminist if we're all just a bunch of hairy man-haters? The bad news, however, trumps all. If this campaign is successful, American women will suffer. We'll be under the thumb of yet another administration that thinks nothing of rolling back women's rights.

No matter how many times feminists point out the hypocrisy of Republicans playing the F-card, however, the bigger truth is that it's not Palin's antifeminist bona fides alone that matter. While Palin is bad for women's rights, she's terrible for America. In addition to being investigated by her own legislature for abuse of power, she is also reported to have asked a librarian about the process for banning books in Wasilla, doesn't support sex education, and has made lying about her record unusually central to her candidacy—even for a politician. These are big warning signs that cut across gender lines.

So while the McCain campaign holds Palin up as a shining example of feminism in action, let's not forget the truth about who's doing the spinning and what they're selling. Because the last thing America needs is another corrupt and lying politician—man or woman.

Sarah's Steel Ones

Amy Alexander

Since the Republican vice presidential candidate's approval rating appears to be immune to facts—notably, that she is entirely unprepared to hold the second-highest office in the land—let's admit that ballsiness is an essential part of Sarah Palin's "relatability."

Nation columnist Patricia J. Williams examined the "frontierswoman" aspect of Palin's profile, and astutely took apart the reasons why that can-do, gun-toting, Annie Oakley image so quickly and firmly grabbed hold of GOP convention delegates and the press. In record time, the number of references to Palin as a g-droppin', huntin', fishin' Wal-Mart Mom, has transported us back to the era of Manifest Destiny, when America's Western expansion (and a hankerin' for gold) required women to man up or die.

This does have some appeal, and maybe it is time we stop fretting about Palin's hypocrisy and contradictions and acknowledge the positive part of her persona. It does exist, and recognizing it does not require you to dismiss her obvious shortcomings.

As Williams points out, there are probably more than a few of us who drift off, from time to time, on the delicious fantasy of what it would feel like to draw down with shotgun on the misbehaving men in our lives. We don't know if Palin has ever done such a thing, but it appears she sure as hell could. I have to own up to the part of me that admires that. After watching her with Gibson, it's safe to say that it took a spine of titanium to stay upright in that chair as "Charlie" scowled at her over the top of his reading glasses: I, too, am a graduate of a state university and instantly recognized Palin's ginned-up bravado and cramming-before-finals anxiety. Watching her struggle to stay on message—she never did answer the question of whether it is OK for U.S. forces to launch raids in Pakistan without that government's knowledge or approval—a small part of me was rooting for her to pull it off. Does that qualify as situational ethics on my part? I don't know. But I do know that by over-intellectualizing this steeliness factor, and by underestimating its power to sway voters, we are not being true to our cultural history.

It is no accident that in the last century, the women authors who changed the literary game, and the heroines they created, are all of the ballsy variety—Zora Neale Hurston, Eudora Welty, Margaret Mitchell, Maya Angelou. Fiction writers and journalists are mere scribblers of history, while politicians are the high-stakes actors in our national drama. But I think we risk throwing shade across a part of our political future by failing to acknowledge the value of Sarah Palin's abundant moxie.

Is this critique sexist? Should I turn in my feminist card? I'm happy to entertain any charges of sexism that may result from my deconstruction of the catnip part of the Palin aesthetic. Yes, we're entering the rabbit hole of the "Why is it OK for blacks to call each other the N-word but not OK for whites?" territory of feminist critique, but I've got thick skin, and I am also consistent: I'm black, I don't call other blacks the N-word, and I don't want other blacks to use that word, either. I'm a woman who doesn't call other women the B-word, and I will call out anyone who is foolish enough to direct either of those words at me.

As for feminist street cred, eh: I'm more concerned with being scrupulous—and pragmatic—enough to recognize the whirl of ambiguities that make humans so interesting. Dick Cheney manages to love his lesbian daughter, which is good. And yes, the self-disciplined Condoleezza Rice is an appropriate role model for black girls. Plus, as we learned from the Hillary Clinton presidential candidacy, charges of sexism can be the red herring in a procedural crime drama worthy of P. D. James.

Progressives and feminists who sneer at women unwilling to separate that stimulus-response "I heart ballsy women!" from the business at hand—"Does she have the intellect and experience to be vice president?"—are spinning their wheels. They also conveniently overlook the possibility that Palin's raw ambition is very close to the self-confidence we want to encourage in our daughters. Sarah Palin is a strong woman, and that is good. Her politics, and what they may lead her to create for our democracy... not so much.

Sarah Palin, Mean Girl
Linda Hirshman

I have been feeling really guilty about not liking Sarah Palin.
She's independent, her husband helps raise the kids, she's
worked most of her life. I should *luv* her. But the minute she
minced on stage in St. Louis Thursday, with her shoulder-
length hair and stiletto heels, I realized why I don't: she's the
Rules Girl.

Remember *The Rules: Time-Tested Secrets for Capturing
the Heart of Mr. Right*, Ellen Fein and Sherry Schneider's
explosively controversial 1995 book that upended thirty
years of feminist teaching about dating? Forget all that
equality and intelligence stuff, *The Rules* advised. Who wants
to be Hillary Clinton? Men are simple, attracted to sexual
symbols and bright, shiny objects. If you want them, they
argued, you must sport long hair and wear sexy, attention-
getting clothes. The suit Palin wore for the debate was some
amazingly iridescent material, and she sported an eye-
popping sparkly rhinestone flag pin. The governor as the It
Girl of the '90s singles scene.

As the capital-letter *Rules* recommend, Palin knows she
must Never Leave the House without Makeup. And, so far
in this campaign, she has scrupulously followed the *Rules*
for dealing with mainstream-media suitors: Rarely Return
Their Calls. Always End the Date First. Never Make a Date for
Saturday Night after a Wednesday Date. Never Make a Date
for *Meet the Press* At All.

Palin follows all the *Rules* most indigestible to feminists.
Let Him Take the Lead. ("Bush Doctrine? In what respect,
Charlie?") Never Tell Him What to Do or Try to Change Him.
(John McCain: "Governor Palin and I agree that you don't
announce that you're going to attack another country." Palin:

"Well, as Senator McCain is suggesting here, also, never would our administration get out there and show our cards to terrorists, in this case, to enemies and let them know what the game plan was, not when that could ultimately adversely affect a plan to keep America secure.")

The Rules provides a perfect model for GOP media prep. How a *Rules* Girl acts does not have to reflect what she really believes—or even what she knows, so long as it's effective with the target audience. As with all such disconnected systems, a practitioner must keep *The Rules* nearby for reference. If you watch the video of Thursday's debate, you'll see that Palin constantly consulted her notecards. Fein and Schneider recommend keeping a copy of their book on the bedside table, hidden from view but close enough to consult if you're tempted to, for example, linger on a phone call with a boyfriend beyond the prescribed time.

The danger is, of course, when a situation arises for which the notecards do not have an answer. When Gwen Ifill asked a question Palin did not have a notecard answer for—whether she agreed with Vice President Cheney's egregiously overreaching interpretation of the constitutional role of the vice president—the answer was ladled up straight from the Palin linguistic smorgasbord:

"Well, our founding fathers were very wise there in allowing through the Constitution much flexibility there in the office of the vice president. And we will do what is best for the American people in tapping into that position and ushering in an agenda that is supportive and cooperative with the president's agenda in that position. Yeah, so I do agree with him that we have a lot of flexibility in there, and we'll do what we have to do to administer very appropriately the plans that are needed for this nation. And it is my executive experience that is partly to be attributed to my pick as VP with McCain, not only as a governor, but earlier on as a mayor, as an oil and gas regulator, as a business owner. It is those years of experience on an executive level that will be put to good use in the White House, also."

In its day, *The Rules* was a best seller on the *New York Times* self-help list. But using it as a guide for political behavior is a dangerous game in 2008. By setting Palin up as the *Rules* Girl—the gorgeous, fecund non-Hillary, equipped with all the right answers—Republicans forget that *The Rules* is a manual for how to attract men.

But for decades, the voting-age population has been predominantly female: Women vote at a greater rate and usually a little differently from men. Despite all the talk of disaffected Hillary supporters crossing over to the GOP after Obama's nomination, serious pollsters found no such thing. Some pundits say Palin did fine last night, but thanks to CNN, we were able to test in real time exactly how the Palin performance played with women voters. CNN provided a little chart that shows how the debaters were faring with a focus group of independent voters from the swing state of Ohio. On the chart, the men's reactions show up in green; women's, in orange. Guess what? Palin really tanked among those women. There were times when the line showing the women's disapproval of her answers sank so low it threatened to leap off the screen and start crawling down the wall behind the TV. I'm imagining those Ohio independents as having a vivid picture of a fully made-up, dimpled, winking woman trying to work the crowd from her tattered copy of *The Rules*.

In the weeks ahead, expect Palin to keep following *The Rules* to be the bright, shiny object McCain needs in his charisma-challenged campaign. No matter how well she does this, however, it may not make a bit of difference. It pains me to say this, but in 2001, just as the book's happily married, perfectly coiffed, complaisant co-author Ellen Fein was releasing a sequel, *The Rules for a Happy Marriage*, her husband left her.

The "Bitch" and the "Ditz"
Amanda Fortini

In the past few weeks, Sarah Palin has been variously
described as a diva who engaged in paperwork-throwing
tantrums, a shopaholic who spent $150,000 on clothing,
a seductress who provocatively welcomed staffers while
wearing only a towel, and a "whack-job"—contemporary
code for hysteric. Worse, she was accused by a suspiciously
gleeful Fox News reporter named Carl Cameron of not
knowing Africa was a continent, of being unable to name
the members of NAFTA, indeed of being unable to name the
countries of North America at all. ("But she can be tutored,"
Bill O'Reilly told Cameron, as though speaking of a small
child.) More significant than the dubious origins of these
leaks, or the fact that the campaign that cried "sexism" at
every criticism of its vice presidential nominee was engaging
in its own misogynistic warfare, is the fact that all of the
allegations were so believable. After all, Palin had earned
herself a reputation as, in the words of one Fox News blogger,
"something of a policy ditz."
    It's hard to get too worked up on Palin's behalf,
of course; she was complicit in her crucifixion. But it is
disappointing to watch what some have called the "year
of the woman" come to such an embarrassing conclusion.
This was an election cycle in which candidates pandered to
female voters, newsweeklies tried to figure out "what women
want," and Hillary Clinton garnered 18 million votes toward
winning the Democratic nomination. The assumption was
that these "18 million cracks in the highest glass ceiling,"
as Clinton put it, would advance the prospects of female
achievement and gender equality. It hasn't exactly worked
out that way.

In the grand passion play that was this election, both Clinton and Palin came to represent—and, at times, reinforce—two of the most pernicious stereotypes that are applied to women: the bitch and the ditz. Clinton took the first label, even though she tried valiantly, some would say misguidedly, to run a campaign that ignored gender until the very end. "Now, I'm not running because I'm a woman," she would say. "I'm running because I think I'm the best-qualified and experienced person to hit the ground running." She was highly competent, serious, diligent, prepared (sometimes overly so)—a woman who cloaked her femininity in hawkishness and pantsuits. But she had, to use an unfortunate term, likability issues, and she inspired in her detractors an upwelling of sexist animus: She was likened to Tracy Flick for her irritating entitlement, to Lady Macbeth for her boundless ambition. She was a grind, scold, harpy, shrew, priss, teacher's pet, killjoy—you get the idea. She was repeatedly called a bitch (as in: "How do we beat the...") and a buster of balls. Tucker Carlson deemed her "castrating, overbearing, and scary" and said, memorably, "Every time I hear Hillary Clinton speak, I involuntarily cross my legs."

Career women, especially those of a certain age, recognized themselves in Clinton and the reactions she provoked. "Maybe what bothers me most is that people say Hillary is a bitch," said Tina Fey in her now-famous "Bitch Is the New Black" skit. "Let me say something about that: Yeah, she is. So am I... You know what? Bitches get stuff done." At least being called a bitch implies power. As bad as Clinton's treatment was, the McCain campaign's cynical decision to put a woman—any woman—on the ticket was worse for the havoc it would wreak on gender politics. It was far more destructive, we would learn, for a woman to be labeled a fool.

When Sarah Palin first stepped onto the national stage, I was, like many women, intrigued by her. Here was a woman who—even if you didn't agree with her politics—seemed to have achieved what so many of us were struggling for: an enviable balance between career and family. She was "a brisk, glam multitasker," to quote the *Observer*'s Doree Shafrir, with a good-natured stay-at-home husband at her side and several adorable young children in tow. She was running a state and breast-feeding a newborn and yet, amazingly, did not seem exhausted. There was something inspiring about seeing a woman so at ease with her choices, even as both liberal and conservative critics chided her for running for vice president when her family needed her. Politics aside, when, at the convention, she delivered a politically deft speech like a pro, it was pleasing to witness the first woman on a Republican ticket perform so well.

Of course, the myth of Sarah Palin unraveled almost as quickly as it was spun. By now, her bizarre filibustering, discomfiting blank stares, weird locutions, and general tendency to trip over herself verbally are familiar. First, there was the painful Charles Gibson interview, in which Palin adopted a Toastmasters-style technique of repeating her interlocutor's name in a vain attempt to sound authoritative. Then Katie Couric, with a newfound air of gravitas, smothered Palin with her simple questions and soothing manner: Palin appeared stunningly uninformed, lacking a basic fluency in foreign policy and economic theory. Even if she had frozen up out of nervousness, or fell into the category of smart-but-inarticulate, it was still unacceptable that she couldn't recall Supreme Court decisions she disagreed with or name a single periodical she reads. *Time*? *Newsweek*? Hello?

Palin was recast as the charmer, the glider, the dim beauty queen, the kind of woman who floats along on a little luck and the favor of men. In the *New Yorker,* Jane Mayer recounted how a handful of conservative Washington thinkers became besotted with Palin during a trip to Alaska and subsequently began to promote her in Washington: *National Review*'s Jay Nordlinger described the governor as "a former beauty-pageant contestant, and a real honey, too"; Bill Kristol called her "my heartthrob"; and Fred Barnes noted she was "exceptionally pretty." While it's obviously not Palin's fault that men find her attractive, it is fair to criticize her for campaigning on a platform of charm rather than substance. In what Michelle Goldberg called a "brazen attempt to flirt [her] way into the good graces of the voting public," she waved and winked and smiled—even during the debate—and called herself "just your average hockey mom." (Never mind that it's impossible to imagine a male candidate mentioning fatherhood as the source of his readiness to be the nation's second-in-command.) Her running mate called her "a direct counterpoint to the liberal feminist agenda for America," and her "Joe Six-Pack" fans seemed to appreciate her nonthreatening approach. To quote a former truck driver named Larry Hawkins who was interviewed by the *New York Times* at a Palin rally: "They bear us children, they risk their lives to give us birth, so maybe it's time we let a woman lead us."

It was enough to incense those of us who related to Hillary Clinton and her plight. "What's infuriating, and perhaps rage-inducing, about Palin, is that she has always embodied that perfectly pleasing female archetype," Jessica Grose wrote on Jezebel, in a post titled "Why Sarah Palin Incites Near-Violent Rage in Normally Reasonable Women." Palin had taken a match and set fire to our meritocratic notions that hard work and accumulated experience would be rewarded. "As has been known to happen in less exalted workplaces," Katha Pollitt wrote, "Palin got the promotion because the boss just liked her." Her blithe ignorance extended from foreign policy to the symbolic value of her candidacy. By stepping into the spotlight unprepared, Palin reinforced some of the most damaging and sexist ideas of all: that women are undisciplined in their thinking; that we are distracted by domestic concerns or frivolous pursuits like shopping; that we are not smart enough, or not serious enough, for the important jobs.

In a rare moment of sympathy for Palin, Judith Warner, writing in the *New York Times*, noted that Palin's admirers must "know she can't possibly do it all—the kids, the special-needs baby, the big job, the big conversations with foreign leaders. And neither could they." But many women do manage to do it all, or pretty close to all. They at least manage to come prepared for the big conversations and the critical meetings, no matter what they have going on at home. "Do we have to drag out a list of women who miraculously have found a way to balance many of these factors—Hillary Clinton? Nancy Pelosi? Michelle Bachelet?—and could still explain the Bush Doctrine without breaking out in hives?" wrote Rebecca Traister in Salon. Why then must Palin's operatic failure be the example that leaves a lasting imprint?

And so, here we are, nearly two years after Hillary Clinton declared her candidacy. While it's true that societal change comes in fits and starts and the Clinton campaign went a long way toward helping voters imagine a female commander in chief, I can't help but think that our historic step forward was followed by more than a few in the opposite direction.

In August, after Clinton had dropped out of the race but before Palin was selected as the vice presidential nominee, the Pew Research Center published a study on gender and leadership. A remarkable 69 percent of respondents believed that men and women made equally good leaders. In fact, women were rated equal to or better than men in seven of eight "leadership traits," such as honesty, intelligence, ambition, creativity, compassion—the only quality on which men scored higher was decisiveness.

Two months later, when voters were asked to rate the leadership ability of one particular woman, the results were just as striking. According to exit polls, 60 percent of voters thought Palin was not qualified to be president if necessary. It's true that Sarah Palin is only one woman, and we've seen male candidates of questionable readiness, like the oft-mentioned Dan Quayle, and even presidents of questionable intelligence, such as George W. Bush and Ronald Reagan, whom Clark Clifford once called "an amiable dunce." But because so few women are present at the highest levels of government, they carry the burden of representing their gender more so than men. In politics as in business, an unqualified woman does more damage than no women at all. She serves to fortify the stereotypes that the next woman will have to surmount.

In the end, women can take pride in the fact that we helped break another set of retrograde stereotypes and prejudices with the election of Barack Obama. Harvard sociologist Orlando Patterson notes that "for the first time since enfranchisement, [women] voted in greater numbers, and more progressively, than men," favoring Obama by a 13 percent margin, while men were almost evenly split. In doing so, we selected a candidate whose views on issues like health care and equal pay and reproductive rights align with our interests.

But among the darker revelations of this election is the fact that the vise-grip of female stereotypes remains suffocatingly tight. On the national political stage and in office buildings across the country, women regularly find themselves divided into dualities that are the modern equivalent of the Madonna-whore complex: the hard-ass or the lightweight; the battle-ax or the bubblehead; the serious, pursed-lipped shrew or the silly, ineffectual girl. It is exceedingly difficult to sidestep this trap. Michelle Obama began the campaign as a bold, outspoken woman with a career of her own, and she was called a hard-ass. Now, as she prepares to move into the White House, she appears poised to recede into a fifties-era role of "mom in chief." It will be heartbreaking if, in an effort to avoid the kind of criticism that followed Hillary Clinton, the first lady is reduced to a lightweight.

Many will say we've come a long way this year. The truth is we have a long way to go.

5/ THE PALIN PAGEANT
Sex, God, and Country First

The Elephant in the Room
Dana Goldstein

You have to feel sorry for Bristol Palin. Because of her
mother's place on the Republican ticket, the biggest
challenges of Bristol's life thus far—becoming a parent and
a wife before she has even graduated high school—will
now play out on the national stage, opening her up to the
judgments of hundreds of millions of gossipy Americans,
not to mention election-watchers across the globe. Barack
Obama was right to react with disgust Monday when asked if
his campaign would make an issue out of Bristol's pregnancy.
Everyone recognizes that Bristol doesn't deserve that.

At the Republican National Convention in St. Paul
Monday, outside of a Lifetime Television event honoring
young women leaders, a Lifetime staffer breathlessly relayed
the story to GOP Congresswoman Cathy McMorris Rodgers
of Washington State. "So she's keeping the baby. And she's
getting married to her boyfriend. And apparently the McCain
people knew." The congresswoman furrowed her brow.

"Wow," McMorris Rodgers replied, taking it all in.
"Oh my." She paused. "Politically, I think it would be fine.
Personally, I think it would be draining."

In conservative circles, the pregnancy news is
more than just fine—politically, it is playing like a dream
among Republican delegates in St. Paul. The idea that the
Christian right would have judged Sarah Palin a failure in
imparting proper values to her sexually active daughter
is silly, a typical liberal misreading of contemporary
conservative ideology. Though the religious right promotes
abstinence-only sex education, vows of chastity, and dances
at which prepubescent girls pledge their virginity to dad,
conservatives do live in twenty-first-century America, just

like the rest of us. They know teen sex happens. They just also happen to believe, against all common sense, that it can be eradicated.

The truth is, conservatives are more familiar with teen parenthood than are secular liberals. On the whole, red states have higher teen pregnancy and birth rates than blue states. In Texas, the state with the highest teen birth rate, sixty-three out of every 1,000 young women aged fifteen to nineteen has had a baby. California has the lowest teen birth rate; only thirty-nine of every 1,000 fifteen- to nineteen-year-old girls there have carried a pregnancy to term. Alaska, where Bristol Palin grew up, has a typical teen birth rate of about forty-two.

Here at the convention, self-described family-values conservatives say they are even more thrilled with Sarah Palin since they learned her daughter is pregnant, marrying, and will keep the child. They are convinced that not only is the Alaska governor a paragon of the pro-life movement, unafraid to live out her values in the public eye, but that she is the very epitome of conservative professional motherhood, a woman who pursued her career without limiting her family size (five kids!), teaching her offspring about the sacredness of pregnancy along the way.

Christine Potocki, a GOP activist from upstate New York, says folks from her area have been energized by the addition of Palin to the ticket and won't be distracted by the news of Bristol's pregnancy. "I think it fits right into who Sarah Palin is," Potocki said, "and I think people will relate." Potocki's own husband, a convention delegate, has a son from a previous relationship who was conceived out of wedlock. "My husband is pro-life because when he was nineteen years old, he found himself in the same situation and made the decision to have a family," Potocki confides. "It speaks to the importance of keeping families intact and supporting those who have a choice to make, and they choose life."

The underlying message is that pregnancy is a gift you should never turn down—even when it's unexpected, even when you are seventeen, even when you haven't had the chance to get an education, or a job, or learn to live as an adult away from your parents. (And even if you're the victim of domestic violence or have been raped.) In other words, choice, schmoice.

Grace Woodson, a senior at Jerry Falwell's Liberty University in Virginia, is attending the convention with a group of classmates and explained that Christian conservatives won't judge Sarah Palin or her family for Bristol's sexual activity. "Everyone is normal and I think they'll realize [hard times are] a normal part of life, no matter if you're conservative or a Democrat," Woodson said. But like all the conservative women I interviewed, Woodson completely avoided the topic of contraception. "If anything, the way she's dealing with it is by respecting her daughter and respecting her daughter's unborn baby."

Obviously, many Americans are shuddering at the thought of parents encouraging their seventeen-year-old to become a mother and are wondering whether Bristol got a stern talking to about birth control, or if she considered abortion at all. In March, Obama, himself the son of a teen mom, was excoriated by the right when he said, in support of comprehensive sex ed, "Look, I got two daughters, nine years old and six years old. I am going to teach them first about values and morals, but if they make a mistake, I don't want them punished with a baby. I don't want them punished with an STD at age sixteen, so it doesn't make sense to not give them information."

The outrage spurred by the "punishment" language was completely predictable, and evidence of just how wide the cultural chasm remains between conservatives and liberals in America. Amid a failing economy and a foreign war, nothing gets people's blood boiling quite like discussions of sex and abortion. They are still some of the most animating issues in American political life.

Like many conservatives, Jo Howard, a convention delegate from the Houston area, sees Bristol's pregnancy as an argument for abstinence-only education. That is in spite of the fact that Howard's own state teaches abstinence-only in every public school, yet boasts the fifth-highest teen pregnancy rate and highest teen birth rate in the nation. "The more we talk about sex, the more kids want to do it," Howard argues. "What you're going to see on the Democratic side is that they're going to push sex education. I think sex education is the problem, and they see it as the solution. These two parties are just totally, totally opposite as far as the issues are concerned. And I think this pregnancy highlights the differences in the two parties."

That it does. If there's any larger societal benefit to Bristol Palin becoming the new face of American teen pregnancy, it might be that her story, alongside that of Britney Spears's kid sister, Jamie Lynn, cuts into stereotypes of all teen moms being black or Latina, or coming from poor families. And if Bistol, with support from her parents, is able to raise her child, make her marriage work, and still get a college education and begin a career, she might even be able to prove to many skeptics that teen pregnancy does not have to leave a young woman's life in ruins.

It is unfortunate, though, that this normal American teen will have her life choices and outcomes placed under a microscope. One wonders, once again, exactly what John

McCain was thinking when he named Sarah Palin his running mate. If McCain wanted to turn this election into a debate over divisive cultural issues, though, it seems he made a very savvy move.

What Scarlet Letter?
Hanna Rosin

When I first heard about Sarah Palin's, uh, domestic irregularities, I expected social conservatives to react with a kind of qualified, patronizing support—we are all sinners, there but for the grace of God, something like that. Instead, they are embracing her with unbridled admiration. The Family Research Council praised her for "choosing life in the midst of a difficult situation." Cathie Adams of the Eagle Forum, a conservative women's group, called her "the kind of woman I've been looking for all along." The two difficult pregnancies—Palin's with a Down syndrome baby and now her unmarried teenage daughter's—are just proof that "they're doing everything right," gushes Adams. Even the stern religious right godfather James Dobson doted: "A lot of people were praying, and I believe Sarah Palin is God's answer."

Some of this reaction can be explained just by listing the religious right's priorities in order. In the pantheon of family values, avoiding abortion sits at the top, above marriage or staying home to raise your children. Conservatives have spent the last thirty years seeding the country with crisis pregnancy centers dedicated to convincing young women not to abort their babies, regardless of their personal situations. The fact that Britney Spears's younger sister made the same decision to keep her pregnancy at seventeen and that *Juno* was a hit movie only adds an unexpected glamour to the choice.

But this explanation takes you only so far. What's missing from the conservative reaction is still remarkable. Just fifteen years ago, a different Republican vice president was ripping into the creators of *Murphy Brown* for flaunting a working woman who chose to become a single mother. This time around, there's no stigma, no shame, no sin attached to what Dan Quayle would once have mockingly called Bristol Palin's "lifestyle" choices. In fact, so cavalier are conservatives about Sarah Palin's wreck of a home life that they make the rest of us look stuffy and slow-witted by comparison. "I think a hard-working, well-organized CEO type can handle it very well," said Phyllis Schlafly, of the Eagle Forum.

Suddenly it's the Obamas, with their oh-so-perfect marriage and their Dick Van Dyke in the evenings and their two boringly innocent young girls, who seem like the fuddy-duddies.

What happened? How did the culture war get flipped on its head? Of course, conservatives are partly lining up behind Palin just so they can stay in the game. But it's not all crass opportunism. To any religious conservative, Palin, with all her contradictions and hypocrisies, is a very familiar type in this peculiar moment in evangelical history.

Starting in the 1970s, leaders such as Dobson began rewriting the rules of the traditional Christian marriage to make it more palatable in an age of feminism. Domestic work was elevated to a special calling; Christian women were told their child-rearing decisions had national implications, as they were raising a generation of righteous soldiers. Mom took on a political tinge. Homeschooling mothers dragged their large broods to volunteer in campaigns. Like with many Christian moms of her generation, Palin's résumé starts with the PTA.

In the Gingrich era, a few of the Christian mom-types, including Palin, broke out and started their own political careers. Andrea Seastrand was an elementary school teacher elected to Congress in California in those years. Linda Smith, of Washington State, kept a blown-up picture of her granddaughters in her congressional office. I remember interviewing her one day while her husband, Vern, sat in a hard chair in a corner and gave words to the obvious contradiction: "One of the reasons we got into politics, we wanted to preserve some of the traditional lifestyle we'd grown up with," Vern told me. "It's funny, with Linda away, we end up sacrificing some of that traditional family life to pass some of that heritage to our children."

Conservative women became a powerful tool for the party, and everyone was willing to overlook the cost to their personal lives. If a conservative Christian mother chose to pursue a full-time career in, say, landscape gardening or the law, she was abandoning her family. But if she chose public service, she was furthering the godly cause. No one discussed the sticky domestic details: Did she have a (gasp!) nanny? Did her husband really rule the roost anymore? Who said prayers with the kids every night? As long as she was seen now and again with her children, she could get away with any amount of power.

The larger Palin clan, meanwhile, reflects a different trend among evangelicals. The stereotype we associate with evangelicals—intact marriage, wife at home, teenage daughter saves it for marriage—actually applies only to the small minority who attend church weekly.

The rest of the 30 percent of Americans who call themselves evangelical have started to slip in their morals and now actually poll worse than the rest of America on traditional measures of upstanding behavior—they are just as likely to live together and have kids out of wedlock, and their teenage daughters lose their virginities at an earlier age than the girls of most Americans. University of Virginia sociologist W. Bradford Wilcox blames this partly on class differences and particularly on a lingering "redneck" Appalachian strain in evangelical culture. (I'm a "fucking redneck," wrote Levi, the father of Bristol's baby, on his MySpace page, before it was taken down.)

In that way, Bristol's pregnancy can be spun as just another one of the Palins' impeccable working-class credentials—salmon fisherman, union member, DWI, hockey mom, soldier son, pregnant teenage daughter.

The most remarkable differences between the large mass of evangelicals and the rest of Americans are in divorce statistics. Since the seventies, evangelicals and the coastal elites have effectively switched places. Evangelicals are now far more likely to get divorced, whereas couples with four years of college education have cut their divorce rates in half. An intact happy marriage that produces well-behaved children, it turns out, is becoming a luxury of the elites— bad news for the Obamas.

Sarah Palin's Shotgun Politics
Gary Younge

Let's hear it for Bristol Palin. The pregnant seventeen-year-old daughter of John McCain's vice presidential pick, Sarah Palin, is going to have her baby and marry her beau, Levi Johnston. That's a brave move, and she deserves all the support she can get. It looks like she'll need it. Her eighteen-year-old husband-to-be describes himself as a "fuckin' redneck." His MySpace page (which has since been taken down) said he is in a relationship and doesn't want kids. Bristol's mom and dad, we are told, are delighted. We know because they issued a statement. "We're proud of Bristol's decision to have her baby and even prouder to become grandparents." Good for them. Now they would like us to talk about something else. "We ask the media to respect our daughter and Levi's privacy," they said. Not so fast.

The fact is, Bristol could make the decision to keep the baby only because, in legal terms at least, she had a choice. A choice, as it happens, that her mother wants to criminalize. Contrary to popular wisdom, the decisive issue in Sarah Palin's vice presidential nomination was not her gender but her views on abortion. Had she not been anti-choice she never would have made it onto the ticket. The principal objection to McCain's purported favorites for the job—Joseph Lieberman and Tom Ridge—was that they support abortion rights. The woman who would like us to keep her daughter's pregnancy a private matter is running for office so that she can make the pregnancies of other people's daughters an affair of the state.

There is precious little to gloat about here. It is depressing how quickly attacks on Palin and her family descend into misogyny, as was the case with Hillary Clinton.

Speculation as to how Palin could possibly balance her responsibilities as a mother of five with the vice presidency, or whether her daughter "strayed" because her mother was too preoccupied with work, is inappropriate and offensive. McCain has seven children—two of whom are older than Sarah Palin—and those questions are never asked about him. Bristol Palin is not fair game.

But that does not mean that her pregnancy is not worthy of comment, for two reasons. First, as a public official her mother has embraced positions that would deny others the options her daughter has enjoyed, would deny access to information about preventing unplanned pregnancies and deny support for those in a similar situation. In Alaska, she opposed programs that teach teenagers about contraception and slashed funding for a shelter for teenage mothers. Meanwhile, her running mate has voted to increase funding for abstinence-only education and to terminate the federal family-planning program, and he voted against funding teen-pregnancy-prevention programs. He has also voted to require teenagers seeking birth control at federally funded clinics to obtain parental consent. Unfortunately for Bristol, her mother's public positions make her personal predicament a teachable moment.

Second, Palin decided to showcase her personal life, and particularly her motherhood, as a centerpiece of her candidacy. McCain introduced her to the country in Dayton, Ohio, as "someone who grew up in a decent, hardworking middle-class family." He went on to say, "I am especially proud to say in the week we celebrate the anniversary of women's suffrage, [she is a] devoted wife and mother of five," as though you should see being married and giving birth to a slew of kids as somehow connected to having the vote. Palin then took time to introduce "four out of five" of her "blessings" (including Bristol) and herself as a "hockey mom" and the "mother of one of those troops" fighting in Iraq.

If she doesn't want her children in the line of fire, she shouldn't introduce them to the battlefield or use her parenting as a weapon. That goes for Barack Obama, John McCain, and Joe Biden as well.

When news of Bristol's pregnancy broke, Obama said, "I think people's families are off limits. I think people's children are especially off limits. This shouldn't be part of our politics. It has no relevance to Governor Palin's performance as governor or her potential performance as a vice president."

Mostly true and fair enough (one shudders to think what the right wing would make of it if the Obama girls were to find themselves in a similar situation ten years from now). But if family and children are off limits, then do us all a favor and keep them the hell off the stage and away from the microphones. Public office seems to be the only career for which people think it is not only acceptable but necessary to interview the spouse and view the brood for the job. The notion that Americans might elect someone single, let alone gay, to the presidency seems far less likely than the chances of electing a black man or a white woman. And so we are force-fed this hetero-fest with tales of first dates and familial bliss and then asked to look the other way when the facade cracks. If politicians really don't want the public to examine their families, they should follow a new code: Don't tell, then we won't have to ask.

In the meantime, the party of abstinence-only programs did not miss a beat as it stepped up to suffocate Bristol in its embrace. After all, she is having the child and getting married. Only the timing is off. "Now she's a typical American family," Kris Bowen, an alternate delegate from Indiana, told the *New York Times*, referring to Palin. "On an individual level, every single person is thinking, 'Oh my gosh, that has happened to me or someone I know or I'm afraid it will.' " It is heartening to know that under all of those vile policies there lies some human compassion. But that does not make the policies any less vile or their consequences any less dire. That Bristol's situation should become national news is unfortunate. She is not the first seventeen-year-old to have to make this kind of decision. But if her mom has her way, she could be one of the last.

Sarah Palin's Frontier Justice
Patricia J. Williams

Long before any of us knew about Sarah Palin's daughter's baby-daddy, the stage was being set. And the narrative that preceded her apotheosis was one of life and death. The Palin family "chose not to murder that beautiful soul," said an evangelical friend, as she closed her eyes and lifted her palms heavenward.

"Choosing not" to "murder" is an interesting and controversial cooptation within the abortion debate, but this particular locution had an additional resonance for me. Only weeks before, this very friend had been going on and on about the marital infidelities of John Edwards and Eliot Spitzer and Bill Clinton. "I'd kill my husband if he ever did something like that. In a New York minute." I'd heard this sentiment before, of course—I believe Representative Larry Craig's wife had said something similar in public, some years before her husband was arrested in Minneapolis, in the very same airport bathroom through which so many Republican delegates are no doubt traipsing all this week. That Mrs. Craig did not in fact murder her husband was a source of some barely suppressed disappointment to my friend. She herself is loaded for bear.

In a nation where one-third of teenage girls will get pregnant (though few bear them to term) and half of all marriages will end in divorce, we nevertheless do love the litany of how shocked! and outraged! we are at the loose morals of others. Hidden within these repetitive passion plays about cheating and betrayal, however, is a narrative that is quite confining when it comes to complex notions of women as autonomous or liberated. Here's a paraphrased but no doubt familiar progression of the discussion about cheating politicians: Men are dogs. How can they be so stupid? They have no brains. Their nether organs do their thinking for them. Why does he do this to his good, honorable, long-suffering wife? Why does she stand beside him, so stoically, so stiff with humiliation? Why doesn't she leave him, let him stand on that podium and apologize to the world by himself? Why doesn't she kill him?

Universally it boils down to that hyperbolic but emphatic refrain: "I swear, I'd kill him."

There's a certain kind of Lorena Bobbitt–ish bottom line in this well-practiced narrative; Lorena, you will recall, just picked up the proverbial kitchen carving knife and chopped off her husband's offending organ. In other Western countries, there is surely scandal, scandal everywhere, just like in the United States. What's different here, I think, is that our political imbroglios are drenched in subliminal desire that the wife murder the husband. Symbolically speaking, of course. In Europe, it seems to me, it's more casual, less deadly; maybe she'll let loose and poison his pasta, but more likely she'll get out there and have a few affairs of her own, like Cecilia Sarkozy or Ségolène Royal.

Here in the United States, there's not merely the element of rage and loss that accompanies any heartbreak, there's also the medievally misogynistic media/cultural assumption that if a husband doesn't love his middle-aged wife, no one else ever will. A woman over forty is dead, love-wise. Her lying, cheating husband didn't just humiliate her, he took away her honor and her life, his fidelity being her only tribute to desirability. If she doesn't have the comforting catharsis of killing him, metaphorically at least, she'll die alone, shriveled and prunelike, and covered in bristles.

I think this is the deeply coded reason so many women identified with Hillary Clinton at a certain point in time—not just in the wake of her husband's legendary adventures but also when the likes of Rush Limbaugh were cackling about how wrinkled and haglike they thought she was. If only she had been the nominee, she would have had a chance for vengeance, for comeback, for sweet irony, for the strength of resurrection. When she didn't win, she lost more than the election. She broke the hearts of many emotionally invested women of a certain age who want to kill their duplicitous husbands, ex-husbands, or anyone like them.

Karl Rove clearly understands this. I'm pretty sure that's the real reason Sarah Palin is the Republican vice presidential nominee. This is a woman whose nickname in high school was "Barracuda," who shoots her own moose meat and, as governor of Alaska, proposed a $150 bounty for those citizens who bring in the foreleg of a wolf as a way of eliminating the animals. She is a lifelong member of the NRA and favors shooting grizzlies and polar bears from helicopters, to hell with whether the EPA thinks they're endangered. She is being investigated for a possible breach of ethics when she apparently used her public position to pressure state law enforcement officials after she felt that they didn't sufficiently punish her brother-in-law, a state trooper, for allegedly battering her sister and tasering her eleven-year-old nephew. Her office is decorated wall-to-wall with dead animal skins, heads, carcasses.

I suspect this is at least partly why so many otherwise "feminist" women are willing to overlook the ironic contradiction inherent in Bristol's situation, given her mother's public posturing regarding "abstinence only" and "just say no." It's as though they've got pixie dust in their eyes, blinding them to the reality that, regardless of sexual politics, there's a lot else to worry about in what Palin endorses. She wants creationism taught in public schools.

She doesn't believe in global warming. But all that potentially vital controversy is treated as secondary to the fact that she is a peppily suggestive version of Thelma or Louise. She is no long-suffering, good-wifely sort. You get the distinct impression that she'd pick up a gun and shoot Bill or Larry or Eliot or John in a heartbeat.

Surely there's something deeply visceral going on in Palin's apparent appeal to women who've "been done wrong." But there's more than mere sentiment: For too many people, this translates into a deep, antidemocratic, ultralibertarian failure of ethical engagement. What is putatively most wrong about our accumulated scandals, in other words, is not the sex per se but any breach of fiduciary relationship in the political realm, rather than in the domestic or religious realm.

With regard to the matter of her allegedly battering brother-in-law, for example, Sarah Palin could have done what Senators Obama, Clinton, and Biden did: work to write, pass, and enforce laws like the Violence Against Women Act. Instead she did the vigilante thing—she apparently took the law into her own hands, using her role as governor to pressure and ultimately fire the head of her state public safety commission. However sympathetic one may be to her sister's plight, what Palin is alleged to have done is corrupt. Yet in an age when movies extol the lonely righteous outlaw, the line she crossed is so often trampled that we don't see it or appreciate it anymore.

But the ethics of executive responsibility mean that you can't use or abuse the enhanced power of your public or fiduciary authority for personal ends. There is a rationale, a logic, behind the due process that is at the heart of our justice system. Our institutions of governance require that there be distance between the meting out of either reward or punishment and the passions of overly-emotionally-involved decision-makers—whether amorously smitten (as in instances of nepotism) or furiously wounded and "bitter" (as in Palin's sister's divorce).

The term "frontier justice" is always put in quotes for a reason. It is not the mark of a great civilization. It is messy and often results in mistakes of terrible magnitude. Ultimately, this is what worries me about men or women in public life, whether married or single, who engage in the conceit of indulging personal ends by taking advantage of the power of their positions. Clarence Thomas evaded answering questions about his behavior toward Anita Hill by declaring that it was none of anyone's business what he did in the bedroom, as opposed to the boardroom. But however the media framed it, the ethical concern in that hearing was precisely founded upon the fact that the encounters did not occur in the bedroom; furthermore, at the time of the alleged misbehavior, Thomas was the head of the Equal Employment Opportunities Commission—the very agency charged with prosecution of harassment in the workplace.

My evangelical friend believes that "sinning" is a public matter, and that the government has a responsibility to discourage all premarital sex. She wants to recognize fertilized ova as persons with full legal rights. She also believes that a husband's straying is adequate defense in a court of law when his wife hops in her SUV and drives over him a few times. I do not.

Here's my bottom line. John Edwards, Larry Craig, and Bristol Palin may have committed excruciatingly painful breaches of "family values," but that's a private matter. It's really none of my business.

What is impermissible, however, is the use of public power either as a personal weapon or a personal reward system—for example, using public funds to pay for one's prostitute, as Governor Eliot Spitzer is alleged to have done. Or promoting one's mistress to a cushy job, as Mayor Kwame Kilpatrick is said to have done. Or demoting someone for failure to do your private bidding, which is exactly what Sarah Palin seems to have done. For that is the ideology of banditry. No matter how well-intentioned, such deployment is irresponsible, because responsibility to others is the first rule of representative government. And this, rather than the prurient details of who boinked whom, is what we need be most concerned about. The kind of narcissistic entitlement that hides in, wallows in or takes actual pride in unaccountability is the antithesis of the role demanded of a public servant.

The Sexy Puritan
Tom Perrotta

In the weeks since Sarah Palin made her entertaining and highly polarizing entrance onto the national stage, journalists have been scrambling to get a fix on her, attaching label after label onto the Alaska governor in the hope that one of them might stick. Is Palin a hockey mom, "a working-class heroine juggling career and family and living out her religious convictions," in the words of conservative writer Ross Douthat? Or is she, as Katha Pollitt would have it, "a right-wing-Christian anti-choice extremist"? Other observers have focused on Palin's appearance, calling her a "babe" (Rush Limbaugh), a "MILF" (Tina Fey), a "stewardess" (Bill Maher), and the ubiquitous "sexy librarian" (only Google knows). The sheer amount of head-scratching expended on Palin might lead you to believe that she's something new and puzzling on the American scene. But she isn't quite as novel as she seems. Caribou-hunting aside, Sarah Palin represents the state-of-the-art version of a particular type of woman—let's call her the Sexy Puritan—that's become a familiar and potent figure in the culture war in recent years.

Sexy Puritans have been around for a while. Anita Bryant, the Miss America runner-up turned antigay crusader in the 1970s, was an early exemplar of the trend. The young Britney Spears, provocatively dressed and loudly proclaiming her virginity, is a more modern version, though that didn't turn out so well. Elisabeth Hasselbeck, the most conservative member of *The View*, has a bit of the Sexy Puritan about her, as does Monica Goodling, the former aide to Attorney General Alberto Gonzales who admitted to engaging in improperly political hiring practices, including the dismissal of a career prosecutor Goodling believed to be a lesbian. (Puritanical footnote: Goodling is reputed to have been responsible for the draping of nude statues at the Department of Justice.)

Sexy Puritans engage in the culture war on two levels—not simply by advocating conservative positions on hot-button social issues but by embodying nonthreatening mainstream standards of female beauty and behavior at the same time. The net result is a paradox, a bit of cognitive dissonance very useful to the cultural right: You get a little thrill along with your traditional values, a wink along with the wagging finger. Somehow, you don't feel quite as much like a prig as you expected to.

I didn't think too much about Sexy Puritans as a type until I began looking into the abstinence-only sex-education movement while researching my novel *The Abstinence Teacher*. I expected to encounter a lot of stern James Dobson–style scolds warning teenagers about the dangers of premarital sex—and there were a few of those—but what I found over and over again were thoughtful, attractive, downright sexy young women talking about their personal decision to remain pure until marriage. Erika Harold, Miss America of 2003 (the right sure loves beauty queens), is probably the best-known to the wider public, but no abstinence rally is complete without the testimony of a very pretty virgin in her early- to mid-twenties. At a Silver Ring Thing event I attended in New Jersey in 2007, a slender young blond woman in tight jeans and a form-fitting T-shirt—she wouldn't have looked out of place at a frat kegger—bragged about all the college boys who'd tried and failed to talk her into their beds. She reveled in her ability to resist them, to stand alone until she'd found the perfect guy, the fiancé with whom she would soon share a lifetime full of amazing sex. While her explicit message was forceful and empowering—virginity is a form of strength and self-sufficiency—the implicit one was clear as well: Abstinence isn't just sour grapes for losers, a consolation prize for girls who can't get a date anyway.

There's a sophisticated strategy of cooptation at work here—not so different from the one employed by Christian rock bands that look and sound almost exactly like their secular counterparts—an attempt to separate "sexiness," which is both cool and permissible, from actual sex, which is not. This is a challenging line to walk in practice, as Britney can attest, quite different from the simpler and more consistent "return to modesty" approach advocated by Wendy Shalit, in which girls are encouraged to downplay their sexuality across the board. What the Sexy Puritan movement represents, I think, is the realization on the part of some cultural warriors on the right that to be seen as anti-sex—and especially to be seen as unsexy—is a losing proposition in contemporary America, even among evangelical Christians most troubled by the fallout from the sexual revolution. Apparently nobody likes the Church Lady anymore, not even the churchgoers. If you don't believe me, you should take a look at the Web site Christian Nymphos, whose authors cheerfully proclaim, "We are women with excessive sexual desire for our husbands!" and offer candid how-to advice on anal sex, fisting, and "masturbating for your husband."

God knows, I'm not trying to link Palin to the Christian Nymphos; I'm only trying to locate her within the context of the great American culture war, which she seems to have single-handedly reignited during an election season that was supposed to have been dominated by other issues (and may well be again, now that Wall Street has imploded). With the selection of Palin, McCain succeeded not only in thrilling the Christian right but in scrambling the categories of the campaign. It used to be perfectly clear which ticket represented youth and change, which seemed old and boring, and which had more appeal to women voters. For a moment, at least, Palin seems to have turned these certainties into open questions.

The right has understood for a long time that harsh social messages seem a lot more palatable coming from an attractive young woman than a glowering old man. What's most striking about Palin thus far is her reluctance to engage in explicit cultural warfare, given some of the extreme positions she's taken in the past. Her recent public statements on homosexuality and global warming are more conciliatory than one might have expected, designed to reassure socially moderate swing voters. And she's in no position to pontificate on the benefits of abstinence-only sex education. For now, her role in the culture war is mainly symbolic. Millions of Americans clearly see her as "one of us"—a devout, working-class, "Bible-believing" Christian whose values and opinions and way of speaking reflect their own—and their exhilaration at having a kindred spirit on the GOP ticket has given the McCain campaign a jolt of populist energy.

In the weeks remaining before November 4, the Obama campaign faces the challenging job of restoring clarity to the election, making people look at Palin and see not just a plucky, surprisingly hot, pro-life mom who made her way from the PTA to the governor's office, but a "Young Earth" creationist who opposes abortion even in the case of rape or incest and thinks a natural-gas pipeline is an expression of God's will. In the meantime, though, she remains a perfect emblem for a stealth culture war: a sexy librarian who would be more than happy to ban a few books.

The Witch-Hunter Anoints Sarah Palin
Max Blumenthal

On September 20 and 21, 2008, I attended services at the church Sarah Palin belonged to since she was an adolescent, the Wasilla Assembly of God. Though Palin officially left the church in 2002, she is listed on its Web site as "a friend," and spoke there as recently as June 8 of this year.

I went specifically to see a pastor visiting from Kiambu, Kenya, named Thomas Muthee. Muthee gained fame within Pentecostal circles by claiming that he defeated a local witch, Mama Jane, in a great spiritual battle, thus liberating his town from sin and opening its people to the spirit of Jesus.

Muthee's mounting stardom took him to Wasilla Assembly of God in May 2005, where he prayed over Palin and called upon Jesus to propel her into the governor's mansion—and beyond. Muthee also implored Jesus to protect Palin from "the spirit of witchcraft." The video archive of that startling sermon was scrubbed from Wasilla Assembly of God's Web site, but now it has reappeared.

Since Palin was nominated as vice president, Wasilla Assembly of God has taken a draconian line with reporters. The church now forbids members of the media from filming, taking notes, or bringing voice recorders to its services. I was able to record Muthee's recent sermons only by deploying an array of tiny cameras and hidden microphones. Though the quality and comprehensiveness of my footage was severely compromised by the church's closed-door policy to the press, I was not going to be deterred.

By the end of the second day of Muthee's sermons, the church had been tipped off about me, the liberal media member in its midst. An associate pastor told me he had received an e-mail from an anonymous source warning him about me. When I tried to interview members of the congregation in the church parking lot, my questions were either met with silence or open hostility. I strongly suspect the McCain campaign has mobilized the Wasilla Assembly of God against perceived threats from the media.

But they hardly needed encouragement. On the first night of services, Muthee implored his audience to wage "spiritual warfare" against "the enemy." As I filmed, a nervous church staffer approached from behind and told me to put my camera away. I acceded to his demand, but as Muthee urged the church to crush "the python spirit" of the unbeliever enemies by stomping on their necks, I pulled out a smaller camera and filmed from a more discreet position. Now, church members were in deep prayer, speaking in tongues and raising their hands. Muthee exclaimed, "We come against the spirit of witchcraft! We come against the python spirits!" Then, a local pastor took the mic from Muthee and added, "We stomp on the heads of the enemy!"

Behind the Christian right's enthusiasm for Palin's conservative credentials is a visceral sense that that she has come from them, not to them. Some right-wing evangelicals even believe she has messianic potential. As former Christian Broadcasting Network vice president Jim Bramlett wrote, "Sarah is that standard God has raised up to stop the flood. She has the anointing."

The Christian right's analysis is accurate to a certain degree. While Palin may not be the One, she is certainly one of them. Her social policy views, from her rejection of scientific evidence on global warming to her opposition to publicly funding emergency contraception for rape victims, are explicitly influenced by the sectarian theology she has subscribed to since she was a teenager. There is no better evidence of the depth of Palin's radical convictions than her startling encounter with the witch-hunter, Bishop Muthee.

Sarah Palin, American
Jeff Sharlet

Religion writers listened to Sarah Palin's convention address expecting heavy religious code, the scriptural allusions that have come to be standard fare in speeches by Republicans and Barack Obama. There wasn't much—"a servant's heart," a prayer for her son sent off to war. But there was, for those with ears to hear it, a far more disturbing allusion: to Westbrook Pegler, a midcentury Rush Limbaugh and then some. At the height of his popularity, he was more powerful; as he faded, he fell back on such rank anti-Semitism that even anti-Semites considered him tacky. One conservative paper begged him to come up with fresh material and lay off "1) New Deal and Roosevelts; 2) Kennedys; 3) Jews." He was a homophobe, too—he once described a critic who'd crossed him as "the bull butterfly of the literary teas"—but he expressed his hatred of homosexuality in such queeny terms that even those who shared his bile turned a blind eye to their man's evident relish for a certain campy rhetorical style.

Pegler was meaner than Limbaugh, but there was also more to him than Limbaugh. Peg hated fascists, until he became one. He despised fat cats, which may be why he came to loathe himself and anyone who reminded him of his past, including his once-beloved Newspaper Guild. He was contemptuous of political platitudes, unless they were his own. His populism was real, even if his expression of it was not.

Heywood Broun, the leftist columnist with whom he shared the front page of the *New York World-Telegram* beginning in 1932, once observed of the angry man to his right, "Some day somebody should take the hide off Peg because the stuff inside is so much better than the varnished surface which blinks in the sunlight of public approval." That's not to say Peg was a sweetie underneath. He was an angry man through and through, born into hatred of Hearst inherited from his father, responsible for the "Hearst Style," a populist tongue of blood and cliché, expressive of the sentiments of working people but emptied of any real political content, and forever ashamed of that invention; he'd damn it in its own terms, describing Hearst papers as resembling a "screaming whore running down the street with her throat cut." Pegler was like that, too; he filled the coffers of his publishers, but he hated them more than he loved the money they paid him. He hated authority, simply put; and when he wrote from the "stuff inside" he channeled that hate into blistering condemnations of corruption that resulted in at least two prison sentences for the deserving.

When Sarah Palin, reading a speech by McCain speechwriter Michael Scully, declared, "A writer declared: 'We grow good people in our small towns, with honesty and sincerity and dignity,' " she passed right over the stuff inside to stand blinking behind her $365 rimless Kazuo Kawasaki glasses in the sunlight of public approval.

In 1999 I spent several weeks poring over Pegler's columns for a profile of the long-dead columnist in the *Baffler*, the now defunct journal founded by Tom Frank, author of *What's the Matter with Kansas?* Tom's already done a better job than I could of taking apart Palin's pander, ugly in its implication that those who don't live in small towns—80 percent of America, according to the United Nations—are somehow morally deficient, and insulting in its disregard for the actual facts of life in the very small towns ill-served by the policies championed by Palin. [See "The GOP Loves the Heartland to Death," in this volume.] So I'll stick to Peg, and see if he doesn't carry back round to Palin, by way of her curiously geographic theology.

Pegler wasn't a small-town man himself until the end of his days. Even when he wrote of the mythical little people—no, not fairies; the common folk—he did so in terms that sounded distinctly urban. Forgive me for quoting my own work; it's the only piece of Pegler's work I have available to me:

> Pegler carried on his campaigns in the name of one particular "little guy" known as George Spelvin, American. "Spelvin" was the stage name an actor used at the the time when, in addition to his main role, he doubled in a small part. The Spelvins of the world were servants, butlers, messengers, clerks, men-on-the-street, and passersby. Pegler's Spelvin, though, was an early Archie Bunker. Union men, uppity women, swells, bubbleheads, and, eventually, foreigners, blacks, and Jews all gave George Spelvin a stomachache.
>
> In 1942, Spelvin went looking for a job because "Mrs. R." (Roosevelt) had "said she thought everyone should be ordered what to do by the government," and her orders were to fit into the war effort anywhere you can. Turns out, though, there were no more jobs in America that didn't require a union card, and "Bigod nobody is going to make him join anything whether it is the Elks or the Moose or the Mice or the Muskrats or whatever. It is the principle of the thing with George, and, moreover, being a native American and a veteran of the last war, he has a rather narrow prejudice against being ordered around by guys who talk like they just got off the boat."

Spelvin's borough of bubbleheads sounds more like Brooklyn than Mayberry. His anxieties, his bigotries—organized labor, immigrants—are those most commonly attendant to urban living. Even his name is a sly joke for working-class sophisticates, common men who'd know enough about culture to be able to whistle "Fanfare for the Common Man," another populist delusion penned in 1942.

That doesn't sound like Sarah Palin. Too many Obama supporters have been too quick to prove Palin right when she spoke of the snobs who look down on people like her. Palin is from a small town, and her interests are those of a small-town citizen; her churches are small-town congregations, suddenly being scrutinized by an army of blogger theologians. Like Pegler, they're homing in on the wrong targets, angling in from the left instead of the right with aim just as shaky. There's nothing wrong with being a moose hunter, or a snow-machine racer, or a redneck, or a holy roller. The gift of tongues is not a form of political expression. At least, not one easily intelligible.

What should be worrisome about Palin's religion and her small-town roots is the way they seem to merge, the territorial spiritual warfare of her churches phrased in secular terms through her channeling of Pegler. "Territorial spiritual warfare" is the idea, embraced by Palin's pastors, that entire cities can be possessed by demons. Small towns, too, theoretically, but that's not usually how it works. The first time I encountered it was at Ted Haggard's New Life Church, in Colorado Springs. When I asked for a restaurant recommendation, I was warned to steer clear of downtown, no matter what I did; urban areas, New Lifers told me, are rife with demons. It was no accident, one New Lifer told me this past spring, that Pastor Ted's downfall occurred up in Denver, surely a sister city of Sodom.

That view, it should be remembered, is very much a minority perspective within conservative Christianity. Indeed, there's just as strong a movement toward cities, as hipster evangelicals plant new churches in New York, Chicago, and Los Angeles with names like The Journey, The Awakening, and Revolution. But Palin is not a hipster evangelical. She is, as she tells us over and over, a small-town girl. And she grew up in a small-town church, one with a fondness for spiritual war and a wariness of cosmopolitanism. "We grow good people in our small towns, with honesty and sincerity and dignity." Palin didn't put that in her speech, a professional speechwriter did. But in her mouth, the fever that filled all of Pegler's words becomes the spirit, and an imaginary municipality, Smalltown, USA, becomes a site of rhetorical pilgrimage, an invocation of place as faith.

The only time Pegler ever lived in a small town was during his last years, when he moved to the desert outside Tucson. Much of what he wrote was no longer publishable, but he sat in his empty, pure, American landscape pounding out more and more of it, trying to get at the monster he couldn't name. Nearly forty years after his death, Palin has dragged Pegler into the spotlight again and resurrected his blinking words. In his mind, they were hate, but in her speech, they were theology. Palin, for all her bigotries, is not a hater. She's too holy for that. Her religion allows her the luxury of sincerity. Which is why it's worth considering the words with which the late Oliver Pilat began his 1963 biography of Pegler, *The Angry Man of the Press*: "By his own standards, he was incorruptible, honorable, and sincere, but sincerity is only an effort to gauge reality and conform to it, and his tools for that effort were inadequate."

Mad Dog Palin
Matt Taibbi

I'm standing outside the Xcel Energy Center in St. Paul, Minnesota. Sarah Palin has just finished her speech to the Republican National Convention, accepting the party's nomination for vice president. If I hadn't quit my two-packs-a-day habit earlier this year, I'd be chain-smoking now. So the only thing left is to stand mute against the fit-for-a-cheap-dog-kennel crowd-control fencing you see everywhere at these idiotic conventions and gnaw on weird new feelings of shock and anarchist rage as one would a rawhide chew toy.

All around me, a million cops in their absurd post-9/11 space-combat get-ups stand guard as assholes in papier-mâché puppet heads scramble around for one last moment of network face time before the coverage goes dark. Four-chinned delegates from places like Arkansas and Georgia are pouring joyously out the gates in search of bars where they can load up on Zombies and Scorpion Bowls and other "wild" drinks and extramaritally grope their turkey-necked female companions in bathroom stalls as part of the "unbelievable time" they will inevitably report to their pals back home. Only twenty-first-century Americans can pass through a metal detector six times in an hour and still think they're at a party.

The defining moment for me came shortly after Palin and her family stepped down from the stage to uproarious applause, looking happy enough to throw a whole library full of books into a sewer. In the crush to exit the stadium, a middle-aged woman wearing a cowboy hat, a red-white-and-blue shirt and an obvious eye job gushed to a male colleague—they were both wearing badges identifying them as members of the Colorado delegation—at the Xcel gates.

"She totally reminds me of my cousin!" the delegate screeched. "She's a real woman! The real thing!"

I stared at her open-mouthed. In that moment, the rank cynicism of the whole sorry deal was laid bare. Here's the thing about Americans. You can send their kids off by the thousands to get their balls blown off in foreign lands for no reason at all, saddle them with billions in debt year after congressional year while they spend their winters cheerfully watching game shows and football, pull the rug out from under their mortgages, and leave them living off their credit cards and their Wal-Mart salaries while you move their jobs to China and Bangalore.

And none of it matters, so long as you remember a few months before Election Day to offer them a two-bit caricature culled from some cutting-room-floor episode of *Roseanne* as part of your presidential ticket. And if she's a good enough likeness of a loudmouthed Middle American archetype, as Sarah Palin is, John Q. Public will drop his giant-size bag of Doritos in gratitude, wipe the Sizzlin' Picante dust from his lips and rush to the booth to vote for her. Not because it makes sense, or because it has a chance of improving his life or anyone else's, but simply because it appeals to the low-humming narcissism that substitutes for his personality, because the image on TV reminds him of the mean, brainless slob he sees in the mirror every morning.

Sarah Palin is a symbol of everything that is wrong with the modern United States. As a representative of our political system, she's a new low in reptilian villainy, the ultimate cynical masterwork of puppeteers like Karl Rove. But more than that, she is a horrifying symbol of how little we ask for in return for the total surrender of our political power. Not only is Sarah Palin a fraud, she's the tawdriest, most half-assed fraud imaginable, twenty floors below the lowest common denominator, a character too dumb even for daytime TV—and this country is going to eat her up, cheering her every step of the way. All because most Americans no longer have the energy to do anything but lie back and allow ourselves to be jacked off by the calculating thieves who run this grasping consumer paradise we call a nation.

The Palin speech was a political masterpiece, one of the most ingenious pieces of electoral theater this country has ever seen. Never before has a single televised image turned a party's fortunes around faster.

Until the Alaska governor actually ascended to the podium that night, I was convinced that John McCain had made one of the all-time campaign-season blunders, that he had acted impulsively and out of utter desperation in choosing a cross-eyed political neophyte just two years removed from running a town smaller than the bleacher section at Fenway Park. It even crossed my mind that there was an element of weirdly self-destructive pique in McCain's decision to cave in to his party's right-wing base in this fashion, that perhaps he was responding to being ordered by party elders away from a tepid, ideologically promiscuous hack like Joe Lieberman—reportedly his real preference—by picking the most obviously unqualified, doomed-to-fail joke of a Bible-thumping buffoon. As in: You want me to rally the base? Fine, I'll rally the base. Here, I'll choose this rifle-toting, serially pregnant moose killer who thinks God lobbies for oil pipelines. Happy now?

But watching Palin's speech, I had no doubt that I was witnessing a historic, iconic performance. The candidate sauntered to the lectern with the assurance of a sleepwalker—and immediately launched into a symphony of snorting and sneering remarks, taking time out in between the superior invective to present herself as just a humble gal with a beefcake husband and a brood of healthy, combat-ready spawn who just happened to be the innocent targets of a communist and probably also homosexual media conspiracy. She appeared to be completely without shame and utterly full of shit, awing a room full of hardened reporters with her sickly-sweet line about the high-school-flame-turned-hubby who, "five children later," is "still my guy." It was like watching Gidget address the Reichstag.

Within minutes, Palin had given TV audiences a character infinitely recognizable to virtually every American: the small-town girl with just enough looks and a defiantly incurious mind who thinks the PTA minutes are Holy Writ, and to whom injustice means the woman next door owning a slightly nicer set of drapes or flatware. Or the governorship, as it were.

Right-wingers of the Bush-Rove ilk have had a tough time finding a human face to put on their failed, inhuman, mean-as-hell policies. But it was hard not to recognize the genius of wedding that faltering brand of institutionalized greed to the image of the suburban-American supermom. It's the perfect cover, for there is almost nothing in the world meaner than this species of provincial tyrant.

Palin herself burned this political symbiosis into the pages of history with her seminal crack about the "difference between a hockey mom and a pit bull: lipstick," blurring once and for all the lines between meanness on the grand political scale as understood by the Roves and Bushes of the world, and meanness of the small-town variety as understood by pretty much anyone who has ever sat around in his ranch-house den dreaming of a fourth plasma-screen TV or an extra set of KC HiLites for his truck, while some ghetto family a few miles away shares a husk of government cheese.

In her speech, Palin presented herself as a raging baby-making furnace of middle-class ambition next to whom the yuppies of the Obama set—who never want anything all that badly except maybe a few afternoons with someone else's wife, or a few kind words in the *New York Times Book Review*—seem like weak, self-doubting celibates, the kind of people who certainly cannot be trusted to believe in the right God or to defend a nation. We're used to seeing such blatant cultural caricaturing in our politicians. But Sarah Palin is something new. She's all caricature. As the candidate of a party whose positions on individual issues are poll losers almost across the board, her shtick is not even designed to sell a line of policies. It's just designed to sell her. The thing was as much as admitted in the on-air gaffe by former Reagan speechwriter Peggy Noonan, who was inadvertently caught saying on MSNBC that Palin wasn't the most qualified candidate, that the party "went for this, excuse me, political bullshit about narratives."

The great insight of the Palin VP choice is that huge chunks of American voters no longer even demand that their candidates actually have policy positions; they simply consume them as media entertainment, rooting for or against them according to the reflexive prejudices of their demographic, as they would for reality-show contestants or sitcom characters. Hicks root for hicks, moms for moms, born-agains for born-agains. Sure, there was politics in the Palin speech, but it was all either silly lies or merely incidental fluffery buttressing the theatrical performance. A classic example of what was at work here came when Palin proudly introduced her Down syndrome baby, Trig, then stared into the camera and somberly promised parents of special-needs kids that they would "have a friend and advocate in the White House." This was about a half-hour before she raised her hands in triumph with McCain, a man who voted against increasing funding for special-needs education.

Palin's charge that "government is too big" and that Obama "wants to grow it" was similarly preposterous. Not only did her party just preside over the largest government expansion since LBJ, but Palin herself has been a typical Bush-era Republican, borrowing and spending beyond her means. Her great legacy as mayor of Wasilla was the construction of a $15 million hockey arena in a city with an annual budget of $20 million; Palin OK'd a bond issue for the project before the land had been secured, leading to a protracted legal mess that ultimately forced taxpayers to pay more than six times the original market price for property the city ended up having to seize from a private citizen using eminent domain. Better yet, Palin ended up paying for the fucking thing with a 25 percent increase in the city sales tax. But in her speech, of course, Palin presented herself as the enemy of tax increases, righteously bemoaning that "taxes are too high" and Obama "wants to raise them."

Palin hasn't been too worried about federal taxes as governor of a state that ranks number one in the nation in federal spending per resident ($13,950), even as it sits just eighteenth in federal taxes paid per resident ($5,434). That means all us taxpaying non-Alaskans spend $8,500 a year on each and every resident of Palin's paradise of rugged self-sufficiency. Not that this sworn enemy of taxes doesn't collect from her own: Alaska currently collects the most taxes per resident of any state in the nation.

The rest of Palin's speech was the same dog-whistle crap Republicans have been railing about for decades. Palin's crack about a mayor being "like a community organizer, except that you have actual responsibilities" testified to the

Republicans' apparent belief that they can win elections till the end of time running against the sixties. (They're probably right.) The incessant grousing about the media was likewise par for the course, red meat for those tens of millions of patriotic flag-waving Americans whose first instinct when things get rough is to whine like bitches and blame other people—reporters, the French, those ungrateful blacks soaking up tax money eating big prison meals, whomever—for their failures.

Add to this the usual lies about Democrats wanting to "forfeit" to our enemies abroad and coddle terrorists, and you had a very run-of-the-mill, almost boring Republican speech from a substance standpoint. What made it exceptional was its utter hypocrisy, its total disregard for reality, its absolute unrelation to the facts of our current political situation. After eight years of unprecedented corruption, incompetence, waste, and greed, the party of Karl Rove understood that 50 million Americans would not demand solutions to any of these problems so long as they were given a new, new thing to beat their meat over.

Sarah Palin is that new, new thing, and in the end it won't matter that she's got an unmarried teenage kid with a bun in the oven. Of course, if the daughter of a black candidate like Barack Obama showed up at his convention with a five-month bump and some sideways-cap-wearing, junior-grade Curtis Jackson holding her hand, the defenders of Traditional Morality would be up in arms. But the thing about being in the reality-making business is that you don't need to worry much about vetting; there are no facts in your candidate's bio that cannot be ignored or overcome.

One of the most amusing things about the Palin nomination has been the reaction of horrified progressives. The Internet has been buzzing at full volume as would-be defenders of sanity and reason pore over the governor's record in search of the Damning Facts. My own telephone began ringing off the hook with calls from ex-Alaskans and friends of Alaskans determined to help get the "truth" about Sarah Palin into the major media. Pretty much anyone with an Internet connection knows by now that Palin was originally for the "Bridge to Nowhere" before she opposed it (she actually endorsed the plan in her 2006 gubernatorial campaign), that even after the project was defeated she kept the money, that she didn't actually sell the Alaska governor's state luxury jet on eBay but instead sold it at a $600,000 loss to a campaign contributor (who is reportedly now seeking $50,000 in taxpayer money to pay maintenance costs).

Then there are the salacious tales of Palin's swinging-meat-cleaver management style, many of which seem to have a common thread: In addition to being ensconced in a messy ethics investigation over her firing of the chief of the Alaska state troopers (dismissed after refusing to sack her sister's ex-husband), Palin also fired a key campaign aide who had an affair with a friend's wife. More ominously, as mayor of Wasilla, Palin tried to fire the town librarian, Mary Ellen Emmons, who had resisted pressure to censor books Palin found objectionable.

Then there's the God stuff: Palin belongs to a church whose pastor, Ed Kalnins, believes that all criticisms of George Bush "come from hell," and wondered aloud if people who voted for John Kerry could be saved. Kalnins, looming as the answer to Obama's Jeremiah Wright, claims that Alaska is going to be a "refuge state" for Christians in the last days, last days which he sometimes speaks of in the present tense. Palin herself has been captured on video mouthing the inevitable born-again idiocies, such as the idea that a recent oil-pipeline deal was "God's will." She also described the

Iraq War as a "task that is from God" and part of a heavenly "plan." She supports teaching creationism and "abstinence only" in public schools, opposes abortion even for victims of rape, has denied the science behind global warming, and attends a church that seeks to convert Jews and cure homosexuals.

All of which tells you about what you'd expect from a raise-the-base choice like Palin: She's a puffed-up dimwit with primitive religious beliefs who had to be educated as to the fact that the Constitution did not exactly envision government executives firing librarians. Judging from the importance progressive critics seem to attach to these revelations, you'd think that these were actually negatives in modern American politics. But Americans like politicians who hate books and see the face of Jesus in every tree stump. They like them stupid and mean and ignorant of the rules. Which is why Palin has only seemed to grow in popularity as more and more of these revelations have come out.

The same goes for the most damning aspect of her biography, her total lack of big-game experience. As governor of Alaska, Palin presides over a state whose entire population is barely the size of Memphis. This kind of thing might matter in a country that actually worried about whether its leader was prepared for his job—but not in America. In America, it takes about two weeks in the limelight for the whole country to think you've been around for years. To a certain extent, this is why Obama is getting a pass on the same issue. He's been on TV every day for two years, and according to the standards of our instant-ramen culture, that's a lifetime of hands-on experience.

It is worth noting that the same criticisms of Palin also hold true for two other candidates in this race, John McCain and Barack Obama. As politicians, both men are more narrative than substance, with McCain rising to prominence on the back of his bio as a suffering war hero and Obama mostly playing the part of the long-lost, future-embracing liberal dreamboat not seen on the national stage since Bobby Kennedy died. If your stomach turns to read how Palin's Kawasaki 704 glasses are flying off the shelves in Middle America, you have to accept that Middle America probably feels the same way when it hears that Donatella Versace dedicated her collection to Obama during Milan Fashion Week. Or sees the throwing-panties-onstage, "I love you, Obama!" ritual at the Democratic nominee's town-hall appearances.

So, sure, Barack Obama might be every bit as much a slick piece of imageering as Sarah Palin. The difference is in what the image represents. The Obama image represents tolerance, intelligence, education, patience with the notion of compromise and negotiation, and a willingness to stare ugly facts right in the face, all qualities we're actually going to need in government if we're going to get out of this huge mess we're in.

Here's what Sarah Palin represents: being a fat fucking pig who pins "Country First" buttons on his man titties and chants "U-S-A! U-S-A!" at the top of his lungs while his kids live off credit cards and Saudis buy up all the mortgages in Kansas.

The truly disgusting thing about Sarah Palin isn't that she's totally unqualified, or a religious zealot, or married to a secessionist, or unable to educate her own daughter about sex, or a fake conservative who raised taxes and horked up earmark millions every chance she got. No, the most disgusting thing about her is what she says about us: that you can ram us in the ass for eight solid years, and we'll not only thank you for your trouble, we'll sign you up for eight more years, if only you promise to stroke us in the right spot for a few hours around election time.

Democracy doesn't require a whole lot of work of its citizens, but it requires some: It requires taking a good look outside once in a while, and considering the bad news and what it might mean, and making the occasional tough choice, and soberly taking stock of what your real interests are.

This is a very different thing from shopping, which involves passively letting sitcoms melt your brain all day long and then jumping straight into the TV screen to buy a Southern Style Chicken Sandwich because the slob singing "I'm Lovin' It!" during the commercial break looks just like you. The joy of being a consumer is that it doesn't require thought, responsibility, self-awareness or shame: All you have to do is obey the first urge that gurgles up from your stomach. And then obey the next. And the next. And the next.

And when it comes time to vote, all you have to do is put your Country First—just like that lady on TV who reminds you of your cousin. U-S-A, baby. U-S-A! U-S-A!

Sarah Palin's Faux Populism
Jim Hightower

It was not my intention to be writing about Sarah Palin, since everyone with a laptop, a No. 2 pencil, or a red crayon seems to be covering that beat. But then came the pundits:

"She's a populist," gushed Karl Rove on Fox TV. Weird, since this right-wing political slime and corporate whore loathes, demonizes, mocks, fears, and tries to destroy real populists.

"Perfect populist pitch," beamed CBS analyst Jeff Greenfield right after Palin's big speech at the GOP fawnfest in St. Paul. In his less infatuated moments, Greenfield surely must realize how ludicrous his comment was, since once, long ago, he co-authored a book that had *populist* in the title, so he has at least had a brush with the authentic people's movement that the term encapsulates.

So they made me do it. Karl, Jeff, and other pundits who are rushing to place the gleaming crown of populism atop the head of this shameless corporate servant—they are the ones who have driven me to write about Palin. Someone has to nail the media establishment for its willing perversion of language, American history, and the substance of today's genuine populism.

Palin might be popular, she might be able to field dress a moose, she might live in a small town, she might enjoy delivering "news flashes" to media elites, she might even become vice president—but none of this makes her a populist. To the contrary, she is to populism what near beer is to beer, only not as close.

You want a taste of the real thing? Try this from another woman who hailed from a town (smaller than Wasilla, Alaska) and was renowned for her political oratory:

Wall Street owns the country. It is no longer a government of the people, by the people, and for the people, but a government of Wall Street, by Wall Street, and for Wall Street.... Our laws are the output of a system which clothes rascals in robes and honesty in rags....

There are thirty men in the United States whose aggregate wealth is over one and one-half billion dollars. There are half a million looking for work.... We want money, land, and transportation. We want the abolition of the National banks, and we want the power to make loans direct from the government. We want the accursed foreclosure system wiped out.... We will stand by our homes and stay by our firesides by force if necessary, and will not pay our debts to the loan-shark companies until the Government pays its debts to us.

The people are at bay, let the bloodhounds of money who have dogged us thus far beware.

That, my media friends, is populism. It comes from Mary Ellen Lease, who was speaking to the national convention of the Populist Party in Topeka, Kansas, in 1890. In a time before women could vote, Lease traveled the countryside to rally a grassroots revolt against the corporate predators of her day, urging farmers to "raise less corn and more hell." She didn't need to brag that she was a pit bull in lipstick, because her message, idealism, and actions made her an actual force for change.

America has been blessed with populist women ever since, including such honest and insistent voices as Ida Tarbell, Mother Jones, Dorothy Day, Rosa Parks, Rachel Carson, Karen Silkwood, Barbara Jordan, Molly Ivins, Barbara Ehrenreich, and Granny D. Measure Sarah Palin against these.

Populism was and is a ground-level, democratic movement with the guts and gumption to go right at the moneyed elites. It is unabashedly class-based, confronting the Rockefellers on behalf of the Littlefellers. To be a populist is to challenge the very structure of corporate power that is running roughshod over workers, consumers, the environment, small farmers, poor people, the middle class—and America's historic ideals of economic fairness, social justice, and equal opportunity for all.

Populist is not an empty political buzzword that can be attached to someone like Palin, whose campaigns (lieutenant governor, governor, and now veep) are financed and even run by the lobbyists and executives of Big Oil, Wall Street bankers, drug companies, telecom giants, and other entrenched economic interests.

Populists don't support opening our national parks and coastlines to allow the ExxonMobils to take publicly owned oil and sell it to China. Palin does. Populists favor a windfall profits tax on oil companies that are robbing consumers at the pump while milking taxpayers for billions of dollars in subsidies. Palin doesn't. Populists don't hire corporate lobbyists to deliver a boatload of earmarked federal funds, then turn around and claim to be a heroic opponent of earmarks. Palin did. Populists favor shifting more of America's tax burden from the middle class to the superwealthy, while opposing another huge tax giveaway for corporations. Palin doesn't and doesn't.

Another thing populists don't do is sneer at community organizers, as Palin did in her nationally televised coming-out party. Indeed, populists of old were community organizers, as are today's. They work in communities all across our great land, putting in long days at low pay to help empower ordinary folks who are besieged by the avarice and arrogance of Palin's own corporate backers. Since the governor likes to put her fundamental Christianity on political display, she might give some thought to a new bumper sticker that expresses a bit of Biblical populism: "Jesus was a community organizer while Pontius Pilate was governor."

Environmental-justice groups, ACORN, living wage campaigns, the Bus Project, clean water efforts, union-organizing drives, PIRG, Fighting Bob Fest, Jobs with Justice, Apollo Alliance, United Students Against Sweatshops, the Evangelical Environmental Network, clean election initiatives, stopping mountaintop removal, USAction, community-supported agriculture, Campus Progress, local business alliances, Citizens Trade Campaign, Wellstone Action—these are but a few of those doing terrific community organizing today. They embody the vitality of modern populism, doing the essential grunt-level work of democracy.

What gives Palin any legitimacy to denigrate that? She embraces none of these causes, instead supporting the rich and powerful whom grassroots folks are having to battle. She's a plutocrat, not a populist. Big difference.

The Sarah Palin Smoke Screen
Katrina vanden Heuvel

"Here's the deal: Palin is the latest GOP distraction," Bob Herbert wrote in a *New York Times* op-ed. "She's meant to shift attention away from the real issue of this campaign—the awful state of the nation after eight years of Republican rule. The Republicans are brilliant at distractions."

Herbert's right on target. Barack Obama homed in on that point in Denver, too: "If you don't have any fresh ideas, then you use stale tactics to scare the voters. If you don't have a record to run on, then you paint your opponent as someone people should run from. You make a big election about small things."

On cue, Sarah Palin attempted to paint an absurd caricature of Obama in her speech at the Republican Convention: "What does he actually seek to accomplish, after he's done turning back the waters and healing the planet? The answer is to make government bigger... take more of your money... give you more orders from Washington... and to reduce the strength of America in a dangerous world."

More than anything, this election should be about the big issues of our time—ending a disastrous war, restoring America's reputation in the world, and building an economy that works for more than just the very rich. The challenge for Democrats is to frame these issues in a way that connects with traditional American and progressive values, exposes Republican callousness, and extremism, and in doing so trumps the GOP's political marketing which cynically and cleverly plays on symbolism. As George Lakoff wrote, "Just arguing the realities, the issues, the hard truths should be enough in times this bad, but the political mind and its response to symbolism cannot be ignored.... Democrats, in addition, need to call an extremist an extremist: to shine a light on the shared anti-democratic ideology of McCain and Palin, the same ideology shared by Bush and Cheney. They share values antithetical to our democracy."

In order to have a fighting chance after eight ruinous years of Bush, the Republicans need voters to lose sight of where we are as a nation and how Republican leadership got us there. We saw that with the GOP's politicization of Hurricane Gustav in an attempt to whitewash eight years of hostility to the notion of government's role as a force for public good. We see it with their hypocritical media-bashing. (Let's not forget, as Bloomberg News' Al Hunt told the *New York Times*, "Probably no one in American politics over the last twenty years has had a closer relationship with the national press than John McCain.") And we are seeing it again now. McCain's campaign manager Rick Davis admitted as much when he said, "This election is not about issues. This election is about a composite view of what people take away from these candidates."

That's exactly how Republicans win. Democrats can't let them get away with it. So it was good to see Obama and Joe Biden both calling the Republicans out for the lack of attention being paid to the economy at the Republican Convention in St. Paul.

"You did not hear a single world about the economy," Mr. Obama said. "Not once did they mention the hardships that people are going through."

Harold Meyerson also wrote about the Republicans' failure to address the economy at their convention in an op-ed in the *Washington Post*: "I have combed the schedule of events here without finding a single forum... devoted to what John McCain and the Republican Party propose to do about America's short and long-term economic challenges.... For all these woes, McCain offers only a continuation of Bush's tax cuts for the rich and an ideological bias toward the very kind of deregulation that has wrecked the housing market.... If the election is about the economy, they're cooked—and their silence this week on nearly all things economic means that they know it."

If the Republicans succeed in making this election about something other than the big issues, they are likely to win. If it's about a likable woman governor who can shoot a gun and field dress a moose, or a churchgoing commander of the Alaskan National Guard, they are likely to win. Or if they pull off the feat of making the reactionary right-wing McCain/Palin ticket seem more "connected to the people" than Obama/ Biden, whose stance on the issues is in touch with millions of Americans who seek a more active government in these economically squeezed times, then they are likely to win.

If voters really want real change, rather than Reality Politics TV–style change, here are some important facts to consider: Since 1948 the economy has grown faster on average under Democratic presidents than under Republicans; and income inequality trended "substantially upward under Republican presidents but slightly downward under Democrats," according to Princeton professor of political science Larry M. Bartels, author of *Unequal Democracy.*

These historical trends have serious implications for today's challenges of increasing poverty, stagnating wages, and a greater concentration of wealth than any time since 1928.

Until the election, small-d democrats who are committed to forming a more perfect union will need to do everything we can to stay focused on the big issues, expose Republican callousness and antidemocratic policies for what they are, and lay out the clear choice that lies before us.

The GOP Loves the Heartland to Death

Thomas Frank

It tells us something about Sarah Palin's homage to small-town America, delivered to an enthusiastic GOP convention last week, that she chose to fire it up with an unsourced quotation from the all-time champion of fake populism, the belligerent right-wing columnist Westbrook Pegler.

"We grow good people in our small towns, with honesty and sincerity and dignity," the vice presidential candidate said, quoting an anonymous "writer," which is to say, Pegler, who must have penned that mellifluous line when not writing his more controversial stuff. As the *New York Times* pointed out in its obituary for him in 1969, Pegler once lamented that a would-be assassin "hit the wrong man" when gunning for Franklin Roosevelt.

There's no evidence that Mrs. Palin shares the trademark Pegler bloodlust—except maybe when it comes to moose and wolves. Nevertheless, the red-state myth that Mrs. Palin reiterated for her adoring audience owes far more to the venomous spirit of Pegler than it does to Norman Rockwell.

Small-town people, Mrs. Palin went on, are "the ones who do some of the hardest work in America, who grow our food and run our factories and fight our wars." They are authentic; they are noble; and they are her own: "I grew up with those people."

But what really defines them in Mrs. Palin's telling is their enemies, the people who supposedly "look down" on them. The opposite of the heartland is the loathsome array of snobs and fakers, "reporters and commentators," lobbyists and others who make up "the Washington elite."

Presumably the various elite Washington lobbyists who have guided John McCain's presidential campaign were exempt from Mrs. Palin's criticism. As would be former House speaker Dennis Hastert, now a "senior adviser" to the Dickstein Shapiro lobby firm, who hymned the "Sarah Palin part of the party" thus: "Their kids aren't going to go to Ivy League schools. Their sons leave high school and join the military to serve our country. Their husbands and wives work two jobs to make sure the family is sustained."

Generally speaking, though, when husbands and wives work two jobs each it is not merely because they are virtuous but because working one job doesn't earn them enough to get by. The two-job workers in Middle America aren't spurning the Ivy League and joining the military straight out of high school just because they're people of principle, although many of them are. It is because they can't afford to do otherwise.

Leave the fantasy land of convention rhetoric, and you will find that small-town America, this legendary place of honesty and sincerity and dignity, is not doing very well. If you drive west from Kansas City, Missouri, you will find towns where Main Street is largely boarded up. You will see closed schools and hospitals. You will hear about depleted groundwater and massive depopulation.

And eventually you will ask yourself, How did this happen? Did Hollywood do this? Was it those "reporters and commentators" with their fancy college degrees who wrecked Main Street, USA?

No. For decades now we have been electing people like Sarah Palin who claimed to love and respect the folksy conservatism of small towns, and yet who have unfailingly enacted laws to aid the small town's mortal enemies.

Without raising an antitrust finger they have permitted fantastic concentration in the various industries that buy the farmer's crops. They have undone the New Deal system of agricultural price supports in favor of schemes called "Freedom to Farm" and loan deficiency payments—each reform apparently designed to secure just one thing out of small-town America: cheap commodities for the big food processors. Richard Nixon's agriculture secretary Earl Butz put the conservative attitude toward small farmers most bluntly back in the 1970s when he warned, "Get big or get out."

A few days ago I talked politics with Donn Teske, the president of the Kansas Farmers Union and a former Republican. Barack Obama may come from a big city, he admits, but the Farmers Union gives him a 100 percent rating for his votes in Congress. John McCain gets a 0 percent. "If any farmer in the Plains states looked at McCain's voting record on ag issues," Mr. Teske says, "no one would vote for him."

Now, Mr. McCain is known for his straight talk with industrial workers, telling them their jobs are never coming back, that the almighty market took them away for good, and that retraining is their only hope.

But he seems to think that small-town people can be easily played. Just choose a running mate who knows how to skin a moose and all will be forgiven. Drive them off the land, shutter their towns, toss their life chances into the grinders of big agriculture . . . and praise their values. The TV eminences will coo in appreciation of your in-touch authenticity, and the carnival will move on.

6/ UNPACKING PALINISM
The World According to Sarah

Capitalism, Sarah Palin–Style

Naomi Klein

Adapted from a speech on May 2, 2009

We are in a progressive moment, a moment when the ground is shifting beneath our feet, and anything is possible. What we considered unimaginable about what could be said and hoped for a year ago is now possible. At a time like this, it is absolutely critical that we be as clear as we possibly can be about what it is that we want because we might just get it.

So the stakes are high.

I usually talk about the bailout in speeches these days. We all need to understand it because it is a robbery in progress, the greatest heist in monetary history. But today I'd like to take a different approach: What if the bailout actually works, what if the financial sector is saved and the economy returns to the course it was on before the crisis struck? Is that what we want? And what would that world look like?

The answer is that it would look like Sarah Palin. Hear me out; this is not a joke. I don't think we have given sufficient consideration to the meaning of the Palin moment. Think about it: Sarah Palin stepped onto the world stage as vice presidential candidate on August 29, 2008 at a McCain campaign rally, to much fanfare. Exactly two weeks later, on September 14, Lehman Brothers collapsed, triggering the global financial meltdown.

So in a way, Palin was the last clear expression of capitalism-as-usual before everything went south. That's quite helpful because she showed us—in that plainspoken, down-homey way of hers—the trajectory the U.S. economy was on before its current meltdown. By offering us this glimpse of a future, one narrowly avoided, Palin provides us with an opportunity to ask a core question: Do we want to go there? Do we want to save that pre-crisis system, get it back to where it was in September 2008? Or do we want to use this crisis, and the electoral mandate for serious change delivered by the last election, to radically transform that system? We need to get clear on our answer now because we haven't had the potent combination of a serious crisis and a clear progressive democratic mandate for change since the 1930s. We use this opportunity, or we lose it.

So what was Sarah Palin telling us about capitalism as usual before she was so rudely interrupted by the meltdown? Let's first recall that before she came along, the U.S. public, at long last, was starting to come to grips with the urgency of the climate crisis, with the fact that our economic activity is at war with the planet, that radical change is needed immediately. We were actually having that conversation: Polar bears were on the cover of *Newsweek* magazine. And then in walked Sarah Palin. The core of her message was this: Those environmentalists, those liberals, those do-gooders are all wrong. You don't have to change anything. You don't have to rethink anything. Keep driving your gas-guzzling car, keep going to Wal-Mart, and shop all you want. The reason for that is a magical place called Alaska. Just come up here and take all you want. "Americans," she said at the Republican National Convention, "we need to produce more of our own oil and gas. Take it from a gal who knows the North Slope of Alaska, we've got lots of both."

And the crowd at the convention responded by chanting and chanting: "Drill, baby, drill."

Watching that scene on television, with that weird creepy mixture of sex and oil and jingoism, I remember thinking: "Wow, the RNC has turned into a rally in favor of screwing Planet Earth." Literally.

But what Palin was saying is what is built into the very DNA of capitalism: the idea that the world has no limits.

She was saying that there is no such thing as consequences, or real-world deficits. Because there will always be another frontier, another Alaska, another bubble. Just move on and discover it. Tomorrow will never come.

This is the most comforting and dangerous lie that there is: the lie that perpetual, unending growth is possible on our finite planet. And we have to remember that this message was incredibly popular in those first two weeks, before Lehman collapsed. Despite Bush's record, Palin and McCain were pulling ahead. And if it weren't for the financial crisis, and for the fact that Obama started connecting with working class voters by putting deregulation and trickle-down economics on trial, they might have actually won.

The president tells us he wants to look forward, not backward. But in order to confront the lie of perpetual growth and limitless abundance that is at the center of both the ecological and financial crises, we have to look backward. And we have to look way backward, not just to the past eight years of Bush and Cheney, but to the very founding of this country, to the whole idea of the settler state.

Modern capitalism was born with the so-called discovery of the Americas. It was the pillage of the incredible natural resources of the Americas that generated the excess capital that made the Industrial Revolution possible. Early explorers spoke of this land as a New Jerusalem, a land of such bottomless abundance, there for the taking, so vast that the pillage would never have to end. This mythology is in our biblical stories—of floods and fresh starts, of raptures and rescues—and it is at the center of the American Dream of constant reinvention. What this myth tells us is that we don't have to live with our pasts, with the consequences of our actions. We can always escape, start over.

These stories were always dangerous, of course, to the people who were already living on the "discovered" lands, to the people who worked them through forced labor. But now the planet itself is telling us that we cannot afford these stories of endless new beginnings anymore. That is why it is so significant that at the very moment when some kind of human survival instinct kicked in, and we seemed finally to be coming to grips with the Earth's natural limits, along came Palin, the new and shiny incarnation of the colonial frontierswoman, saying: Come on up to Alaska. There is always more. Don't think, just take.

This is not about Sarah Palin. It's about the meaning of that myth of constant "discovery," and what it tells us about the economic system that they're spending trillions of dollars to save. What it tells us is that capitalism, left to its own devices, will push us past the point from which the climate can recover. And capitalism will avoid a serious accounting— whether of its financial debts or its ecological debts— at all costs. Because there's always more. A new quick fix. A new frontier.

That message was selling, as it always does. It was only when the stock market crashed that people said, "Maybe Sarah Palin isn't a great idea this time around. Let's go with the smart guy to ride out the crisis."

I almost feel like we've been given a last chance, some kind of a reprieve. I try not to be apocalyptic, but the global warming science I read is scary. This economic crisis, as awful as it is, pulled us back from that ecological precipice that we were about to drive over with Sarah Palin and gave us a tiny bit of time and space to change course. And I think it's significant that when the crisis hit, there was almost a sense of relief, as if people knew they were living beyond their means and had gotten caught. We suddenly had permission to do things together other than shop, and that spoke to something deep.

But we are not free from the myth. The willful blindness to consequences that Sarah Palin represents so well is embedded in the way Washington is responding to the financial crisis. There is just an absolute refusal to look at how bad it is. Washington would prefer to throw trillions of dollars into a black hole rather than find out how deep the hole actually is. That's how willful the desire is not to know.

And we see lots of other signs of the old logic returning. Wall Street salaries are almost back to 2007 levels. There's a certain kind of electricity in the claims that the stock market is rebounding. "Can we stop feeling guilty yet?" you can practically hear the cable commentators asking. "Is the bubble back yet?"

And they may well be right. This crisis isn't going to kill capitalism or even change it substantively. Without huge popular pressure for structural reform, the crisis will prove to have been nothing more than a very wrenching adjustment. The result will be even greater inequality than before the crisis. Because the millions of people losing their jobs and their homes aren't all going to be getting them back, not by a long shot. And manufacturing capacity is very difficult to rebuild once it's auctioned off.

It's appropriate that we call this a "bailout." Financial markets are being bailed out to keep the ship of finance capitalism from sinking, but what is being scooped out is not water. It's people. It's people who are being thrown overboard in the name of "stabilization." The result will be a vessel that is leaner and meaner. Much meaner. Because great inequality—the super rich living side by side with the economically desperate—requires a hardening of the hearts. We need to believe ourselves superior to those who are excluded in order to get through the day. So this is the system that is being saved: the same old one, only meaner.

And the question that we face is: Should our job be to bail out this ship, the biggest pirate ship that ever was, or to sink it and replace it with a sturdier vessel, one with space for everyone? One that doesn't require these ritual purges, during which we throw our friends and our neighbors overboard to save the people in first class. One that understands that the Earth doesn't have the capacity for all of us to live better and better.

But it does have the capacity, as Bolivian President Evo Morales said recently at the United Nations, "for all of us to live well."

Because make no mistake: Capitalism will be back. And the same message will return, though there may be someone new selling that message: You don't need to change. Keep consuming all you want. There's plenty more. Drill, baby, drill. Maybe there will be some technological fix that will make all our problems disappear.

And that is why we need to be absolutely clear right now.

Capitalism can survive this crisis. But the world can't survive another capitalist comeback.

Drill, Drill, Drill
By Eve Ensler

I am having Sarah Palin nightmares. I dreamt last night that she was a member of a club where they rode snowmobiles and wore the claws of drowned and starved polar bears around their necks. I have a particular thing for polar bears. Maybe it's their snowy whiteness or their bigness or the fact that they live in the Arctic or that I have never seen one in person or touched one. Maybe it is the fact that they live so comfortably on ice. Whatever it is, I need the polar bears.

I don't like raging at women. I am a feminist and have spent my life trying to build community, help empower women, and stop violence against them. It is hard to write about Sarah Palin. This is why the Sarah Palin choice was all the more insidious and cynical. The people who made this choice count on the goodness and solidarity of feminists.

But everything Sarah Palin believes in and practices is antithetical to feminism, which for me is part of one story— connected to saving the earth, ending racism, empowering women, giving young girls options, opening our minds, deepening tolerance, and ending violence and war.

Sarah Palin does not believe in evolution. I take this as a metaphor. In her world and the world of fundamentalists nothing changes or gets better or evolves. She does not believe in global warming. The melting of the Arctic, the storms that are destroying our cities, the pollution and rise of cancers, are all part of God's plan. She is fighting to take the polar bears off the endangered species list. The earth, in Palin's view, is here to be taken and plundered. The wolves and the bears are here to be shot and plundered. The oil is here to be taken and plundered. Iraq is here to be taken and plundered. As she said herself of the Iraq War, "It was a task from God."

Sarah Palin does not believe in abortion. She does not believe women who are raped and incested and ripped open against their will should have a right to determine whether they have their rapist's baby or not.

She obviously does not believe in sex education or birth control. I imagine her daughter was practicing abstinence, and we know how many babies that makes.

Sarah Palin does not much believe in thinking. From what I gather she has tried to ban books from the library, and has a tendency to dispense with people who think independently. She cannot tolerate an environment of ambiguity and difference.

Sarah believes in guns. She has her own custom Austrian hunting rifle. She has been known to kill forty caribou at a clip. She has shot hundreds of wolves from the air.

Sarah believes in God. That is of course her right, her private right. But when God and guns come together in the public sector, when war is declared in God's name, when the rights of women are denied in his name, that is the end of separation of church and state and the undoing of everything America has ever tried to be.

I write to my sisters. I write because I believe we hold this election in our hands. This vote is a vote that will determine the future not just of the United States, but of the planet. It will determine whether we create policies to save the earth or make it forever uninhabitable for humans. It will determine whether we move toward dialogue and diplomacy in the world or whether we escalate violence through invasion, undermining, and attack. It will determine whether we go for oil, strip mining, and coal burning, or invest our money in alternatives that will free us from dependency and destruction. It will determine if money gets spent on education and health care or whether we build more and more methods of killing. It will determine whether America is a free, open, tolerant society or a closed place of fear, fundamentalism, and aggression.

If the polar bears don't move you to do everything in your power to get Obama elected, then consider the chant that filled the hall after Palin spoke at the Republican National Convention, "Drill, baby, drill." I think of teeth when I think of drills. I think of rape. I think of destruction. I think of domination. I think of military exercises that force mindless repetition, emptying the brain of analysis, doubt, ambiguity, or dissent. I think of pain.

Do we want a future of drilling? More holes in the ozone, in the floor of the sea, more holes in our thinking, in the trust between nations and peoples, more holes in the fabric of this precious thing we call life?

Sarah Palin, Meet Mahmoud Ahmadinejad
Juan Cole

Is Sarah Palin America's Mahmoud Ahmadinejad? The two differ in many key respects, of course, but it is remarkable how similar they are. There are uncanny parallels in their biographies, their domestic politics, and the way they present themselves—even in their rocky relationships with party elders.

Both are former governors of a northwest frontier state with great natural beauty (in Ahmadinejad's case, Ardabil). Both are known for saying things that produce a classic *Scooby-Doo* double take in their audiences. Both appeal to a sort of wounded nationalism, speaking of the sacrifice of dedicated troops for an often feckless public, and identifying themselves with the common soldier. They are vigilant against foreign designs on their countries and insist on energy and other independence.

But above all, both are populists who claim to represent the little people against wily and unscrupulous elites, and against pampered upper-middle-class yuppies pretending to be the voice of democracy. Together, they tell us something about dangerous competing populisms in an age of globalization.

Both politicians glory in being mavericks, as a way of underlining their credentials as representatives of the ordinary person. Former beauty queen Palin calls herself a hockey mom and plays up her avocation of wolf and moose hunting, to rally her rural supporters and, perhaps, to disconcert squeamish urbanites. Ahmadinejad, who earned a Ph.D. in civil engineering with top grades, is said to have once dressed up as a janitor and swept the streets when campaigning for mayor of Tehran. Most recently, his supporters have dismissed the Iranian protesters as pampered young people from the wealthy neighborhoods of North Tehran. In fact, both figures are themselves quite comfortable.

Palin portrays herself as the small-town outsider. "I'm not a member of the permanent political establishment," she proclaimed last fall. She blamed her bad press on not being in the "Washington elite," when, in fact, self-inflicted debacles such as her deer-in-the-headlights interview with Katie Couric, in which she demonstrated a shaky grasp of world politics, are a better explanation for media questions about her qualifications. In his debates with rivals for the presidency this spring, Ahmadinejad apparently damaged his standing with voters by attacking the wife of his electoral rival, Mir Hossein Mousavi, and tarring previous presidents of the Islamic Republic from the centrist and reform factions as having been corrupt. On June 5, 2009 he said on Iranian radio that since he was not a part of that closed "power circle," he had been targeted for both a domestic and an international media "smear campaign." Actually, Ahmadinejad was raked over the coals during the campaign by Mousavi for his ignorant and bigoted statements about Israel, which, Mousavi pointed out, had damaged Iran's standing in the international community.

Both so-called mavericks have had tense relations with their party elders at times. Many Republicans have made withering statements about Palin and consider her a "train wreck," and her conflicts with the camp of her former running mate, Senator John McCain, are legend. Ahmadinejad got into hot water with his patron, Supreme Leader Ali Khamenei, for appointing an overly liberal relative as his first vice president. Ahmadinejad dragged his feet on firing the man, but in the end bowed to pressure from his fellow hard-liners. On Friday, the president was forced to deny that there was any rift between him and Khamenei. For a maverick populist, such conflicts with the party elders are useful in emphasizing their independence from the establishment even as they remain largely within it.

Both leaders see press criticisms as coordinated attempts to discredit them not from the media's duty to examine a political figure's policies or public statements, but from an elite conspiracy. In her farewell address as governor, Palin fell into a Shakespearean soliloquy directed at the media, saying, "Democracy depends on you, and that is why, that's why our troops are willing to die for you. So, how 'bout in honor of the American soldier, ya quit makin' things up." Palin did not say what exactly she thought the media was making up about the American soldier. On June 16, in his first news conference after his officially announced victory in Iran's June 12 presidential election, Ahmadinejad complained, "During these elections, our nation was faced with a widespread psychological war and propaganda by some of mass media which have not learned from the past." The people, he boasted, followed not the media but the path of "the martyrs [in war]...."

An armed citizenry is important to Palin's conception of the republic, and she warned in her farewell address, "You're going to see anti-hunting, anti–Second Amendment circuses from Hollywood...." She continued, "Stand strong, and remind them patriots will protect our guaranteed, individual right to bear arms...." By talking about "patriots" "protecting" the individual right to bear arms, Palin skated awfully close to the militia or "patriot" movement on the right-wing American fringe (and not for the first time). Ahmadinejad is not similarly in favor of all citizens having guns, but he comes out of a popular militia, the Basij, which consists of hundreds of thousands of ordinary citizen patriots, armed and pledged to defend the Constitution of the Islamic Republic.

Right-wing populism, rooted in the religion, culture, and aspirations of the lower middle class, is often caricatured as insane by its critics. That judgment is unfair. But it is true that such movements often encourage a political style of exhibitionism, disregard for the facts as understood by the mainstream media, and exaltation of the values of people who feel themselves marginalized by the political system. Not all forms of protest, however, are healthy, even if the protesters have legitimate grievances. Right-wing populism is centered on a theory of media conspiracy, a "my country right or wrong" chauvinism, a fascination with an armed citizenry, an intolerance of dissent, and a willingness to declare political opponents mere terrorists. It is cavalier in its disregard of elementary facts and arrogant about the self-evident rightness of its religious and political doctrines. It therefore holds dangers both for the country in which it grows up and for the international community. Palin is polling well at the moment against other Republican front-runners such as Mitt Romney, and so, astonishingly, is a plausible future president. At least Iranians only got Ahmadinejad because of rigged elections, and they had the decency to mount massive protests against the result.

Sarah Palin's Nine Most Disturbing Beliefs
AlterNet Staff

Let's forget for a moment that Sarah Palin likes to kill moose, has lots of children, and was once voted the second-prettiest lady in Alaska; that's all part of the gusher of sensationalist, but not particularly substantive, news that has dominated coverage of the Alaska governor's addition to the Republican ticket.

Before the next news cycle brings the shocking information that Palin was actually impregnated by Bigfoot, we need to shift the discussion to what really matters about her in the context of the White House: her dangerous views.

AlterNet has compiled a list of Palin's most shocking beliefs, ranging from her positions on the economy to her views on reproductive rights. This list has nothing to do with her personal life, her looks, or her gender. It's the stuff that voters need to know: what Sarah Palin really believes.

1. Despite problems at home, Sarah Palin does not believe in giving teenagers information about sex.

The McCain campaign is spinning Bristol Palin's pregnancy as a neat, shiny example of the unbreakable bonds of family. But while Bristol's actions and choices should not be attacked, teen pregnancy is no cause for celebration, either. To state the very obvious, it is not a good thing when teenagers have unprotected sex. And U.S. teens appear to have unprotected sex a lot: The United States has some of the highest rates of teen pregnancy in the industrialized world, and one in four American teen girls has a sexually transmitted infection.

Like John McCain's, Palin's approach to the problems of teen pregnancy and STI transmission is abstinence-only education. In a 2006 questionnaire by the conservative group Eagle Forum, Palin stated: "Explicit sex-ed programs will not find my support." Presumably the programs that do find Palin's support are ones that focus on abstinence and only mention contraceptives to talk about their supposed shortcomings.

But someone already tried that. For eight years the Bush administration has thrown its heft behind Title V, a federal program that provides states with funding for abstinence-based sex education. In 2007 an expansive study proved abstinence-until-marriage education does not delay teen sexual activity.

If Palin is elected, she will continue to throw money at a policy that does little besides ensure that a larger number of sexually active teens lack information about how to avoid pregnancy and STIs.

2. Sarah Palin believes the United States Army is on a mission from God.

In June, Palin gave a speech at the Wasilla Assembly of God, her former church, in which she exhorted ministry students to pray for American soldiers in Iraq. "Our national leaders are sending them out on a task that is from God," she told them. "That's what we have to make sure that we're praying for, that there is a plan and that plan is God's plan."

Palin talked about her son, Track, an infantryman in the U.S. Army: "When he turned eighteen, right before he enlisted, he had to get his first tattoo. And I'm like—I don't think that's real cool, son. Until he showed me what it was and I thought, Oh he did something right, 'cause on his calf, he has a big ol' Jesus fish!"

Holy war, holy warriors.

3. Sarah Palin believes in punishing rape victims.

Palin thinks that rape victims should be forced to bear the child of their rapist. She believes this so strongly that she would oppose abortion even if her own daughter were raped.

The Huffington Post reports: "Granting exceptions only if the mother's life was in danger, Palin said that when it came to her daughter, 'I would choose life.' "

At the time, her daughter was fourteen years old. Moreover, Alaska's rape rate was an abysmal 2.2 times the national average, and 25 percent of all rapes resulted in unwanted pregnancies.

If Palin's own daughter was only fourteen when she made that statement, does she think any girl of reproductive age is old enough to have a child? Girls are hitting puberty earlier and earlier. What if the rape victim were only ten? Nine? Eight?

Palin also opposes abortion in cases of incest and would grant an exception only if childbirth would result in the mother's death. She has not made any statements yet about whether she believes a ten-year-old who was raped by her father would be able to actually raise the child once it was born. Perhaps Palin doesn't care.

4. Who's really not in favor of clean water? Sarah Palin.

As The Hill reports, "Governor Palin has... opposed a crucial clean water initiative."

Alaska's KTUU explains: "It is against the law for the governor to officially advocate for or against a ballot measure; however, Palin took what she calls 'personal privilege' to discuss one of this year's most contentious initiatives."

Palin said, "Let me take my governor's hat off just for a minute here and tell you, personally, Prop 4—I vote no on that." And what is that? A state initiative that would have banned metal mines from discharging pollution into salmon streams.

She also approved legislation that let oil and gas companies nearly triple the amount of toxic waste they can dump into Cook Inlet, an important fishery. It looks like being an avid outdoorsperson doesn't mean Palin really has the health of watersheds, natural resources, or our environment at heart.

5. Sarah Palin calls herself a reformer, but on earmarks and the Bridge to Nowhere, she is a hypocrite.

Palin says she's a "conservative Republican" who is "a firm believer in free-market capitalism." She's running as an anti-tax crusader, and she did make deep cuts to Alaska's budget.

So, one would assume she is no borrow-and-spend conservative like George W., right?

Well, there was the time when she served as the mayor of the tiny town of Wasilla, Alaska. According to the Associated Press, "Palin hired a lobbyist and traveled to Washington annually to support earmarks for the town totaling $27 million." You'd think that $27 mil in taxpayers' funds would be enough scratch for a town with a population of 8,000, but you'd be wrong. According to Politico, Palin then "racked up nearly $20 million in long-term debt as mayor of the tiny town of Wasilla—that amounts to $3,000 per resident."

Then there's her current stint as Alaska governor, during which her appetite for federal pork spending has been on clear display. The Associated Press reported, "In her two years as governor, Alaska has requested nearly $750 million in special federal spending, by far the largest per capita request in the nation." While Palin notes she rejected plans to build a $398 million bridge from Ketchikan to an island with fifty residents and an airport, that opposition came only after the plan was ridiculed nationally as a Bridge to Nowhere.

6. Sarah Palin believes creationism should be taught in schools.

Until somebody digs up the remnants of a *T. rex* with an ill-fated caveman dangling from its jaws, the scientific community, along with most of the American public, will be at peace with the theory of evolution. But this isn't true of everyone. More than eighty years after the Scopes "monkey" trial, there are people—and politicians—who do not believe in evolution and lobby for creationism to be taught in schools.

Palin is one of those politicians. When Palin ran for governor, part of her platform called for teaching schoolchildren creationism alongside evolution. Although she did not push hard for this position after she was elected governor, Palin has let her views on evolution be known on many occasions. According to the *Anchorage Daily News*, Palin stated, "Teach both. You know, don't be afraid of information. Healthy debate is so important, and it's so valuable in our schools. I am a proponent of teaching both."

Palin further argued, "It's OK to let kids know that there are theories out there. They gain information just by being in a discussion."

Not when those "theories" are being presented as valid alternatives to a set of principles that most scientists have ascribed to for more than a century.

7. Sarah Palin supports offshore drilling everywhere, even if it doesn't solve our energy problems.

If McCain was hoping to salvage any part of his credibility with environmentalists, he threw that chance out the window by adding Palin to his ticket. Palin is in favor of offshore drilling and drilling in the ecologically sensitive Arctic National Wildlife Refuge.

The *Miami Herald* reported: "The Alaska governor has said that she has tried to persuade McCain to agree with her on drilling in the wildlife refuge. She also has said that she was happy that he changed his position over the summer and now supports offshore oil drilling."

As if that weren't bad enough, in her speech at the Republican National Convention, she said, "Our opponents say, again and again, that drilling will not solve all of America's energy problems—as if we all didn't know that already." Huh. I guess drilling even when it won't help is better than working on renewable energy sources, as Palin also vetoed money for a wind-energy project.

8. Sarah Palin loves oil and nuclear power.

Aside from her "drill here, drill there, drill everywhere" approach to our energy crisis, the only other things we know about Palin's energy policy, especially given her Bush-like love of avoiding the press, comes from her acceptance speech: "Starting in January, in a McCain/Palin administration, we're going to lay more pipelines, build more nuclear plants, create jobs with clean coal, and move forward on solar, wind, geothermal and other alternative sources."

Nuclear power plants. Interesting. As folks look for alternative fuel sources (and again, Palin loves oil first and foremost, so her commitment to any alternative energy source is suspect at best), nuclear power is enjoying a return to vogue. But here's the problem: Even the U.S. government's own nuclear agency, the Nuclear Regulatory Commission, thinks an atomic renaissance is a bad idea.

Delivered by one of America's most notoriously docile agencies, the NRC's warning essentially says that all cost estimates for new nuclear reactors—and all licensing and construction schedules—are completely up for grabs and have no reliable basis in fact. Thus any comparisons between future atomic reactors and renewable technologies are moot at best.

Not to mention all the other problems with nuclear energy, such as how to dispose of nuclear waste and the possibility of a catastrophic meltdown, to name a couple. Palin has no background with nuclear energy and shows no evidence of having looked into the science behind it or the dangers that come with it.

Also, it's time for Palin to drop another Bush-like tendency: Governor, the word is pronounced "new-clear."

9. Sarah Palin doesn't think much of community activism; she'd much rather play insider political games.

In her Republican convention speech, Palin slammed Barack Obama's early political work, saying, "I guess a small-town mayor is sort of like a community organizer, except you have actual responsibilities." Palin's put-down of grassroots workers, often unpaid or low-paid, demeaned an American tradition of neighbors helping neighbors, according to Deepak Bhargava, executive director of the Center for Community Change. But more revealing is Palin's apparent lack of experience in community change and local volunteer efforts, during her years in Alaska before becoming governor.

Scores of press accounts of her early years as mayor of Wasilla omit any mention of such work. Instead, they note, as mayor and in the intervening years before running for governor, Palin gravitated to those with power, money, or influence. She worked to enlarge Wasilla's Wal-Mart and build a sports center (that went over budget in an eminent domain dispute), and she hired a Washington lobbyist, directed a political fundraising committee for the state's senior U.S. senator, Republican Ted Stevens who was subsequently prosecuted for corruption, and steered $22 million in federal aid to her town. While some of her early community work was undoubtedly centered on her church, perhaps this comment by a blog reader best sums up Palin's political opportunism: "So community organizers [aren't] responsible? Or caring? Or doing anything important[?] What a terrible insult to the greatest community organizer of all time, Jesus Christ."

7/ GOING ROGUE
A Woman's Right to Lose

The Sarah Palin Pity Party

Rebecca Traister

Is this the week that Democrats and Republicans join hands—to heap pity on poor Sarah Palin?

At the moment, all signs point to yes, as some strange bedfellows reveal that they have been feeling sorry for the vice presidential candidate ever since she stopped speaking without the help of a teleprompter. Conservative women like Kathleen Parker and Kathryn Jean Lopez are shuddering with sympathy as they realize that the candidate who thrilled them, just weeks ago, is not in shape for the big game. They're not alone. The *New Republic*'s Christopher Orr feels that Palin has been misused by the team that tapped her. In the *New York Times*, Judith Warner feels for Sarah, too! And over at the *Atlantic*, Ta-Nehisi Coates empathizes with intelligence and nuance, making clear that he's not expressing pity. Salon's own Glenn Greenwald watched the Katie Couric interview and "actually felt sorry for Sarah Palin." Even Amy Poehler, impersonating Katie Couric on last week's *Saturday Night Live*, makes the joke that Palin's cornered-animal ineptitude makes her "increasingly adorable."

I guess I'm one cold dame, because while Palin provokes many unpleasant emotions in me, I just can't seem to summon pity, affection, or remorse.

Don't get me wrong, I'm just like all of the rest of you, part of the bipartisan jumble of viewers that keeps one hand poised above the mute button and the other over my eyes during Palin's disastrous interviews. Like everyone else, I can barely take the waves of embarrassment that come with watching someone do something so badly. Roseanne Barr singing the national anthem, Sofia Coppola acting in *The*

Godfather: Part III, Sarah Palin talking about Russia—they all create the same level of eyeball-squinching discomfort.

But just because I'm human, just because I can feel, just because I did say this weekend that I "almost feel sorry for her" doesn't mean, when I consider the situation rationally, that I do. Yes, as a feminist, it sucks—hard—to watch a woman, no matter how much I hate her politics, unable to answer questions about her running mate during a television interview. And perhaps it's because this experience pains me so much that I feel not sympathy but biting anger. At her, at John McCain, at the misogynistic political mash that has been made of what was otherwise a groundbreaking year for women in presidential politics.

In her "Poor Sarah" column, Warner writes of the wave of "self-recognition and sympathy [that] washed over" her when she saw a photo of Palin talking to Henry Kissinger. Palin—as "a woman fully aware that she was out of her league, scared out of her wits, hanging on for dear life"— apparently reminded Warner of herself. Wow. Putting aside the massively depressing implication that Warner recognizes this attitude because she believes it to be somehow written into the female condition, let's consider that there are any number of women who could have been John McCain's running mate—from Olympia Snowe to Christine Todd Whitman to Kay Bailey Hutchison to Elizabeth Dole to Condoleezza Rice—who would not have provoked this reaction. Democrats might well have been repulsed and infuriated by these women's policy positions. But we would not have been sitting around worrying about how scared they looked.

In her piece, Warner diagnoses Palin with a case of "Impostor Syndrome," positing that admirers who watched her sitting across from world leaders at the United Nations were recognizing that "she can't possibly do it all—the kids, the special-needs baby, the big job, the big conversations with foreign leaders. And neither could they." Seriously? Do we have to drag out a list of women who miraculously have found a way to manage to balance many of these factors—Hillary Clinton? Nancy Pelosi? Michelle Bachelet?—and could still explain the Bush Doctrine without breaking into hives? This is not breaking my heart. It is breaking my spirit.

The *Atlantic*'s Coates takes a far smarter, but ultimately still too gentle, approach to Palin in his blog. He writes, compassionately, "There are a lot of us lefties who are guffawing right now and are happy to see Palin seemingly stumbling drunkenly from occasional interview to occasional interview." Coates asserts that McCain "[tossed] her to the wolves" and notes that while she surely had some agency in this whole mess, "where I am from the elders protect you, and pull you back when you've gone too far, when your head has gotten too big."

Where I come from, a woman—and especially a woman governor with executive experience—doesn't have to rely on any elder or any man to protect her and pull her ass out of the fire. She can make a decision all on her own. (Palin was more than happy to tell Charles Gibson that she made her decision to join the McCain ticket without blinking.) I agree with Coates that the McCain camp was craven, sexist, and disrespectful in its choice of Palin, but I don't agree that the Alaska governor was a passive victim of their Machiavellian plotting. A very successful woman, Palin has the wherewithal to move forward consciously. What she did was move forward thoughtlessly and overconfidently, without considering that her abilities or qualifications would ever be questioned.

Christopher Orr writes sympathetically about the scenario that Palin may have envisioned, in which she tours the country on the wave of adoration that buoyed her out of St. Paul and through a post-convention victory lap. In his mind, she might well have continued to give winning, grinning interviews, charming the pants off regular folks all across the country, if the accursed McCain campaign hadn't nervously locked her in a no-press-allowed tower. Orr compares Palin to a talented athlete who, as a result of being overcoached, doesn't soar to new physical heights but instead gets "broken down, [loses] confidence in his game, [becomes] tentative, second guessing himself even to the point of paralysis."

Surely if Palin's political muscles were as taut and supple as Orr suspects, the campaign would not have been so quick to put her on a special training regimen.

It was so predictable that we would get to a pity-poor-helpless-Sarah phase. The press was already warming up for it on the day McCain announced her as his running mate, when NBC reporter Andrea Mitchell speculated that McCain's choice was designed to declaw scrappy Joe Biden, whose aggressive style would come off as bullying next to the sweet hockey mom from Alaska. Now, of course, we know about the hockey moms and the pit bulls; the more-powerful-than-expected Palin juggernaut forestalled the pity/victim/mean-boy/poor-Sarah phase.

So here it is, finally. And as unpleasant as it may be to watch the humiliation of a woman who waltzed into a spotlight too strong to withstand, I flat out refuse to be manipulated into another stage of gendered regress— back to the pre-Pelosi, pre-Hillary days when girls couldn't stand the heat and so were shooed back to the kitchen.

Sarah Palin is no wilting flower. She is a politician who took the national stage and sneered at the work of community activists. She boldly tries to pass off incuriosity and lassitude as regular-people qualities, thereby doing a disservice to all those Americans who also work two jobs and do not come from families that hand out passports and backpacking trips, yet still manage to pick up a paper and read about their government and seek out experience and knowledge.

When you stage a train wreck of this magnitude—trying to pass one underqualified chick off as another highly qualified chick with the lame hope that no one will notice—well then, I don't feel bad for you.

When you treat women as your toys, as gullible and insensate pawns in your Big Fat Presidential Bid—or in Palin's case, in your Big Fat Chance to Be the First Woman Vice President Thanks to All the Cracks Hillary Put in the Ceiling—I don't feel bad for you.

When you don't take your own career and reputation seriously enough to pause before striding onto a national stage and lying about your record of opposing a Bridge to Nowhere or using your special-needs child to garner the support of Americans in need of health care reform you don't support, I don't feel bad for you.

When you don't have enough regard for your country or its politics to cram effectively for the test—a test that helps determine whether or not you get to run that country and participate in its politics—I don't feel bad for you.

When your project is reliant on gaining the support of women whose reproductive rights you would limit, whose access to birth control and sex education you would curtail, whose health care options you would decrease, whose civil liberties you would take away, and whose children and husbands and brothers (and sisters and daughters and friends) you would send to war in Iraq, Iran, Pakistan, Russia, and wherever else you saw fit without actually understanding international relations, I don't feel bad for you.

I don't want to be played by the girl-strings anymore. Shaking our heads and wringing our hands in sympathy with Sarah Palin is a disservice to every woman who has ever been unfairly dismissed based on her gender, because this is an utterly fair dismissal, based on an utter lack of ability and readiness. It's a disservice to minority populations of every stripe whose place in the political spectrum has been unfairly spotlighted as mere tokenism; it is a disservice to women throughout this country who have gone from watching a woman who—love her or hate her—was able to show us what female leadership could look like to squirming in front of their televisions as they watch the woman sent to replace her struggle to string a complete sentence together.

In fact, the only people I feel sorry for are Americans who invested in a hopeful, progressive vision of female leadership, but who are now stuck watching, verbatim, a *Saturday Night Live* skit.

Palin is tough as nails. She will bite the head off a moose and move on. So, no, I don't feel sorry for her. I feel sorry for women who have to live with what she and her running mate have wrought.

The Un-Hillary: Why Watching Sarah Palin Is Agony for Women

Emily Bazelon

When Harriet Miers blew her murder boards—days spent grilling in preparation for her Senate confirmation hearings—she yanked her own nomination to the Supreme Court. Her "uncertain, underwhelming responses" made her handlers panic, and so Miers and the Bush administration called off the show.

Sarah Palin's murder boards have taken place in public. We've all watched her stumped and stumbling in her interviews with Katie Couric. When asked about the Supreme Court, Palin mentioned *Roe v. Wade* and then couldn't name another case. This time, she didn't repeat stock phrases. She just went silent. Kathleen Parker at National Review Online and Fareed Zakaria in *Newsweek* have called for her to follow Miers and pull out. But Palin isn't expendable—the Republican base that mistrusted Miers loves her. So instead of bowing out, she heads into her debate with Joe Biden with expectations so low either she or her opponent seems bound to trip over them.

For women who are watching this all unfold, this means a lot of analysis, much of it angst-ridden. Conservatives express straightforward disappointment. "I watch her interviews with the held breath of an anxious parent, my finger poised over the mute button in case it gets too painful," Parker writes glumly. "Unfortunately, it often does. My cringe reflex is exhausted."

Many more-liberal women, meanwhile, make the point that Palin's poverty of knowledge is a big reason to doubt John McCain's judgment, as Ruth Marcus drives home in her column in the *Washington Post* this week. The problem is that Palin is a vice presidential candidate who is not ready to be president, not that she's a woman who isn't ready. Given that, let her fail now, before she does real damage in office.

But Palin's gender is at the center of another set of reactions I've been hearing and reading among women who don't support her ticket, who are filled with ambivalence over how bad she is. Laugh at the Tina Fey parodies that make Palin ridiculous just by quoting her verbatim. And then cry. When Palin tanks, it's good for the country if you want Obama and Biden to win, but it's bad for the future of women in national politics. I'm in this boat, too. Should we feel sorry for Sarah Palin? No. But if she fails miserably, we might be excused for feeling a bit sorry for ourselves.

Palin is the most prominent woman on the political stage at the moment. By taking unprepared hesitancy and lack of preparation to a sentence-stopping level, she's yanking us back to the old assumption that women can't hack it at these heights. We know that's not true—we've just watched Hillary Clinton power through a campaign with a masterful grasp of policy and detail. Clinton lost in part because she was the girl grind. Complex sentences, the names of Supreme Court cases, and bizarre warnings about foreign heads of state invading our airspace weren't her problem. The fear now is that Palin is the anti-Hillary and that her lack of competence threatens to undo what the Democratic primary did for women. Palin won't bust through the ceiling that has Hillary's 18 million cracks in it. She'll give men an excuse to replace it with a new one.

Worrying about this can lead you to an odd, even self-contradictory amalgam of anger and pity. Judith Warner embodied this in the *New York Times* when she described watching Palin smile while sitting down with Henry Kissinger and feeling a "wave of self-recognition and sympathy" and an "upsurge of concern and kinship." In the next breath, in proper feminist fashion, she points out that glamorizing incompetence "means that any woman who exudes competence will necessarily be excluded from the circle of sisterhood." But then Warner loops back to her opening sympathy and ends by casting Palin's nomination as not only "an insult to the women (and men) of America" but "an act of cruelty toward her as well." The suggestion is that John McCain inflicted the cruelty when he picked her.

As Rebecca Traister points out in Salon, there's an obvious feminist comeback here. Shut down the "Palin pity party," Traister urges. "Shaking our heads and wringing our hands in sympathy with Sarah Palin is a disservice to every woman who has ever been unfairly dismissed based on her gender, because this is an utterly fair dismissal, based on an utter lack of ability and readiness." Good point. And an especially pertinent one on the eve of the vice presidential debate. Traister's argument refutes the McCain campaign's effort to spin the justified attacks on Palin as sexism. The campaign can't rightly dismiss Palin's critics as sexist for jumping on her thin, stock-phrase-laden answers to reasonable questions. It would be sexist—and destructive for the country—to demand less of a vice presidential candidate. But the answer isn't necessarily to throw the sexism line back in the campaign's face, as Campbell Brown did on CNN last week. Brown scolded the campaign for treating Palin as if she's too delicate to handle the press. But where is Palin in this equation? Doesn't she have to account for the way she's been shielded from questions that shouldn't be hard for her to answer?

Traister is right that this is on Palin at least as much as it's on John McCain. Palin put herself in line for the presidency; she could have turned down the invitation to join the ticket. She gains from this campaign no matter what— before it, she had no national profile, now she has an outsize one, and all the criticism will just make her true fans love her more. (They're ready to eat Kathleen Parker alive.) She has cannily based her appeal on scorning the media, so it hardly makes sense to feel pity for her when the media scorn *her*, given all the fodder she's provided.

For all of these reasons, I should take Traister's advice and stop agonizing. I'm not ambivalent about Palin's positions on taxes, stem-cell research, or offshore drilling. Why should I be ambivalent about how she performs in the debate? What if Palin does unexpectedly well and gives McCain another boost in the polls? Better she should go down hard for knowing nothing about the Supreme Court than that the court should move ever rightward because the Republicans get to pick the next justices.

And yet. When I watch Palin, I can't help but cringe along with Parker. Call it women's solidarity, however misplaced. I keep coming back to this prim phrase: Please, don't make a spectacle of yourself. String some coherent sentences together. Your efforts to wrap yourself in Hillary's mantle make no sense in terms of what you'd actually do in office. But if you could pull off just a bit of her debating prowess—just a bit—I'll step a little lighter when I wake up Friday morning.

Flirting Her Way to Victory

Michelle Goldberg

At least three times in her debate with Joe Biden, Sarah
Palin, the adorable, preposterous vice presidential candidate,
winked at the audience. Had a male candidate with a similar
reputation for attractive vapidity made such a brazen
attempt to flirt his way into the good graces of the voting
public, it would have been universally noted, discussed, and
mocked. Palin, however, has single-handedly so lowered
the standards both for female candidates and American
political discourse that, with her newfound ability to speak
in more-or-less full sentences, she is now deemed to have
performed acceptably.

By any normal standard, including the ones applied
to male presidential candidates of either party, she did not.
Early on, she made the astonishing announcement that
she had no intentions of actually answering the queries
put to her. "I may not answer the questions that either the
moderator or you want to hear, but I'm going to talk straight
to the American people and let them know my track record
also," she said.

And so she proceeded, with an almost surreal disregard
for the subjects she was supposed to be discussing, to unleash
fusillades of scripted attack lines, platitudes, lies, gibberish,
and grating references to her own pseudo-folksy authenticity.

It was an appalling display. The only reason it was not
widely described as such is that too many American pundits
don't even try to judge the truth, wisdom or reasonableness
of the political rhetoric they are paid to pronounce upon.
Instead, they imagine themselves as interpreters of a
mythical mass of "average Americans" whom they both
venerate and despise.

In pronouncing upon a debate, they don't try to determine whether a candidate's responses correspond to existing reality, or whether he or she is capable of talking about subjects such as the deregulation of the financial markets or the devolution of the war in Afghanistan. The criteria are far more vaporous. In this case, it was whether Palin could avoid utterly humiliating herself for ninety minutes, and whether urbane commentators would believe that she had connected to a public that they see as ignorant and sentimental. For the Alaska governor, mission accomplished.

There is indeed something mesmerizing about Palin, with her manic beaming and fulsome confidence in her own charm. The force of her personality managed to slightly obscure the insulting emptiness of her answers in the debate. It's worth reading the transcript of the encounter, where it becomes clearer how bizarre much of what she said was. Here, for example, is how she responded to Biden's comments about how the middle class has been short-changed during the Bush administration, and how McCain will continue Bush's policies:

> Say it ain't so, Joe, there you go again pointing backwards again. You preferenced [sic] your whole comment with the Bush administration. Now doggone it, let's look ahead and tell Americans what we have to plan to do for them in the future. You mentioned education, and I'm glad you did. I know education you are passionate about with your wife being a teacher for thirty years, and God bless her. Her reward is in heaven, right?... My brother, who I think is the best schoolteacher in the year, and here's a shout-out to all those third graders at Gladys Wood

Elementary School, you get extra credit for watching the debate.

Evidently, Palin's pre-debate handlers judged her incapable of speaking on a fairly wide range of subjects, and so instructed her to simply disregard questions that did not invite memorized talking points or cutesy filibustering. They probably told her to play up her spunky averageness, which she did to the point of shtick—and dishonesty. Asked what her Achilles' heel is—a question she either didn't understand or chose to ignore—she started in on how McCain chose her because of her "connection to the heartland of America. Being a mom, one very concerned about a son in the war, about a special-needs child, about kids heading off to college, how are we going to pay those tuition bills?"

None of Palin's children, it should be noted, is heading off to college. Her son is on the way to Iraq, and her pregnant seventeen-year-old daughter is engaged to be married to a high school dropout and self-described "fuckin' redneck." Palin is a woman who can't even tell the truth about the most quotidian and public details of her own life, never mind about matters of major public import. In her only vice presidential debate, she was shallow, mendacious, and phony. What kind of maverick, after all, keeps harping on what a maverick she is? That her performance was considered anything but a farce doesn't show how high Palin has risen, but how low we all have sunk.

Sayonara, Sarah
Katha Pollitt

And so we bid farewell to Sarah Palin. How I'll miss her daily presence in my life! The mooseburgers, the wolf hunts, the kids named after bays and sports and trees and airplanes and who did not seem to go to school at all, the winks and blinks, the cute Alaska accent, the witch-hunting pastor and those great little flared jackets, especially the gray stripey one. People say she was a dingbat, but that is just sexist: The woman read everything, she said so herself; her knowledge of geography was unreal—she knew just where to find the pro-America part of the country; and don't forget her keen interest in ancient history! Thanks largely to her, Bill Ayers is now the most famous sixtysomething professor in the country—eat your heart out, Ward Churchill! You can snipe all you want, but she was truly God's gift: to Barack Obama, Katie Couric—notice no one's making fun of America's sweetheart now—Tina Fey, and columnists all over America.

She was also a gift to feminism. Seriously. I don't mean she was a feminist—she told Couric she considered herself one, but in a later interview, perhaps after looking up the meaning of the word, coyly wondered why she needed to "label" herself. And I don't mean she had a claim on the votes of feminists or women—why should women who care about equality vote for a woman who wants to take their rights away? Elaine Lafferty, a former editor of Ms., made a splash by revealing in the Daily Beast (Tina Brown's new Web site, for those of you still following the news on paper) that she has been working as a consultant to Palin. In a short but painful piece of public relations called "Sarah Palin's a Brainiac," Lafferty claimed to find in Palin "a mind that is thoughtful, curious, with a discernible pattern of associative thinking and insight," with a "photographic memory," as smart as legendary Senator Sam Ervin, "a woman who knows exactly who she is." According to Lafferty, all that stuff about library censorship and rape kits was just "nonsense"—and feminists who held Palin's wish to criminalize abortion against her were Beltway feminist-establishment elitists who shop at Whole Foods when they should be voting against Barack Obama to make the Dems stop taking women for granted.

So the first way Palin was good for feminism is that she helped us clarify what it isn't: Feminism doesn't mean voting for "the woman" just because she's female, and it doesn't mean confusing self-injury with empowerment, like the Ellen Jamesians in *The World According to Garp.* (I'll vote for the forced-childbirth candidate; that'll show Howard Dean!) It isn't just feel-good "you go, girl" appreciation of female moxie, which I cheerfully acknowledge Palin has by the gallon. As I wrote when she was selected, if she were my neighbor I would probably like her—at least until she organized with her fellow Christians to ban abortion at the local hospital, as Palin did in the 1990s. Yes, feminism is about women getting their fair share of power, and that includes the top jobs—but that can't take a backseat to policies that benefit all women: equality on the job and the legal framework that undergirds it, antiviolence, reproductive self-determination, health care, education, childcare, and so on. Fortunately, women who care about equality get this—dead-enders like the comically clueless Lynn Forester de Rothschild got lots of press, but in the end Obama won the support of the vast majority of women who had supported Hillary Clinton.

Second, Palin's presence on the Republican ticket forced family-values conservatives to give public support to working mothers, equal marriages, pregnant teens, and their much-maligned parents. Talk-show frothers, Christian zealots, and professional antifeminists—Rush Limbaugh and Phyllis Schlafly—insisted that a mother of five, including a "special-needs" newborn, could perfectly well manage governing a state (a really big state, as we were frequently reminded), while simultaneously running for veep and, who knows, field dressing a moose. No one said she belonged at home. No one said she was neglecting her husband or failing to be appropriately submissive to him. No one blamed her for seventeen-year-old Bristol's out-of-wedlock pregnancy or hard-partying high-school-dropout boyfriend. No one even wondered out loud why Bristol wasn't getting married before the baby arrived. All these things have officially morphed from sins to "challenges," just part of normal family life. No matter how strategic this newfound broadmindedness is, it will not be easy to row away from it. Thanks to Sarah, ladies, we can do just about anything we want as long as we don't have an abortion.

Third, while Palin did not win the Hillary vote, the love she got from Republican women, including very conservative, traditional women, shows that what I like to call the feminism of everyday life is taking hold across the spectrum. That old frilly-doormat model of femininity is gone: Even women who stay home and attend churches that bar women from the clergy thrill to the idea of women being all that they can be and taking their rightful place in the public realm. Like everyone else, they want respect and power, and now, finally, thanks to the women's movement they despise, they may actually get some.

Finally, Palin completed the task Hillary Clinton began: Running in different parties across a single political season, they have normalized the idea of a woman in the White House. It is hard even to remember now how iconoclastic

Hillary was—how hard it was for her to negotiate femininity and ambition, to be warm but not weak, smart but not cold, attractive but not sexy, dynamic but not threatening. Only a year ago, it was a real question whether men would vote for a woman or, for that matter, whether women would. Palin may have been unfit for high office, but just by running she showed there was more than one mode for a female politician. After almost two years of the whole country watching two very different women in the White House race, it finally seems normal.

So thanks, Sarah. And now, please—back to your iceberg.

Lost in Translation: Why Sarah Palin Really Quit Us

Dahlia Lithwick

When America is finally ready to reckon with the phenomenon that was Sarah Palin, I suspect we will discover that whatever she represents actually had less to do with her gender, class, or ideology than we now believe. It's easy to look at the soon-to-be-former governor of Alaska as an iconic feminist, a pathbreaking working mother, or noble rabble-rousing populist. But when the dust settles, the lesson may be that she was simply a woman who made no sense. Her meteoric rise and dubious fall will say less about America than you think, beyond the fact that America likes its politicians to communicate their ideas clearly. We will someday come to realize that while it's all well and good to be mavericky with one's policies, it's never smart to be mavericky with one's message.

Whatever you may think of Sarah Palin, she's widely celebrated as a rare and perhaps raw political talent. She's gorgeous, charismatic, warm, and funny. She has a remarkable ability to connect with her listeners. But—with the exception of a well-scripted performance at the Republican National Convention—it's tough to find an extemporaneous Palin speech, statement, or tweet that contains a coherent message. From her acceptance speech last August in Dayton, Ohio, when McCain first tapped her as a running mate, to her circular and swooping prime-time interviews, Palin's political skill lies in selling a persona but not a message. And in the end, this may explain why she quit.

Palin's completely inscrutable resignation speech last week was only the most recent example of a lengthy political communication from her that explained nothing, clarified nothing, and expounded upon nothing, save for the fact that she speaks in riddles and koans. Watch it as many times as you like; you still come away feeling you've been treated to a cozy chat with the Mad Hatter. The media are bad. Those ethics complaints are expensive. Alaska was a great idea. She is not a dead fish. Put it all together and what do you get? A born fighter who has given us no sense whatsoever of what she's fighting for.

Had Palin simply quit without giving a press conference, there might have been a lesson in this exercise. Feminists would be free to say there are double standards for women, and conservatives could argue she was too visionary for her time. But Palin's act of explaining her resignation to us in a torrent of unconnected sentence fragments left everyone wondering, What was the point of Sarah Palin? If she cannot even communicate a simple idea ("I'm quitting because ..."), why should we care that she's quitting?

That's why the strangest part of the Sarah Palin saga will always be her loathing of the media. She never failed to remind us that she didn't like being "filtered." She only wanted to talk directly to us, her listeners. Yet the reason Sarah Palin continues to have any kind of political force at all in this country is because of the media "filter." The media helped refine and define her Dada statements and arguments into something that briefly sounded like a coherent worldview. Governor Palin excoriated Andrea Mitchell for "not listening to me" in an NBC interview. You have to go back and watch the clip before you can apprehend that Mitchell was indeed listening. It was Palin who was speaking in half-expressed thoughts and internal contradictions.

It's too easy to characterize Sarah Palin as an irrational bundle of bristling grievance. But I think it's more complicated than her simple love for playing the victim all the time. If you think of Palin as someone who never felt herself to be fully heard or understood, not truly politically realized in the eyes of the American public, then her rage toward the country, the media, and those of us who fail to love and understand her is easier to comprehend. Think of an American visiting France who believes that if he just speaks louder, he will be speaking French. Palin has done everything in her power to explain herself to us, and still we fail to appreciate what she is all about. I'd be frustrated, too, if I thought I was offering up straight talk and nobody was getting the message. Especially if I held a degree in communications.

Once you understand that Palin's only actual message is the importance of loving and understanding Palin, it becomes easier to understand why she quit. The more Palin tries to explain herself, the more we all fail to get her. Every time she goes off script, she makes less sense. No wonder she didn't want to do debate prep or be coached by the McCain communications team. Instead of thanking those who packaged, explained, and spun her, Palin resents them. And because she believes she has been crystal clear all along, she's come to resent us, too. The enduring political lesson of Sarah Palin may simply be that for most of her political career she's been lost in translation, without fully appreciating that only in translation was she ever, briefly found.

8/ PALIN'S POISON
Lingering in the Body Politic

She Broke the GOP and Now She Owns It
Frank Rich

Sarah Palin and Al Sharpton don't ordinarily have much in common, but they achieved a rare harmonic convergence at Michael Jackson's memorial service. When Sharpton told the singer's children it was their daddy's adversaries, not their daddy, who were "strange," he was channeling the pugnacious argument the Alaska governor had made the week before. There was nothing strange about her decision to quit in midterm, Palin told America. What's strange— or "insane," in her lingo— are the critics who dare question her erratic behavior on the national stage.

Sharpton's bashing of Jackson's naysayers received the biggest ovation of the entire show. Palin's combative resignation soliloquy, though much mocked by prognosticators of all political persuasions, has an equally vociferous and more powerful constituency. In the aftermath of her decision to drop out and cash in, Palin's standing in the GOP actually rose in the *USA Today*/Gallup poll. No less than 71 percent of Republicans said they would vote for her for president. That overwhelming majority isn't just the "base" of the Republican Party that liberals and conservatives alike tend to ghettoize as a rump backwater minority. It is the party, or pretty much what remains of it in the Barack Obama era.

That's why Palin won't go gently into the good night, much as some Republicans in Washington might wish. She is not just the party's biggest star and most charismatic television performer; she is its only star and charismatic performer. Most important, she stands for a genuine movement: a dwindling white nonurban America that is aflame with grievances and awash in self-pity as the country hurtles into the twenty-first century and leaves it behind. Palin gives this movement a major party brand and political plausibility that its open-throated media auxiliary, exemplified by Glenn Beck, cannot. She loves the spotlight, can raise millions of dollars and has no discernible reason to go fishing now except for self-promotional photo ops.

The essence of Palinism is emotional, not ideological. Yes, she is of the religious right, even if she winks literally and figuratively at her own daughter's flagrant disregard of abstinence and marriage. But family-values politics, now more devalued than the dollar by the philandering of ostentatiously Christian Republican politicians, can only take her so far. The real wave she's riding is a loud, resonant surge of resentment and victimization that's larger than issues like abortion and gay civil rights.

That resentment is in part about race, of course. When Palin referred to Alaska as "a microcosm of America" during the 2008 campaign, it was in defiance of the statistical reality that her state's tiny black and Hispanic populations are unrepresentative of her nation. She stood for the "real America," she insisted, and the identity of the unreal America didn't have to be stated explicitly for audiences to catch her drift. Her convention speech's signature line was a deftly coded putdown of her presumably shiftless big-city opponent: "I guess a small-town mayor is sort of like a community organizer, except that you have actual responsibilities." (Funny how this wisdom has been forgotten by her supporters now that she has abandoned her own actual responsibilities in public office.)

The latest flashpoint for this kind of animus is the near-certain elevation to the Supreme Court of Sonia Sotomayor, whose Senate confirmation hearings arrive this week. Prominent Palinists were fast to demean Sotomayor as a dim-witted affirmative-action baby. Fred Barnes of the *Weekly Standard*, the Palinist hymnal, labeled Sotomayor "not the smartest" and suggested that Princeton awards academic honors on a curve. Karl Rove said, "I'm not really certain how intellectually strong she would be." Those maligning the long and accomplished career of an Ivy League–educated judge do believe in affirmative action—but only for white people like Palin, whom they boosted for vice president despite her minimal achievements and knowledge of policy, the written word, or even geography.

The politics of resentment are impervious to facts. Palinists regard their star as an icon of working-class America even though the Palins' combined reported income ($211,000) puts them in the top 3.6 percent of American households. They see her as a champion of conservative fiscal principles even though she said yes to the Bridge to Nowhere and presided over a state that ranks number one in federal pork.

Nowhere is the power of resentment to trump reason more flagrantly illustrated than in the incessant complaint by Palin and her troops that she is victimized by a double standard in the "mainstream media." In truth, the commentators at ABC, NBC, and CNN—often the same ones who judged Michelle Obama a drag on her husband—all tried to outdo each other in praise for Palin when she emerged at the Republican convention. Even now, the so-called mainstream media can grade Palin on a curve: at MSNBC's *Morning Joe* last week, Palin's self-proclaimed representation of the "real America" was accepted as a given, as if white rural America actually still was the nation's baseline.

The Palinists' bogus beefs about double standards reached farcical proportions at Fox News on the sleepy pre-Fourth Friday afternoon when word of her abdication hit the

East. The fill-in anchor demanded that his token Democratic stooge name another female politician who had suffered such "disgraceful attacks" as Palin. When the obvious answer arrived—Hillary Clinton—the Fox host angrily protested that Clinton had never been attacked in "a sexual way" or "about her children."

Americans have short memories, but it's hardly ancient history that conservative magazines portrayed Hillary Clinton as both a dominatrix cracking a whip and a broomstick-riding witch. Or that Rush Limbaugh held up a picture of Chelsea Clinton on television to identify the "White House dog." Or that Palin's running mate, John McCain, told a sexual joke linking Hillary and Chelsea and Janet Reno. Yet the same conservative commentariat that vilified both Clintons 24/7 now whines that Palin is receiving "the kind of mauling" that the media "always reserve for conservative Republicans." So said the *Wall Street Journal* editorial page last week. You'd never guess that the *Journal* had published six innuendo-laden books on real and imagined Clinton scandals, or that the Clintons had been a leading target of both Letterman and Leno monologues, not to mention many liberal editorial pages (including that of the *New York Times*), for much of a decade.

Those Republicans who have not drunk the Palin Kool-Aid are apocalyptic for good reason. She could well be their last presidential candidate standing. Such would-be competitors as Mark Sanford, John Ensign, and Newt Gingrich are too carnally compromised for the un-Clinton party. Mike Huckabee is Palin Lite. Tim Pawlenty, Bobby Jindal—really? That leaves the charisma-challenged Mitt Romney, precisely the kind of card-carrying Ivy League elitist Palinists loathe, no matter how hard he tries to cosmetically alter his history as a socially liberal fat-cat banker. Palin would crush him like a bug. She has the Teflon-coated stature among Republicans that Romney can only fantasize about.

Were Palin actually to secure the 2012 nomination, the result would be a fiasco for the GOP akin to Goldwater 1964, as the most relentless conservative Palin critic, David Frum, has predicted. Or would it? No one thought Richard Nixon—a far less personable commodity than Palin—would come back either after his sour-grapes "last press conference" of 1962. But Democratic divisions and failures gave him his opportunity in 1968. With unemployment approaching 10 percent and a seemingly bottomless war in Afghanistan, you never know, as Palin likes to say, what doors might open.

It's more likely that she will never get anywhere near the White House, and not just because of her own limitations. The Palinist "real America" is demographically doomed to keep shrinking. But the emotion it represents is disproportionately powerful for its numbers. It's an anger that Palin enjoyed stoking during her "palling around with terrorists" crusade against Obama on the campaign trail. It's an anger that's curdled into self-martyrdom since Inauguration Day.

Its voice can be found in the postings at a Web site maintained by the fans of Mark Levin, the Obama hater who is, at this writing, the number-two best-selling hardcover nonfiction writer in America. (Glenn Beck is number one in paperback nonfiction.) *Politico* surveyed them last week. "Bottomline, do you know of any way we can remove these idiots before this country goes down the crapper?" wrote one Levin fan. "I WILL HELP!!! Should I buy a gun?" Another called for a new American revolution, promising "there will be blood."

These are the cries of a constituency that feels disenfranchised—by the powerful and the well-educated who gamed the housing bubble, by a news media it keeps being told is hateful, by the immigrants who have taken some of their jobs, by the African-American who has ended a white monopoly on the White House. Palin is their born avatar. She puts a happy, sexy face on ugly emotions, and she can solidify her followers' hold on a GOP that has no leaders with the guts or alternative vision to stand up to them or to her.

For a week now, critics in both parties have had a blast railing at Palin. It's good sport. But just as the media muttering about those unseemly "controversies" rallied the fans of the King of Pop, so are Palin's political obituaries likely to jump-start her lucrative afterlife.

The Losers Who Gave Us Sarah Palin
Joe Conason

Disaster is often followed by recrimination, a bitter aspect of human nature that can be observed among the Republicans as the Sarah Palin fiasco continues to unfold. The Alaska governor's surprise resignation, amid negative press coverage in *Vanity Fair* and elsewhere, suddenly revived dormant feuding among campaign operatives and conservative media figures—notably between Steve Schmidt, the former campaign manager, and Bill Kristol, the *Weekly Standard* editor and Fox News commentator.

In ordinary circumstances, all their bitchy backbiting, spinning, and fabricating would be of little interest except as comic entertainment for political junkies. Who first called Palin a "diva"? Who insinuated that she might suffer from postpartum depression? Who searched computer files to find out which staffer was leaking these bilious tidbits to the press? And who cares now, eight months later, except for these losers?

Plainly there is no reason why anyone should care, except for one small nagging concern. It is worth remembering that these are the same people who chose Palin, a manifestly unqualified and incompetent politician unable to string together a series of coherent sentences, as the potential presidential successor to a seventy-two-year-old cancer survivor. So it would be refreshing and salubrious to see the perpetrators of that contemptuous and cynical tactic held accountable for endangering the country.

The latest eruptions from Kristol, Schmidt, and all the lesser actors in the Republican reality show echo similar complaints from the closing days of the campaign last fall, when they were blaming each other for the obvious mistake of Palin's nomination. Back then, Schmidt and other top figures in the McCain orbit—including lobbyists Rick Davis and Charles Black and speechwriter Mark Salter—started to seek distance from the Wasilla phenomenon as soon as they realized that their ticket was going to lose the election, and that her nomination might well be counted among the reasons. In assigning responsibility for impending doom, these gentlemen criticized not only Palin herself but her cheerleaders on the right, the most vocal of whom had been Kristol.

But in late October 2008, the *New York Times Magazine* published an extraordinary and timely story that explained exactly how McCain had come to select Palin. According to that article, Schmidt had collaborated with Davis and Salter to promote Palin over several more qualified candidates— after a cursory background investigation that revealed almost nothing about her lack of knowledge, bizarre official conduct, and narcissistic temperament. When the three insiders presented her to a smitten, impetuous McCain, he accepted their judgment, ratified by Charlie Black, one of the most experienced Republican operatives in Washington, who told him that if he chose her, he might win—and otherwise he would surely lose.

It is true, of course, that Kristol had been pushing Palin forward with almost puppyish enthusiasm, ever since his infatuating luncheon with her at the governor's mansion in Juneau during a summer cruise sponsored by his magazine in 2007. "She could be both an effective vice presidential candidate and an effective president," he gushed on *Fox News Sunday*. "She's young, energetic." It is also true, however, that McCain, Schmidt, Davis, and Salter chose to listen to Kristol, almost always a political mistake with consequences ranging from the merely absurd to the utterly dire. (The latter category includes the invasion of Iraq, with an astronomical cost in lives and treasure that should be charged to him and his magazine, as he used to boast.)

Enormous as Kristol's errors in judgment surely were, at least he can plausibly claim to be loyal. If anything he is too steadfast, still insisting that Palin deserves to be considered a serious candidate for the presidency and that her qualifications for that position are comparable to those of Barack Obama.

If that sounds ridiculous—and it does to most sane people—then let's not forget that Schmidt and many other Republicans were making the same argument on Palin's behalf, at least publicly, not so long ago. When journalists dared to question her qualifications, after the excited flush faded from her convention debut, Schmidt was belligerent—as befitted a protégé of Karl Rove.

"Her selection came after a six-month-long, rigorous vetting process where her extraordinary credentials and exceptionalism became clear," he barked. "This vetting controversy is a faux media scandal designed to destroy the first female Republican nominee for vice president of the United States who has never been a part of the old boys' network that has come to dominate the news establishment in this country."

Schmidt was lying—about the process, about her credentials, about the confidence he and his cronies supposedly had in her, and about the media questions that he knew to be legitimate.

Rarely is anyone in Washington, from politicians to operatives to journalists, held accountable for the damage they inflict on the body politic. Those who banged the drum for disastrous war flit from one editorial page to the next; those who insisted on ruinous deregulation return as economic advisers to the president. The men who told us that Sarah Palin should be next in line of succession to the presidency may quarrel among themselves now, but they will all be back with yet more stupid advice—and we can only blame ourselves if we listen.

Beyond the Palin
Rick Perlstein

The conservative opinion elite is divided—irreconcilably so—
about Sarah Palin's decision to quit the Alaska governorship.
One faction says good riddance: The *Washington Post*'s
Charles Krauthammer had already judged her unfit for
national office twenty-four hours before her announcement,
and the *New York Times*'s Ross Douthat now refers to her
"brief sojourn on the national stage" in the past tense. On the
other side, the *Post*'s William Kristol called Palin's quitting a
"high-risk move" designed to catapult her to greater public
prominence. Taking the longer view, though, the clash is
symptomatic of the deepest strategic debate in Republican
circles since the disciples of the Reagan revolution captured
Congress in 1994.

For decades it has remained a Republican article
of faith: White, lower-middle-class, "heartland" masses,
fundamentally socially conservative, were an inexhaustible
electoral resource. So much so that Bill Clinton made
re-earning their trust—he called them the Americans
who "worked hard and played by the rules"—the central
challenge in rebuilding Democratic fortunes in the 1990s.
And in 2008 the somewhat aristocratic John McCain seemed
to regard bringing these folks back into the Republican fold
so imperative that he was moved to make the election's most
exciting strategic move: drafting churchgoing, gun-toting
unknown Sarah Palin onto the GOP ticket.

But beneath the surface, some Republicans have been
chafing at the ideological wages of right-wing populism. In
intellectual circles, writers like David Brooks and Richard
Brookhiser have argued for a conservatism inspired by
Alexander Hamilton, the least democratic of the Founding

Fathers, over one spiritually rooted in Thomas Jefferson, the most democratic. After Barack Obama's victory, you heard thinkers like author and federal judge Richard Posner lamenting on his blog that "the face of the Republican Party had become Sarah Palin and Joe the Plumber. Conservative intellectuals had no party."

Such discomfort has been dormant for some time. Under the influence of philosophical gurus like Leo Strauss and Irving Kristol, the sotto voce tradition arose of flattering the sort of voter who drove a pickup truck even if he wasn't the sort you might want to socialize with. (Take, for example, "jes' folks" Mark Sanford of South Carolina. Long before his jet-setting affair, after all, he met the jet-setting, Georgetown-educated Yankee investment banker who became Mrs. Sanford at a Hamptons beach party.) But Palin has raised the "class" question publicly among conservatives as seldom before.

Michael Barone, writing in March on *U.S. News*'s Thomas Jefferson Street blog, noted that the electorate's portion of "under-30 downscale whites" has been stagnating, while the participation of both young upscale whites and African-Americans generally has spiked upward. The pool is shrinking; thus he thinks Republicans should now focus on wooing upscale whites, banking on their disenchantment with Obama's moves to fix the economy. Author and former Bush speechwriter David Frum recently made the argument, on the occasion of the split between Palin's single eighteen-year-old daughter, Bristol, and the nineteen-year-old father of her child, that "it is marriage that creates culturally conservative voters—and young downscale Americans are not getting married. When they do marry, they do not stay married: While divorce rates among the college educated have declined sharply since the 1970s, divorce rates among high school graduates remain ominously high." In a much-discussed blog post titled "Bristol's Myth," Frum cited statistics showing that white women without a college degree are far more likely to have a child out of wedlock than their college-educated counterparts. He concluded that "the socially conservative downscale voter is increasingly becoming a mirage—and a Republican politics based on that mirage will only lead us deeper into the desert."

It was a strange argument to make. This is the kind of statistical story liberals frequently tell: They will note that the states that vote most heavily Republican are the ones with the highest divorce rates, teenage births, and usage of online pornography—the highest rates of sin. They mean to sting conservatives with the charge of hypocrisy: "See? Conservatives aren't more 'moral' after all." Such claims, though, misunderstand a basic underpinning of conservative philosophy: Human beings become civilized not through the absence of sin but the conscious struggle with sin. Sin is bad; but the true offense is sin in the absence of guilt—an indifference to the notion that there are moral boundaries even worth recognizing. Conservatism is usually most politically successful in religiously orthodox precincts where anxiety over the modern-day collapse of visible moral boundaries is most evident. That Americans sin a lot so we can't hope for them to vote conservatively is a new claim.

Why the change? For one thing, populism has never been an entirely comfortable fit for elite conservatives. Majorities of middle-class Americans can be persuaded to support tax cuts for the rich—even repeal of the estate tax—out of an optimism that they may eventually become rich themselves. But they are also susceptible to appeals like the one George Wallace made in the recession year of 1976. He built his campaign on both hellfire-and-brimstone moralism and a pledge of soak-the-rich tax policies. The elite conservative fears that the temptation to woo working-class voters will, you know, shade into policies that actually advantage the working class. That fear surfaced recently when Rush Limbaugh—whom Frum himself has singled out as one of the dangerous populists dragging the Republicans down—dismissed those who criticized the AIG bonuses as "peasants with their pitchforks" who must be silenced for the sake of conservative orthodoxy. But it's harder to persuade the economically less fortunate to respect conservative orthodoxy during a recession. That's starting to make some conservatives nervous.

Another thing that makes some elite conservatives nervous in this recession is the sheer level of unhinged, even violent irrationality at the grassroots. In postwar America, a panicky, violence-prone underbrush has always been revealed in moments of liberal ascendency. In the Kennedy years, the right-wing militia known as the Minutemen armed for what they believed would be an imminent Russian takeover. In the Carter years it was the Posse Comitatus; Bill Clinton's rise saw six antiabortion murders and the Oklahoma City bombing. Each time, the conservative mainstream was able to adroitly hive off the embarrassing fringe while laying claim to some of the grassroots anger that inspired it. Now the violence is back. But this time, the line between the violent fringe and the on-air harvesters of righteous rage has been harder to find. This spring the alleged white-supremacist cop killer in Pittsburgh, Richard Poplawski, professed allegiance to conspiracist Alex Jones, whose theories Fox TV host Glenn Beck had recently been promoting. And when Kansas doctor George Tiller was murdered in church, Fox star Bill O'Reilly was forced to devote airtime to defending himself against a charge many observers found self-evident: that O'Reilly's claim that "Tiller the baby killer" was getting away with "Nazi stuff" helped contribute to an atmosphere in which Tiller's alleged assassin believed he was doing something heroic.

At least in the past, those who wished to represent their movement as cosmopolitan and urbane could simply point to William F. Buckley as the right's most prominent spokesman. Now Buckley is gone, and the most prominent spokesmen—the Limbaughs and O'Reillys and Becks—can be heard mouthing attitudes once confined to the violent fringe. For the second time in three months, Fox heavily promoted anti-administration "tea party" events this past Fourth of July—rallies in praise of secession and the Articles of Confederation, at which speakers "joked" about a coup against the communist Muslim Barack Obama like the one against Manuel Zelaya in Honduras. "What's going on at Fox News?" Frum recently asked, excoriating Beck for passing out to followers books by the nutty far-right conspiracy theorist W. Cleon Skousen. If you were an elite conservative, you might be embarrassed too.

The conservative intellectuals once were able to work together more effectively with the conservative unwashed. Now, more and more, their irritation renders them akin to the Stalinist commissars mocked by poet Bertolt Brecht, who asked if they might "dissolve the people/And elect another." The bargain the right has offered the downwardly mobile, culturally insecure traditionalist—give us your votes, and we will give you existential certitudes in a world that seems somehow to have gone crazy—is looking less like good politics all the time.

Sarah Palin's Death Panels
Robert Reich

Three years ago, my mother died after a long and painful illness. During her last months she was only partially conscious, and in her brief intervals of awareness was often distraught. At several points my father, sister, and I met with doctors to figure out how to ease her obvious suffering with pain medications, and how we could get her into a hospice facility. We could afford the counseling, but millions of other families cannot—which is why one of the useful health care reforms now moving through Congress authorizes Medicare to reimburse doctors for such voluntary end-of-life consultations. The American Medical Association and the National Hospice and Palliative Care Organization support the provision.

But in a cruel contortion, former Alaska Governor Sarah Palin calls these consultations "death panels," and in a Facebook posting charges that they'll force the elderly to accept minimal end-of-life care in order to reduce health care costs: "It's misleading for the president to describe this section as an entirely voluntary provision that simply increases the information offered to Medicare recipients." She added, "It's all just more evidence that the Democratic legislative proposals will lead to health care rationing."

In her short time on the public stage, we've come to expect this sort of thing from Governor Palin. But listen to other Republicans these days—and if you can bear it, tune in to right-wing Hate Radio—and you'll hear more of the same.

Health care is already rationed, of course. Those who can't afford health care don't get much of it, except in emergency rooms. For those who have insurance, the rationing is done by prepaid medical groups, the legacies of HMOs, that decide what drugs and procedures their members will get. Or it's done by insurance company personnel who decide what will be covered.

But for the scaremongers to say that under the health care reform proposals now being considered, government will do the rationing—and that government bureaucrats will decide whether people live or die—is odious. It's a deliberate lie that preys upon the fears of many people who already scared as hell about loss of their jobs, health care, homes, and savings.

The "town meetings" that are now spewing such anger reflect deep-seated fears that are welling up across America during this economic crisis. Health care reform may ease some of these fears. But the demagogues that are manipulating those fears for political gain don't give a hoot.

Have they no shame?

How Sarah Palin Renewed American Socialism
John Nichols

I am not sure that I will ever be able to convey the depth
and breadth of my appreciation for Sarah Palin. I know that
my sometimes snarky articles and blog posts have probably
made it seem like I do not value the contribution she has
made to the national discourse. But I do. I really do.

So let me say this as plainly as I can: Thank you, Sarah
Palin. Thank you for bringing socialism back from the
wilderness. Thank you for infusing it with the credibility
that can only be conveyed by someone who sees Russia from
her house. The post-ideology crowd may imagine you as just
another clueless candidate spewing stream-of-consciousness
political punch-lines. But you and I know better.

Your obsession with socialism, your determination
to label every government program you come across (with
the possible exception of Alaska's annual redistribution of
the wealth from oil companies to citizens) "socialist," your
willingness to identify your opponents as "socialists"—even
when they most certainly, and most disappointingly, are
not—has renewed the economic and political discourse in a
country where it had pretty much died.

Socialism, the very American ideology that Tom Paine
imagined and that immigrant believers in the utopian
ideals of Robert Owen and Charles Fourier gave shape
and meaning to on the nineteenth-century frontier, had
fallen on exceptionally hard times in a country that had
forgotten its roots in revolt against empire. Even as Latin
America succumbed, country by country, to exciting new
variations on the vision of a cooperative commonwealth,
the dictatorship of the not-so-proletariat so dominated the
United States that liberal Democrats proclaimed their passion

for free-market capitalism with a fervency that would have embarrassed Margaret Thatcher.

Then came you. Late in August of 2008, the Republican Party (itself the spawn of French socialist immigrants who gathered in Wisconsin in 1854 to form a radical antislavery movement) nominated a certain Alaskan governor for the vice presidency. Channeling the "analysis" of *National Review*, Rush Limbaugh and the assorted ideological mentors who had championed a nineteen-month governor as the appropriate running mate of an aging nominee, Sarah Palin immediately began to suggest that Barack Obama might just be a "socialist."

Unfortunately, Obama had no instinct toward socialism. Fortunately, Palin had no instinct toward accuracy. When Palin appeared on CNN (or, as her backers refer to it: the "Communist News Network") she was asked: "Is Barack Obama a socialist?"

She did not dismiss the notion. Rather, with that flirting-with-facts style we had come to love, she announced: "I'm not going to call him a socialist. But as Joe the Plumber has suggested, in fact he came right out and said it, it sounds like socialism to him. And he speaks for so many Americans who are quite concerned now after hearing finally what Barack Obama's true intentions are with his tax and economic plan." It was clear that, even if she was "not going to call him a socialist," Palin obviously sympathized with Plumber Joe's assessment that Obama stood slightly to the left of Hugo Chávez on the ideological continuum.

The governor got over her compunctions about describing Obama and his policies as "socialist" quickly enough. Two days after the CNN appearance, she told a crowd in Roswell, New Mexico—yup, the alien place—that Obama's platform "sounds more like socialism" than she liked.

"Friends," she screeched, in a plea for the rejection of Obama, "now is no time to experiment with socialism."

Wow, there it was again, that word *socialism*. Maybe Palin was right. As a journalist, I had a responsibility to check out whether Obama was some kind of Manchurian candidate—or, maybe, considering the right's obsession with a certain Venezuelan president, some kind of Caracas candidate. So I contacted the Socialists. I got hold of Brian Moore, the 2008 presidential nominee of what remained of America's honorable old Socialist Party. "Is Sarah right?" I inquired. "Is Obama a fellow traveler?"

No such luck, Moore told me. Obama was "bought and sold" by Wall Street, said the Florida peace activist who was carrying the banner that year of the party of Eugene Victor Debs and Norman Thomas. Of course, Moore added, so too was Palin's presidential running mate, John McCain. "The two major candidates cannot move, they are imprisoned by accepting all that corporate money," explained the Socialist candidate.

What would a real socialist be proposing? To begin with, instead of supporting the socialism-for-the-rich bailout by the American taxpayers of bad bankers that both Obama and Palin had recently endorsed, Moore suggested socialism for the rest of us. Congress, he argued, should "nationalize the banking system" and replace it with "a socially owned, democratically controlled independent national banking authority, made up of consumers, workers, accountants, and economists, who will set national policy. It would be a nonprofit national institution, which would operate through credit unions, cooperatives, and state-run banks."

Any chance that Obama and the Democrats might be sitting on a secret plan to do just that? Was it just possible that Palin knew something that we didn't? Not a chance, said

Moore. While "the economic system is collapsing before their very eyes," he explained, "neither major party fully grasps the severity of the situation."

Moore was, of course, correct. But, while economic democracy might not have been in the offering, Sarah Palin was still on to something. She kept telling anyone who would listen that people who asked whether Wall Street's meltdown might suggest a flaw in the capitalist calculus were socialists. As the crisis grew worse, this twenty-first-century Josie McCarthy's campaign-season ranting about socialism undoubtedly helped rather than hurt Obama. Palin was attacking the Democratic candidate for being insufficiently invested in the economic orthodoxy of the Republicans who had run the country for the better part of a decade at precisely the moment when the underpinnings of the financial system went into spectacular collapse, Wall Street was freefalling, and Americans began worrying if they would ever be able to retire.

The prospect that Obama might not be a completely committed capitalist of the Reagan/Bush/Cheney/Palin school seemed to be, if not an argument in and of itself for the Democrat's election then surely a point in his favor. At precisely the point when casino capitalism spun out of control, the Democratic nominee for president was being attacked more vociferously and consistently as a socialist than any party nominee since Franklin Delano Roosevelt. And, like Roosevelt, Americans elected Obama by a landslide.

Obama got more cautious, and capitalist, after his election. But Palin and her posse kept invoking the S-word. Indeed, as the Obama presidency unfolded, Palin quit her governorship to go on the attack full time. Her pal Sean Hannity asked her in mid-2009 whether the Obamanation that America had become was "headed toward socialism."

Why, yes, Palin replied. "If we keep going down these roads nationalizing many of our services, our projects, our businesses, yes, that's where we would head," she said. As it happened, Obama was giving money to corporations, not nationalizing them. But Palin courageously threw off the bondage of facts.

And she kept talking socialism. Even if Obama wasn't keeping up his end of the bargain, Americans were listening. After years when the word "socialism" was barely mentioned in the American media, when pols and pundits never uttered the word, it had been reintroduced by no less a figure than the Republican nominee for vice president.

Palin's determination to present socialism as the alternative to casino capitalism had a remarkable impact. In the spring of 2009, a survey by the Republican-friendly Rasmussen Reports polling group found that one in five Americans viewed socialism was a preferable system to capitalism. Another 27 percent of Americans said they weren't sure whether they preferred socialism or capitalism. A bare majority—53 percent—was still rooting for the system that Americans had for decades been told was "the only alternative." Among young people, the numbers were even more startling. Thirty-three percent of those under thirty told the pollster they preferred socialism to capitalism, while just 37 percent were for capitalism. That's a statistical tie! Add the 33 percent for socialism to the huge undecided group in this survey—30 percent—and you get a whopping 63 percent of the rising generation of Americans refusing to embrace capitalism.

Could numbers like this have been imaginable just a few years ago, when President Bush and his amen corner in the media were beating into the popular consciousness the theory that America had become an "opportunity society" where everyone was going to roll the dice on the free market craps table and hope to come up lucky? No way. It took a revolutionary to break the lockstep mentality. It took a twenty-first-century Margaret Thatcher to tell America that there is an alternative to boom-and-bust, meltdowns, mass unemployment, credit crunches, and foreclosure notices. It took Sarah Palin to give socialism back its good name.

Thank you, Sarah Palin. From America in this time of crisis, and from the rising generation of Americans that you have shown another way, thank you. Thank you for reminding America that socialism is still an option.

Forum: What is Sarah Palin's Future in American Politics?

Jane Hamsher, Christopher Hayes,
Amanda Marcotte, Michael Tomasky

Jane Hamsher

When Sarah Palin called a hasty press conference on a July afternoon and gave a rambling, disjointed speech to announce her resignation as governor of Alaska, tongues instantly began to wag. Surely there must be a scandal, a criminal investigation of some sort looming in the background. Because nobody puts on this kind of erratic spectacle by choice, knowing that the announcement they are about to make will leap straight into banner headlines. No, there surely had to be something else weighing on Sarah Palin's mind that day or she never would stood before the cameras in such a state. This was certainly not the composed woman who had made such an impact at the Republican National Convention less than a year ago.

Palin's response was to promptly threaten to sue anyone who said as much. She apparently didn't realize that the mistake they actually made was to give her far more credit than she deserved. Their conclusions were based on the presumption that this behavior was emanating from an otherwise normal, rational person. The story she crafted to explain her resignation, starring herself as the brave heroine who boldly refuses to half-ass the remainder of her term while her public beckons, was so thoroughly preposterous—so narcissistic and delusional—that nobody could imagine it hadn't been cobbled together under duress.

Sadly, there was no guile there. No attempt to deceive, no rationale that lay beneath the surface. She really is what she appears to be: an ambitious woman with a flair for melodrama who thinks it's the obligation of every governor to resign before the job's over. And moreover, gosh darn it, that she's the only one with the courage, the fortitude, and the moral fiber to do it.

To the surprise of almost no one not named Sarah Palin, her poll numbers took an instant hit. At the time she made her Norma Desmond–esque departure from the governor's office, she was in a three-way tie with Mike Huckabee and Mitt Rommey among likely Republican primary voters who were asked which candidate they favored for the 2012 GOP presidential nomination. Four months later, she trails Romney by eight points and Huckabee by eleven.

Few would dispute that Michael Jackson was a phenomenal talent, but as he made his way into adulthood his need to express himself in the pages of the *National Enquirer* soon eclipsed his talent. Whatever Sarah Palin's talent for governance is, her inability to control that same impulse may soon overwhelm her political career too. Can she hold it together long enough to mount a political campaign? Will she shine as one of the leading lights of the Republican Party, or will her compulsive tango with the tabloids render her Wasilla's once and future Kato Kaelin?

Richard Land, head of the Southern Baptist Convention, is the man credited with suggesting Palin for the vice presidential slot on the 2008 ticket. I asked him once why he had chosen her. He told me that the next Republican presidential candidate had to be pro-life and the next one and the next one. Because the people who staff the phones, make the calls, knock on doors, and do the grunt work to get out the vote for the GOP are antiabortion women, and they just couldn't get worked up over John McCain. They well knew who Palin was, however, and when her name was announced as McCain's running mate, they were dancing in the streets and weeping for joy. She's a powerful symbol for them, and they showed up for her.

The Republicans are now engaged in doing what an opposition party is supposed to do—winding up their base and motivating a strong turnout for the 2010 midterms. It's what the teabag rallies are all about. The political message may be incoherent, and much of the symbolism seems to have a not-so-subtle racial component, but the rallying cry is crystal clear: It's us against them, and they suck. While liberal netizens cynically dismiss her as Caribou Barbie or Bible Spice, right-to-lifers in the GOP base see Sarah Palin as a woman wronged by the "liberal media." She is their hope for the future.

Ultimately her compulsive attraction to tabloid melodrama may undermine any shot Sarah Palin might have at the presidency. People who will tune in to see Tom DeLay on *Dancing with the Stars* don't necessarily want to see him in the White House. But don't underestimate her ability to turn out true believers come election time, because while Rahm Emanuel busies himself with demoralizing the Democratic base, Sarah Palin will be tending to hers.

Christopher Hayes

A friend of mine who is the publisher of a very successful news site has a joke: In the future the Internet will consist entirely of Sarah Palin slide shows. Anyone who's ever had occasion to look at traffic statistics for a news website understands what he's saying. Few things draw in readers and garner clicks more reliably than articles (or, even better, pictures) of Sarah Palin. We can't look away. We can't stop talking about her even when we desperately want to. The very fact that you're holding this book in your hands attests to that.

My first experience of this Sarah Palin effect came during the Republican National Convention in St. Paul. As a progressive opinion journalist who routinely reports on conservatives, you come to develop a kind of practiced disassociative state when behind enemy lines. You'd never be able to gain any understanding whatsoever if you spent all your time arguing with and hectoring people at evangelical colleges or anti-immigration rallies, so it's both psychologically and professionally necessary to put yourself in a state of mind where you simply listen.

On the night Palin gave her big debut national speech, I sat through the speeches that preceded hers in that same slightly removed state. Then Palin came to the stage. The crowd grew more and more raucous, and the room began to feel like a Roman Colosseum. When Palin went after the "reporters and commentators" in the "Washington elite" for having disparaged and condescended to her, the crowd erupted and began pointing and jeering at Tom Brokaw, sitting in the NBC booth. I watched all this still, I thought, with equanimity.

About a third of the way through the speech, when she delivered her infamous potshot at community organizers— "I guess a small-town mayor is sort of like a community organizer, except that you have actual responsibilities"— I suddenly felt like the room was 100 degrees. Realizing my face was burning with heat, I went to touch my cheeks, which felt feverish. I couldn't for the life of me understand what was going on, and was about to get up for a breath of fresh air or water until it hit me: I was furious.

My father is a community organizer and spent years toiling in some of the poorest neighborhoods in New York, doing the painstaking, unglamorous work of attempting to build power among people who were routinely getting screwed over. And Sarah Palin had just spit in his face.

Despite my best efforts, she had gotten to me.

What I was experiencing was a strange kind of dislocation: Palin had managed to bypass one part of my brain and reach down deep into another. There are two kinds of politics: There's politics of the prefrontal cerebral cortex, the politics of analysis and facts and discussion, and there's politics of the limbic system, the sub-rational, emotional, ancient part of the brain that controls the bodily responses like the blood flushing my cheeks in that seat in the Xcel Energy Center.

As degraded as our politics may be, it's impossible for me to imagine a politician as purely limbic as Sarah Palin ever managing to ascend to the White House. But democratic politics in a heterogeneous society like ours is inevitably tribal, and millions of Americans view her as their vessel and their chief. The political potency of someone who can provoke that kind of visceral reaction shouldn't be underestimated.

Amanda Marcotte

Looking at the train wreck that is Sarah Palin, I find myself torn between my partisan desires and my love of country. Palin's continued popularity with the Republican base has the potential to marginalize the GOP even further, as the public at large perceives Palin both as a bimbo and as a right winger who blows past "conservative" straight into militia separatist territory, with a side of speaking in tongues. As a Democratic partisan, I can only hope Palin takes the Republicans further away from the mainstream.

But as a patriot, I'm concerned about Palin's future as a politician. It's not impossible for the American people to have a collective brain fart and vote her into high office; we are the nation that gave Richard Nixon an overwhelming victory and saw George W. Bush as the conquering hero of 9/11. When I hear fellow liberals cheer Palin on with hopes that she'll sink the Republican Party, I find myself cringing in fear. Let's not cheer her all the way to the White House, I think.

But it seems that my greatest Palin hope (that she'll ruin the Republicans) and my greatest Palin fear (that she'll ruin the country) might both amount to nothing. Palin may try to spin her hasty resignation from the Alaska governor's office as a political asset, but that doesn't mean anyone else is under any obligation to believe her. Recent news stories about Palin doing things like signing up for LinkedIn, like any common job searcher, or sniggering jokes about her upcoming memoirs being written a tad too quickly send the message that the political and media establishment can't take Palin seriously enough to let her have any power.

Palin has potential, lurking career-destroying scandals that could put the John Edwards affair to shame. If any of the many rumors floating around about her are true, she's definitely toast. Remember, the same *National Enquirer* that broke the Edwards story has run with rumors about Palin having an affair, rumors that the mainstream media will cease ignoring if Palin stages a successful political comeback.

But for my money, the most amusing danger to Palin's career comes in the form of her grandson's father, Levi Johnston. Johnston is both a publicity hound and an endless fountain of amusing anecdotes about the Palin family that are incompatible with the humble American right-wing populist image Palin cultivates. Johnston has embarrassed the Palin family by mocking their social conservative front and by revealing that Sarah Palin openly spoke about how much more money she'd make as a professional celebrity than as a governor. Not the best things to have out there if you want a serious political career. The man has expressed interest in posing for *Playgirl*. That's the sort of association that's hard to live down.

Not that any of this matters to the hard-core conservative base that loves Sarah Palin. Their unchanging love is based not so much on who Palin actually is, but the role she plays, that of a Bible-thumping, moose-shooting beauty queen who really gets them. Luckily, the majority of the country isn't quite as keen on embracing the fantasy.

Michael Tomasky

Stan Greenberg and James Carville, the Democratic pollsters, released a study in October 2009 in which they reported the results of a focus group they convened of hard-shell (and all white) conservatives in Georgia. You, I suspect, can predict all the things they didn't like: Barack Obama, Democrats, liberalism, socialism, National Socialism (the Obama variety, natch), the media, being called racist, and so on and so forth.

As for what they liked... well, it was a short list. They didn't like the Republicans ("old and out of touch....Weak," said one). They were okay with George W. Bush on a personal level but thought that Washington, that infectious redoubt of pencil-pushers and status-quo-ers, had made him soft (he "tried to reach across the aisle a little too much," said one).

Ah, but there was one person they really liked: *You betcha... Spicy... Honest... Go girl... Forthright. Right up there... Says what she feels.*

I just hope that Sarah Palin has Hillary's backbone because she is going to need it and that is the thing. I would vote for her in a heartbeat. I love Sarah Palin.

I also admired Sarah Palin for being a professional woman and a great mom. She sacrificed and she was you know an

Alaskan woman.... She was a real woman.... You know strong, courageous, almost like the pioneer women.

I think that she has the moral fiber. I believe she's unselfish, really.... I don't think that she's a person who lies or, you know, she's probably not going to be perfect, but I think she's got the moral fiber.

The key words in these encomiums are *forthright, backbone, pioneer* (in its hardy literal meaning, not that gooey liberal "Shirley Chisholm was a pioneer" sense), and *moral fiber.*

These are the people—maybe not literally, but the kind of people—who attend the "tea party" marches. The kind who swooned last year when John McCain pulled Palin away from Russo-proximity and chose her for vice president, and who roared their approval when she said Obama was busy "palling around with terrorists." I'm not a political scientist, and I haven't undertaken an extensive crunching of the data, but even in the absence of empirical proof I think we can safely say that the space where the Palin-devotee set overlaps with the "dawn of socialism" set is f airly large.

I've grown less interested in Palin than in her people. After all, without them, she's nothing. I went to the 9/12 tea party march on the Mall. I observed these folks (lots of Palin signs there) and chatted with a few.

They were incredibly nice and polite. A couple in full America-Is-Doomed regalia stood on a Metro platform consulting a city map, trying to figure out which subway stop was nearest their desired restaurant. I told them. The husband shook my hand as gratefully as if I'd just pulled his dog out from in front of an onrushing bus. If you saw them at the mall—the suburban lower-case one, not the National upper-case one—and started talking to them about football or sitcoms or what was *really* up with Jon and Kate, you'd be able to have a perfectly pleasant conversation.

But... well, you know. What is going on in this land of ours? I have this imaginary conversation that I indulge in every once in a while. I'm talking with a stone-cold Palinite. I try to get through to him. I say, for example:

"But she couldn't name one Supreme Court case in American history beyond *Roe v. Wade*. Not one, sir. I mean, even if all you care about is abortion rights or the absence thereof, wouldn't you at least hope she knew one or two of the other abortion-related decisions—*Casey v. Planned Parenthood*, anyway?

"And not knowing the Bush Doctrine. Doesn't this, you know, bother you? Okay, I understand. You don't know what the Bush Doctrine is exactly, either. I agree—your average citizen would have trouble with that one off the top of her head. But you, sir, and the average citizen, aren't hoping to be the president of the United States. She is. Do you really think the president shouldn't maybe know more about stuff than you do?

"And finally, what about that whole quitting business? I mean, imagine that upon being hired, your boss suggested that he expected you to stay for four years, and you'd pretty much said yes. But what if you quit your job, just said you were tired of it, a year and half in, after having led him to believe you'd stay four? Would you then expect a promotion?"

I win, sometimes, in my imaginings. My foe grunts and says: "Huh. Never thought of it like that." But I know I'm fooling myself. I also sometimes imagine: What could Sarah Palin do that would cause her base to turn on her? Well, she could suddenly embrace evolution or abortion rights, I suppose. But short of that, none of the normal things that usually hurt politicians—scandal, incompetence—would do it. Virtually anything would be seen as a plot by liberals and the media. And once it's that, it's merely another jewel in her tiara, another basis on which to rise to her defense.

This is different from how many on our side adulate Obama, and it's even different from how their side lionized Bush. There's a much deeper sense of protectiveness in it. Maybe it's because she's a woman (and because many conservative males' ardor for her may well emanate, shall we say, from a region about three feet below the brain). The woman above who said she hoped Palin has Hillary's backbone? She sounds to me like she knows Palin may not. But that's only because "that Hillary" is so desperately ambitious that she'll endure anything to get what she wants, while Sarah sets honorable human limits on what she will endure (and therefore quitting was the right thing to do, get it?).

We will never win this Palin argument. If you have relatives or whatever—trust me, don't even try. Just remember: They're 20 percent of the country. Best if we just talk to them about Jon and Kate.

ACKNOWLEDGMENTS

The idea for this book—and its title—came from the clever and enterprising literary agent Deirdre Mullane, who proceeded to nurture *Going Rouge* into its present form with unflagging enthusiasm and resourcefulness through the mad rush to the publishing deadline. We are extremely grateful to her for all of her efforts. It was our amazing luck to have Colin Robinson in our close circle of friends when Deirdre approached us with her concept. He not only understood our vision instantly but enriched it immeasurably with his unique blend of wit, imagination, sharp political insight, and P.R. genius. He worked tirelessly to pull off what at times felt like a Sisyphean task, and inspired us to toil into the night—yet somehow, as if by magic, made it all fun. John Oakes, his partner at OR Books, embraced the book and shepherded it into print (and e-form) with great warmth and impressive efficiency. We're deeply honored that *Going Rouge* is the debut title of OR Books, a bold experiment in publishing and a brilliant response to the industry's current doldrums.

Lena de Casparis donated her time and labor to this project in all sorts of generous and helpful ways. Joana Kelly did a stellar job gathering permissions under extreme time pressure. Sebastian Jones, a crackerjack researcher, has a great career ahead as one of the world's leading Palintologists. Prem Krishnamurthy and Adam Michaels of the design firm Project Projects provided the handsome interior design. Daniel S. Dunham designed the knockout cover; you can insert your own joke about lipstick here. Josh Garrett-Davis is an eagle-eyed and extremely fast proofreader and copy editor. Katrina vanden Heuvel, the editor and publisher of *The Nation* and our beloved boss, supported us, indulged us, and guided us. Ben Wyskida stepped in with crucial publicity assistance. Our friends and families cheerfully tolerated us. But the greatest debt we owe is to the contributors whose work is assembled here. They rose valiantly to the challenge posed by Sarah Palin, and for that the whole world should be thankful.

CONTRIBUTOR BIOGRAPHIES

Amy Alexander's work has appeared in the *Washington Post*, National Public Radio, TheRoot.com, and the *Nation*. Her next book, *Minority Opinion: A Story of Race, Media, and Reinvention* (Beacon Press), will be published January 2010.

Emily Bazelon is a senior editor at Slate and the Truman Capote Fellow at Yale Law School. Her work has appeared in the *New York Times Magazine*, the *Atlantic*, and *Mother Jones*.

Max Blumenthal is a senior writer for the Daily Beast and a contributor to the *Nation*, Al Jazeera English, Salon, AlterNet, the Huffington Post, and the *Washington Monthly*. His new book is *Republican Gomorrah: Inside the Movement that Shattered the Party* (Nation Books). Research support for his article was provided by the Investigative Fund of the Nation Institute.

Juan Cole is Richard P. Mitchell Collegiate Professor of History at the University of Michigan. His most recent books include *Engaging the Muslim World* and *Napoleon's Egypt: Invading the Middle East*. He also has a regular column at Salon and writes the blog Informed Comment.

Joe Conason is national correspondent for the *New York Observer*, a columnist for Salon, and the director of the Nation Institute Investigative Fund. His books indclude *Big Lies: The Right-Wing Propaganda Machine and How It Distorts the Truth*.

Jeanne Devon, based in Alaska, blogs as AKMuckraker and Mudflats.

Eve Ensler is an American playwright, performer, feminist, and activist, best known for her play *The Vagina Monologues*. Her latest work is her first book, *Insecure At Last: Losing It In Our Security-Obsessed World*.

Amanda Fortini has written for the *New Yorker*, *Slate*, *Elle*, and *New York*, among other publications. She contributed to *Going Hungry: Writers on Desire, Self-Denial, and Overcoming Anorexia*.

Thomas Frank is a columnist for the *Wall Street Journal*. He is the founder and editor of *The Baffler* and the author of *The Wrecking Crew: How Conservatives Rule* and *What's the Matter with Kansas?*

Dana Goldstein is an associate editor at the *American Prospect*. Her writing has also appeared in *BusinessWeek, Slate*, the *Guardian*, the *New Republic*, and the *Nation*.

Michelle Goldberg is the author of *Kingdom Coming: The Rise of Christian Nationalism* and *The Means of Reproduction: Sex, Power, and the Future of the World*. She is currently a blogger at the Huffington Post and also writes an online column for the *American Prospect*. Research support for her article was provided by the Investigative Fund of the Nation Institute.

Jane Hamsher is the founder of firedoglake.com and the author of the best-selling book *Killer Instinct*. She has appeared on CNN, MSNBC, Al Jazeera, PBS, and the BBC.

Christopher Hayes is the *Nation's* Washington, D.C., editor. His articles have appeared in the *New York Times Magazine*, the *American Prospect*, the *New Republic*, the *Washington Monthly* and the *Chicago Reader*. He is currently a fellow at the New America Foundation.

Katrina vanden Heuvel is the editor of the *Nation*. She is the co-editor of *Taking Back America—And Taking Down The Radical Right* and editor of *The Dictionary of Republicanisms*. Her articles have appeared in the *Washington Post*, the *Los Angeles Times*, the *New York Times* and the *Boston Globe*.

Jim Hightower writes a nationally syndicated column carried by seventy-five independent weekly newspapers and other publications. He also writes a monthly newsletter, "The Hightower Lowdown."

Mark Hertsgaard is the environment correspondent at the *Nation*. He is the author of five books. His next book is *Living Through the Storm: How We Survive the Next 50 Years of Climate Change*.

Sheila Kaplan is a lecturer in political reporting at the University of California Berkeley Graduate School of Journalism. Her work has appeared in the *Washington Post*, the *Nation*, Salon, *Legal Times*, the *Washington Monthly* and *U.S. News & World Report*.

Naomi Klein is an award-winning journalist, syndicated columnist, and author of *The Shock Doctrine: The Rise of Disaster Capitalism* and *No Logo*. Klein's regular column for the *Nation* and the *Guardian* is distributed internationally by the New York Times Syndicate.

Richard Kim is a senior editor at the *Nation*.

Michael T. Klare is the defense correspondent for the *Nation* and professor of peace and world security studies at Hampshire College. His latest book is *Rising Power, Shrinking Planet: The New Geopolitics of Energy*.

Linda Hirshman is the author of *Get to Work: And Get A Life Before It's Too Late*. She is also a columnist with *Double X*.

Jane Mayer is a staff writer for the *New Yorker* and the author of the best-selling book *The Dark Side: The Inside Story of How the War on Terror Turned Into a War on American Ideals.*

Elstun Lauesen is a rural affairs specialist in Alaska.

Dahlia Lithwick is a senior editor and legal correspondent for *Slate*, and is a weekly legal commentator for the NPR show, *Day to Day.* She is co-author of *Me v. Everybody: Absurd Contracts for an Absurd World.*

Amanda Marcotte is a blogger for Pandagon. Her book is entitled *It's a Jungle Out There: The Feminist Survival Guide to Politically Inhospitable Environments.*

Shannyn Moore is a broadcaster based in Anchorage, Alaska, who has interviewed Sarah Palin numerous times. She has appeared on *Democracy Now! with Amy Goodman*, Keith Olbermann's *Countdown* and the *Rachel Maddow Show.*

Brentin Mock is a Metcalf Institute Fellow for Environmental Reporting at the *American Prospect.* He also writes for *Essence, GOOD*, and *Next American City* magazines. His work has also appeared in *Intelligence Report, Harper's*, the *Source*, and the *Pittsburgh City Paper.*

David Neiwert is the author of *The Eliminationists: How Hate Talk Radicalized the American Right, Death on the Fourth of July: The Story of a Killing, a Trial, and Hate Crime in America*, and *In God's Country: The Patriot Movement*

and the Pacific Northwest. Research support for his article was provided by the Investigative Fund of the Nation Institute.

John Nichols writes the Online Beat at TheNation.com. He also writes for the *Nation* as its Washington correspondent and is a contributing writer for the *Progressive* and *In These Times.* He is the author of *The Genius of Impeachment, Jews for Buchanan*, and *Dick: The Man Who Is President.*

Katha Pollitt is a columnist at the *Nation.* Her work has been compiled in: *Reasonable Creatures: Essays on Women and Feminism; Subject to Debate: Sense and Dissents on Women, Politics, and Culture*; and *Virginity or Death! And Other Social and Political Issues of Our Time.*

Tom Perrotta is a novelist and screenwriter best known for his novels *Election* and *Little Children*, both of which were made into films. His latest novel, *The Abstinence Teacher*, has just been published in paperback.

Rick Perlstein is the author of *Nixonland: The Rise of a President and the Fracturing of America*, and *Before the Storm: Barry Goldwater and the Unmaking of the American Consensus.* He previously wrote a column for the New Republic Online.

Betsy Reed is the executive editor of the *Nation.* She was the editor of *Unnatural Disaster: The Nation on Hurricane Katrina*, and the anthology *Nothing Sacred: Women Respond to Religious Fundamentalism and Terror.*

Robert Reich is co-founding editor of the *American Prospect* magazine. He has written twelve books, including *The Work of Nations*. His commentaries can be heard weekly on public radio's *Marketplace*.

Frank Rich is an op-ed columnist for the *New York Times*. He has written his childhood memoir, *Ghost Light*; and a collection of Rich's drama reviews, *Hot Seat: Theater Criticism for The New York Times, 1980–1993*, was published in 1998.

Hanna Rosin is a contributing editor at the *Atlantic Monthly* and the author of *God's Harvard: A Christian College on a Mission to Save America*.

Hart Seely is an award-winning reporter for the *Syracuse Post-Standard*. He is the author of *Mrs. Goose Goes to Washington: Nursery Rhymes for the Political Barnyard*.

Jeff Sharlet is a contributing editor for *Harper's* and *Rolling Stone* and the co-creator of two online journals; Killing the Buddha and the Revealer. He authored *The Family: Secret Fundamentalism at the Heart of American Power*.

Marilyn Berlin Snell is a San Francisco–based journalist and editor who has written for the *New York Times, This American Life*, the *New Republic, Discover, Mother Jones, Harper's*, the *Los Angeles Times, NPQ*, and *Sierra*. Research support for her article was provided by the Investigative Fund of the Nation Institute.

Gloria Steinem launched the feminist *Ms.* magazine. She has authored *Revolution from Within: A Book of Self-Esteem* and more recently, *Doing Sixty and Seventy*.

Matt Taibbi works at *Rolling Stone* where he authors a column, "Road Rage." He also recently joined True/Slant as a blogger. His most recent book is titled *The Great Derangement: A Terrifying True Story of War, Politics & Religion at the Twilight of the American Empire*.

Michael Tomasky is the editor in chief of *Democracy: A Journal of Ideas*, editor of *Guardian America*, and a contributing editor for the *American Prospect*.

Rebecca Traister is a senior writer at Salon. She has freelanced for *Elle*, the *Nation*, the *New York Times*, and *Glamour*. Her new book *Big Girls Don't Cry*, about women and the 2008 presidential election, will be published in fall 2010 by the Free Press at Simon & Schuster.

Jessica Valenti is the founder and editor of the popular blog Feministing.com, and the author of: *Full Frontal Feminism: A Young Woman's Guide to Why Feminism Matters* and *He's a Stud, She's a Slut... 49 Other Double Standards Every Woman Should Know*.

Patricia J. Williams is a professor of law at Columbia University. Her publications include *Anthony Burns: The Defeat and Triumph of a Fugitive Slave* and *We Are Not Married: A Journal of Musings on Legal Language and the Ideology of Style*.

JoAnn Wypijewski is a columnist for *Mother Jones* and formerly an editor at the *Nation*. She is the editor of *Painting by Numbers: Komar and Melamid's Scientific Guide to Art*, and *The Thirty Years Wars: Dispatches and Diversions of a Radical Journalist, 1965–1994*.

Gary Younge is a fellow at the Nation Institute. He is also the New York correspondent for the *Guardian* and the author of *No Place Like Home: A Black Briton's Journey through the Deep South* and *Stranger in a Strange Land: Travels in the Disunited States*.

CREDITS

JoAnn Wypijewski's "Beauty and the Beast" reprinted with permission from the September 10, 2008, issue of the *Nation* and TheNation.com.

Jane Mayer's "The Insiders: How John McCain came to pick Sarah Palin" reprinted with permission courtesy of Jane Mayer. Originally published in the October 16, 2008, issue of the *New Yorker.*

Gloria Steinem's "Palin: Wrong Woman, Wrong Message" from September 4, 2008, reprinted with permission courtesy of Gloria Steinem. Originally published in the *LA Times.*

Max Blumenthal and David Neiwert's "Meet Sarah Palin's Radical Right-Wing Pals" first appeared in Salon on October 10, 2008, at www.Salon.com. An online version remains in the Salon archives. Reprinted with permission.

Michelle Goldberg's "Palin's Party: Her Religious Right Roots" reprinted with permission from the September 24, 2008, issue of the *Nation* and TheNation.com.

Mark Hertsgaard's "Our Polar Bears, Ourselves" from September 12, 2008, reprinted with permission courtesy of Mark Hertsgaard. Originally published in the *Nation.*

Michael T. Klare's "Palin's Petropolitics" reprinted with permission from the September 17, 2008, issue of the *Nation* and TheNation.com.

Sheila Kaplan and Marilyn Berlin Snell's "Northern Exposure: Sarah Palin's Toxic Paradise" from October 22, 2008, reprinted by permission of the *New Republic,* © 2008, TNR II, LLC.

John Nichols's "Why Troopergate Matters" reprinted with permission from the September 24, 2008, issue of the *Nation* and TheNation.com.

Brentin Mock's "Examining Palin's Record on Violence Against Women," reprinted with permission from the *American Prospect*: September 18, 2008. www.prospect.org. The American Prospect, 1710 Rhode Island Avenue, NW, 12th Floor, Washington, D.C. 20036. All rights reserved.

Elstun Lauesen's "Palin Enthusiastically Practices Socialism, Alaska-Style" from November 7, 2008 reprinted with permission courtesy of Elstun Lauesen.